MARIANNE CONAN
(1795 – 1839)

JOHN DOYLE
(1797 – 1868)

CHARLES
ALTAMONT DOYLE
(1832 – 1893)

CONSTANCE AMELIA
MONICA DOYLE
(1868 – 1924)

JANE ADELAIDE
ROSE DOYLE
(1875 – 1937)

E
YLE
1)

JOHN FRANCIS
INNES HAY DOYLE
(1873 – 1919)

BRYAN MARY
JULIA DOYLE
(1877 – 1927)

NATIUS
OYLE
30)

JEAN ELIZABETH LECKIE
(1874 – 1940)

55)

ADRIAN
(1910 – 1970)

LENA JEAN
(1912 – 1997)

CREATING SHERLOCK HOLMES

The Second Stain

The Solitary Cyclist

The Dancing Men

The Hound of the Baskervilles

The Speckled Band

The Reigate Squire

The Boscombe Valley Mystery

The Red-Headed League

The Norwood Builder

The Abbey Grange

The Final Problem

The Bruce Partington

CREATING SHERLOCK HOLMES

THE REMARKABLE STORY OF SIR ARTHUR CONAN DOYLE

CHARLOTTE MONTAGUE

CHARTWELL
BOOKS

SIR ARTHUR CONAN DOYLE
(1859 – 1930)

Sir Arthur Conan Doyle's full name is Arthur Ignatius Conan Doyle. Conan was originally one of his two middle names. But in honor of his influential godfather, Michael Conan, he adopted Conan as part of his surname in his teenage years. The world-famous author is now very often referred to simply as Conan Doyle.

CONTENTS

INTRODUCTION

Sherlock Holmes is one of the most extraordinary characters in all of literature, a figure instantly recognizable from his deerstalker hat, Aberdeen cape and curved calabash pipe (even though his creator never mentioned any of these in his writings) and his long angular features and disdain for the etiquette of life. He has taken on a life of his own during the 130 years since he first appeared in the novel *A Study in Scarlet*. In film, on television, on stage, in parody and pastiche, Sherlock Holmes is all around us, employing his unique talents to right wrongs and to find answers where the bumbling police can find none.

And yet, what do we know about the great detective? Not a great deal, apart from what we learn of him during his investigations. There are some vague details about his family being country squires and a connection with an obscure French painter, but what we know of Holmes is mostly the day to day, whatever he is engaged upon in whatever story we are gripped by. His chronicler and ineffably loyal lieutenant, Dr. John Watson, gives us the occasional glimpse into Holmes's dark and fairly impenetrable soul but he remains an enigma whose story is told in the fifty-six short stories and four novels crafted over a period of roughly forty years.

On the other hand, Sherlock Holmes's creator, Sir Arthur Conan Doyle, the Scotsman whose family on both sides originated in Ireland, was an increasingly public figure during his life. Starting out as a doctor, his talent for storytelling soon shone through and before long he was

Portrait of Arthur Conan Doyle by George Hutchinson, 1894.

earning enough money to be able to support himself and his family by his pen alone. The reason was Sherlock Holmes—although Sir Arthur Conan Doyle continually expressed regret that he had to rely on such popular writing to maintain his lifestyle. He longed to be taken seriously as a writer of historical fiction, the teller of tales of derring-do from a bygone age, but, to his eternal dismay, that was not where his talents lay. Instead, his skill was in writing superior stories of detection, consummately crafted crime novels for which people would stand in long lines outside magazine offices to get their hands on the next adventure. They would turn out in their thousands around the world not to see the writer of *Sir Nigel*, but to catch a glimpse of the man who had invented one of the greatest and most memorable characters in literary history.

This book as well as chronicling the life and times of both Sir Arthur Conan Doyle and Sherlock Holmes contains summaries—some brief, some longer—of all the stories in the Sherlock Holmes canon. They are collected together in the same running order as when they were published as anthology collections, even though they had all been published earlier as short stories or serialized over several months in *The Strand Magazine* in England or *Collier's Magazine* in the United States. It is a twin biography of the two men whose lives are interlinked forever, one strikingly real and powerful, and the other fictional and brilliant but destined to long outlive his creator. It seems that with

every new generation, Holmes continues to be re-invented, as we see with Benedict Cumberbatch's splendid twenty-first century re-incarnation of the great detective.

Hopefully this book will help to add to the picture of the creator of Sherlock Holmes as well as the character himself and the world in which he first existed. Even though Sir Arthur Conan Doyle tried to kill him off in 1893, Sherlock Holmes is still very much alive in the public's imagination.

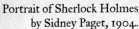

Portrait of Sherlock Holmes by Sidney Paget, 1904.

PART ONE

★ ★ ★

THE ADVENTURE OF THE RESTLESS YOUTH

★ ★ ★

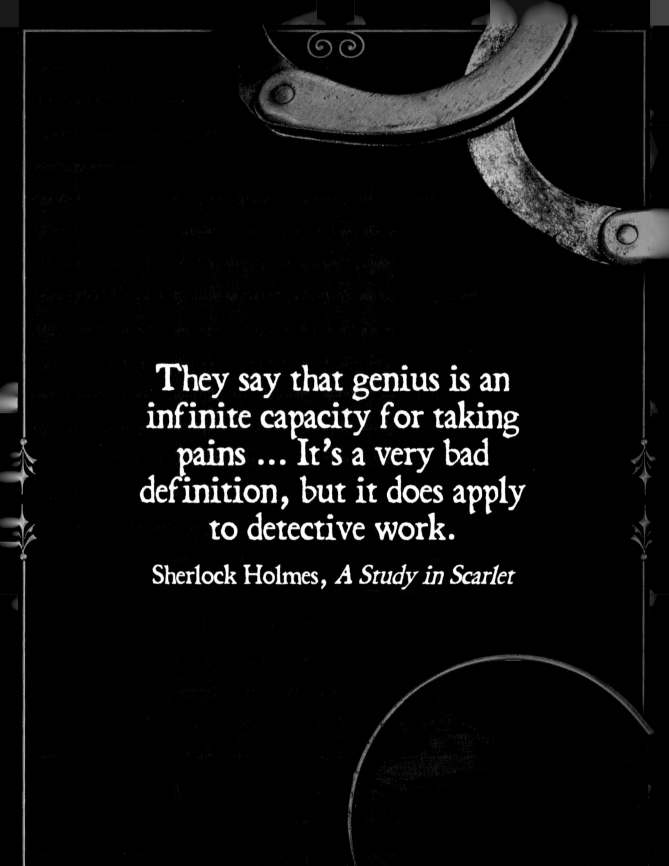

They say that genius is an infinite capacity for taking pains ... It's a very bad definition, but it does apply to detective work.

Sherlock Holmes, *A Study in Scarlet*

CHAPTER 1

AN ARTISTIC FAMILY

AN IRISH BACKGROUND

Both sides of Sir Arthur Conan Doyle's family originated in Ireland although it is difficult to trace his lineage accurately because of the loss of so many records in the Irish Civil War. He liked to believe, however, that the Doyles were descendants of Dubhgall, King of Ulster, and when he was living in the house he named "Undershaw" in Hindhead, between 1897 and 1907, he installed a stained-glass window with crests. Later, however, he believed the Doyles to be a cadet branch of a Roman Catholic family from Staffordshire that relocated to Ireland in the seventeenth century. They were given large estates—possibly in County Offaly or County Laois— but with the Protestants in the ascendancy, they had been persecuted on account of their religion and dispossessed.

Records that have survived show that John Doyle (1797 – 1868), Arthur's grandfather, eldest son of a silk merchant, was a successful equestrian artist working in Dublin. He later moved to London and established himself as an artist and political cartoonist.

SEEKING FAME AND FORTUNE

The Doyle family was devoutly Roman Catholic and John Doyle's two sisters became Roman Catholic nuns while one of his brothers trained as a priest. John's wife, Marianne Conan (1795 – 1839), whom he married in 1820, was also the child of a father who worked in the clothing industry and the Conan family were said to be French in origin, with roots in an ancient dukedom in Brittany. Like many other ambitious Irishmen of his time, John viewed London as offering far more opportunity than Dublin. The United Kingdom of Great Britain and Ireland had been instituted in 1800, after the failure of the Irish Rebellion of 1798 against British rule in Ireland. The successful revolutions that had taken place in France and the United States had persuaded the republican revolutionary group, the United Irishmen, to take up arms but they had failed. Now, Irishmen were beginning to seek fame and fortune in London.

LIFE IN LONDON

John Doyle initially rented a house in Berners Street, among other artists in London's west end, but, with business slow and his family increasing, he was forced to move a few times. In 1833, as his career took off, the Doyle family moved into a large house in Cambridge Terrace, located to the north of Hyde Park, a street that is now known as Sussex Gardens. The Doyles' seven children all showed artistic leanings, to a greater or lesser degree. Ann Martha (1821 – 99), a fine musician, later became a nun. James (1822 – 92) illustrated and wrote about history. Richard (1824 – 83) became a successful illustrator and cartoonist. Henry (1827 – 92) became a cartoonist and then for twenty-three years was director of the Irish National Gallery. Charles Altamont Doyle (1832 – 93) —"Altamont" coming from the subsidiary title, Earl of Altamont of John's client, the Marquess of Sligo—was also a painter. The remaining children, Francis and Adelaide, both died young in the early 1840s.

John had little time for English education and the Doyle children were largely taught at home by a tutor named Street. They also had fencing and dancing teachers. John expected results from this regime, however, the children having to provide illustrated reports of their visits to museums or the theater. On Sundays, they had to stage a play or a concert. Meanwhile, the house was always full of fascinating visitors from Benjamin Disraeli (1804 – 81) to Charles Dickens (1812 – 70).

JOHN DOYLE

John Doyle studied landscape painting under the Italian painter, Gaspare Gabrielli (1770 – 1828) who worked in Dublin for many years. Doyle also attended the Drawing School of the Royal Dublin Society. Among his aristocratic patrons as he launched his professional career were the Marquess of Sligo (1788 – 1845) and the Lord Lieutenant of Ireland, The Earl Talbot (1777 – 1849). He produced a popular series of six prints in 1822 entitled *The Life of a Racehorse* and that same year he and his wife, Marianne Conan, moved to London. In 1825, he exhibited the painting *Turning Out the Stag* which was well received by the critics and the public.

Just before Christmas 1839, Marianne died of heart disease and, while Doyle continued to paint miniatures, by 1835 he was enjoying greater success as a political cartoonist. Using the brand new printing technology of lithography he published his work once a month during parliamentary sessions. He continued in this work for the next twenty-two years. His political sketches were identified by the initials "H.B." which was contrived from Doyle's initials—two Js and two Ds. The true identity of H.B., however, remained a secret until Doyle wrote in an 1843 letter to Prime Minister Sir Robert Peel (1788 – 1850) that he was, indeed, the political cartoonist.

Eventually, H.B.'s style softened and Doyle's reputation waned. He died in obscurity but is now recognized to have been the progenitor of a school of cartoonists that includes John Leech (1817 – 64), and John Tenniel (1820 – 1914) celebrated for his illustrations of Lewis Carroll's *Alice in Wonderland*. Doyle formed a bridge between the harsh Regency satire of George Cruikshank (1792 – 1878) and James Gillray (1756 or 57 – 1815) and the altogether more polite work of Tenniel and Leech.

Arthur's grandfather, John Doyle.

RICHARD DOYLE

Known as Dicky as well as by his pseudonym, "Dick Kitcat," Richard Doyle was a very popular and successful illustrator. He is remembered for his social satire, reminiscent of the great English caricaturist and book illustrator, George Cruikshank. But he was also an illustrator of books of fairy tales and other subjects, establishing his reputation in that genre with illustrations in 1846 for *The Fairy Ring*, a new translation of tales by the Brothers Grimm.

In 1840, at age sixteen, Doyle published a series of humorous envelopes for the newly established Post Office and in the same year he produced a series of cartoons called *The Tournament*, satirizing Victorian neo-medievalism. In 1843, he joined the staff of the satirical magazine *Punch*, and a year later, designed the front cover of the sixth edition of the magazine, showing fairies and elves revolving around a rusticated title. This was used as the magazine's front cover format until 1954. After the magazine ran an attack on the Catholic Church in 1850, the devout Dicky Doyle resigned.

He became an illustrator of children's fantasy books and in 1869, he produced what is considered his greatest work—*In Fairyland, a series of Pictures from the Elf World*—his illustrations accompanied by a poem by Irish poet, William Allingham (1824 – 89).

Although undoubtedly an artist of some brilliance, Doyle was also decidedly unreliable. His illustrations regularly arrived late, especially those he provided for William Makepeace Thackeray's serial novel, *The Newcomes*. Thackeray threatened to give the work to another artist, so frustrated was he with Doyle's disregard for deadlines. His career was indeed hampered by his lack of professionalism, but his work is now widely collected.

Arthur's uncle, Richard Doyle (1824 – 83).

AN EARLY DEATH

Everything was changed by Marianne's early death in 1839 which forced John Doyle to cut back on work commitments in order to concentrate on his children's upbringing. Richard adapted well to the new situation, focusing his attention on his considerable skills as an artist. Charles was less engaged in the artistic hothouse that the Doyle residence had become. Interestingly, Richard was a particular fan of the historical paintings of the French artist, Paul Delaroche (1797 – 1856) who was the son-in-law of another French painter, Horace Vernet (1789 – 1863). Sir Arthur Conan Doyle's fictional detective, Sherlock Holmes, claims in the 1893 story "The Adventure of the Greek Interpreter" to be related to Vernet, saying: "My ancestors were country squires ... my grandmother ... was the sister of Vernet, the French artist." There were several Vernets in what was, like the Doyles, something of an artistic dynasty.

AN INFLUENTIAL UNCLE

Marianne Doyle's brother, Michael Conan, moved into Cambridge Terrace around the time of his sister's death. He had been educated at Trinity College, Dublin, which was highly unusual for a Roman Catholic as that institution was staunchly Protestant. In fact, he was permitted to be a student there only after gaining special permission from his bishop. Conan, who had moved to London after graduation, and had qualified as a barrister, was also a painter and moved in artistic circles. But he opted for a career in journalism, working first for the *Morning Herald*. In 1832, he was sent to cover the French siege of Antwerp that followed the Belgian Revolution. The French *Armée du Nord*, commanded by Maréchal Étienne Gérard, besieged the occupying Dutch troops. Sir Arthur Conan Doyle would later appropriate this name for his *Brigadier Gerard* stories. Michael Conan later moved to a job writing for the *Art Journal*.

CHARLES DOYLE MOVES TO EDINBURGH

Arthur's father, Charles, was perhaps less artistic than his brothers and was probably an altogether quieter and more sensitive boy. He enjoyed fishing and his favorite books were the Gothic romances of the English novelist, G.P.R. James (1799 – 1860). He was conservative, both in nature and politics. Meanwhile, his brother Richard was developing the humor and fantasy skills in his drawing that later stood him in good stead.

Charles did not appear to be making the kind of headway in life that his brothers were. The decision was taken, therefore, to send him to Edinburgh where he could exploit his draftsmanship and design skills as assistant to Robert Matheson (1808 – 77), Clerk of Works for Scotland. Charles's salary was two hundred and twenty pounds a year.

THE MOTHER'S SIDE

Arthur's mother was Mary Josephine Foley (1837 – 1920) whose family were mainly Protestant. They owned land around Lismore in County Wexford and made grand claims about having arrived with the English invaders in the seventeenth century. Mary's grandfather, Thomas Foley, was agent of the estate of the Duke of Devonshire who owned Lismore Castle. He was also a mill-owner, running a mill on the Blackwater river. The river boasted the best salmon fishing in Ireland and Mary's grandfather owned the rights to eleven miles of it.

Thomas Foley married three times, and had nine children although not all survived into adulthood. The oldest son, Patrick inherited the mill and the fishing rights on the Blackwater. Thomas, son of his father's second wife, became a lawyer while William (1807 – 41) the first-born of Thomas Foley's third marriage, to a Cardiff woman named Hannah Lowe, went to Trinity College, Dublin to study medicine. Thomas Foley had originally been a Catholic, converting to Protestantism out of convenience when he married his first wife. By the time William came along, however, he seems to have reverted to Catholicism and William was recorded at Trinity as being Roman Catholic.

CONAN DOYLE'S MATERNAL GRANDMOTHER

William Foley graduated as a doctor and in 1835 married Catherine Pack (1808 – 62) who co-owned a girls' boarding school. Part of the Anglo-Irish establishment, they hailed from Kilkenny where Catherine's mother had originally established the school. Catherine's ancestral ranks were filled with doctors, clergymen, and soldiers. Her grandfather and an uncle had both been headmaster of Kilkenny College which was Ireland's pre-eminent Protestant secondary school. They even had aristocratic connections, having married into an illegitimate branch of the Duke of Northumberland's family, the Percys. Surrounded by successful progenitors and relatives Catherine's father William was less prosperous, working in Kilkenny as a grocer and wine merchant. His wife came from a good background, however. Her father, Matthew Scott, owned a woollen mill.

On marrying William Foley in 1835, Catherine chose to take his Catholic religion but he died in 1841 in his early thirties and she returned with her two young daughters, Mary and Catherine (1839 – ?), to her family in Kilkenny where she started a girls' school. It was not an easy time to launch a new venture. The potato famine devastating Ireland closed her school down and in April 1847 she sold her property in Kilkenny and moved with her children to Edinburgh.

A QUIET LODGER

Catherine and her two girls were among many Irish people who emigrated during the famine to Scotland where work was plentiful. Most went to Glasgow but Catherine had a link with Edinburgh where her grandfather Matthew knew the great Scottish novelist, Sir Walter Scott (1771 – 1832). This may or may not be true but it certainly was an exciting place to move to. It was teeming with people who had relocated from Scotland's countryside as well as those who had come from Ireland. The railway had opened up the city to travelers and Edinburgh had rapidly expanded both in population and area. Catherine and her daughters moved into lodgings on the edge of Edinburgh's New Town at 27 Clyde Street, where she established a new business—the Governesses' Institution—supplying governesses to schools and families. Her income was initially insufficient, leading her to find a lodger. The newly arrived seventeen-year-old Charles Doyle knocked on her door and was soon ensconced in Clyde Street.

Charles's stay was brief but he liked the family whom he described in a letter to a friend as "Very pleasant people and very Irish." He was working hard to establish himself but was not happy in Edinburgh, finding the people uncouth and he was shocked by the drunkenness and violence he encountered. His brother Richard had resigned from *Punch* in protest at what he saw as its anti-Catholic coverage of the Ecclesiastical Titles Bill and Charles also turned to his Catholic faith during a time that was tumultuous for the Church of Rome. In March 1851 he attended a meeting protesting against anti-Catholic measures passed by Lord Russell's government. He even seconded the resolutions that were to be sent to Parliament.

END OF AN ERA

Back in London, Michael Conan had moved out of the Doyle house in Cambridge Terrace with his wife and sister. In 1851, John Doyle, at age fifty-four, drew his last political sketch and, failing to find employment, started inundating the government with mad inventions he believed would benefit the British troops in the Crimea. His grandson Arthur later did much the same during the Boer War. Meanwhile, John's daughter Ann Martha became a nun, although she was still able to live at Cambridge Terrace and look after John. Michael Conan's sister-in-law Anne also took religious orders and Conan and his wife moved to Paris where he continued writing for the *Art Journal*.

NOTHING LESS THAN BOSH

In Edinburgh, Charles Doyle was at a low ebb and although Richard tried to cheer him up, his family worried about him. He lacked confidence and when he entered a competition to design stained glass windows for Glasgow Cathedral, he first sent his designs to Cambridge Terrace for approval before submission. Again, when he was commissioned to design a scroll marking Cardinal Wiseman's links with Scotland, he turned to his family for advice and approval, telling them that he was not up to the job. His brother James gave him short shrift, "Allow me to say that your remark about your not being equal to the job is nothing less than 'bosh.'"

SHERLOCK HOLMES'S FAMILY AND EARLY YEARS

Details about Sherlock Holmes's family are scant. Even aging him presents problems, but in "His Last Bow. The War Service of Sherlock Holmes," Holmes posing as an Irish-American who is passing secrets to a German spy is described as "a tall, gaunt man of sixty." As this was supposed to be 1914, we can deduce that Sherlock Holmes was born in 1854.

As to the family into which he was born, we are thrown a crumb by the detective in the story "The Adventure of the Greek Interpreter:"

My ancestors were country squires, who appear to have led much the same life as is natural to their class.

And he expands talk about a family connection with an artistic French family that may have helped to make him the man he was:

But, none the less, my turn that way is in my veins, and may have come with my grandmother, who was the sister of Vernet, the French artist. Art in the blood is liable to take the strangest forms.

However, Holmes never specified to which of the three Vernet brothers—Claude Joseph, Carle or Horace—he was referring. During the same discussion he also tells us, for the first time, that he was not an only child. He had a brother, Mycroft, who "possesses it in a larger degree than I do." Mycroft Holmes, we learn, was seven years older than Sherlock and worked as a government official.

Sherlock Holmes illustrated by Erberto Carboni.

A JULY WEDDING

While Charles had been lodging at Clyde Street, he had been taken, somewhat, by the twelve-year-old Mary Foley. She had been sent away to a school in France before Charles had really got to know her but on her return in 1854, now seventeen, the young woman captivated him. Catherine Foley was delighted. Charles sent a photograph of her to Dicky who made a sketch of her and expressed his approval which was all the encouragement Charles needed. On July 31, 1855, he and Mary were married at St. Mary's Church, Edinburgh. They honeymooned at an inn just outside the city before moving into a rented apartment. Just under a year later, on July 22, 1856, their first child, a daughter was born and named Annette Conan Doyle in honor of Charles's mother's family.

THINGS LOOK UP FOR CHARLES

Richard Doyle tried to obtain additional income for Charles to help him and his young family. He provided him with contacts at magazines in London and proposed that Charles become his agent in Edinburgh.

John Doyle, meanwhile, tried to get Charles transferred to London but that notion did not please Charles, as he wrote to his sister Ann Martha:

> *I have the greatest horror of being herded with a set of snobs in the London office, who would certainly not understand and probably laugh at the whole theory of construction, as also the technical terms in use among the builders here, to whom brick is an unknown quantity.*

He was drawing more however, with his comic work appearing in magazines such as the *Illustrated Times*. Things were also improving at work where he had languished for a decade in the shadow of Robert Matheson. He was now allowed some credit for his designs, although that was not always a good thing. His work on the fountain in the forecourt of Holyrood Palace in Edinburgh was described by the trade magazine *The Builder* as a "confused and miserable mixture, ugly in outline and puerile in detail." Charles was further depressed when his and Mary's second daughter, six month-old Catherine, died in October 1858 from water on the brain.

Dicky Doyle's sketch of Mary Foley, Arthur's mother, at age 17.

Arthur (right) at age 6, with his sister Annette at age 9, in 1865.

CHAPTER 2

AN EDINBURGH CHILDHOOD

Picardy Place was a quiet street to be found just off the main road out of Edinburgh to the port of Leith, the street so-named because French linen-weavers had settled there in 1729. It was at number 11 Picardy Place that Arthur Ignatius Conan Doyle was born on May 22, 1859.

Just before the birth of his son, Charles Doyle provided the illustrations for a book entitled *Men Who Have Risen: A Book for Boys*, a volume designed to demonstrate to young boys the virtues of hard work and the desire for self-improvement. By the time of Arthur's birth there was a dark cloud over Picardy Place, however. Charles had started to drink heavily and could often be found selling drawings for the price of a drink. Picardy Place was busy as Mary had moved in her mother and sister and the Governesses' Institution was still being run from there. She had time to give birth to a daughter, also called Mary, in late 1861 and, with the house seriously overcrowded, the family moved once again to 3 Tower Bank, Portobello, a coastal suburb of Edinburgh. But it proved to be Catherine's last move as she died in May 1862. She was fifty-four.

A DRINKING PROBLEM

Charles responded well to living in Portobello which is close to the sea and began to paint, but his drinking increased in the winter of 1862. He was incapable of working and while he was absent his salary was halved. He stole from his wife and children and ran up large debts with shopkeepers. It would not have been so bad had Charles become indebted for the sake of his family, but he was selling the goods he bought on the "never-never" in order to finance his drinking habit. Things got so bad that he drank furniture varnish when there was no alcohol to hand.

Arthur and his father, Charles Doyle, May 1865.

17

Meanwhile, in the midst of this desperate situation, Mary did her best for her young family, providing much-needed emotional support for her son Arthur, and taking on the role of father as well as mother. In the autobiography that Arthur wrote later in life, his father's drinking problems were never mentioned only the privations the family endured as a result of Charles's low income.

TALES OF DERRING-DO

Mary, for her part, seems to have moved away from her faith and threw herself into her family history, sharing it with Arthur. She regaled the boy with tales of derring-do enacted by her distant cousin, Major-General Sir Denis Pack (c. 1772 – 1823) who demonstrated conspicuous bravery during the Peninsular War and fought at Waterloo. She also filled the boy's head with Percy family history. If nothing else, it excited his febrile imagination and helped her to escape the drab reality of her life, a reality made all the harsher by the death of the couple's two-year-old daughter Mary in June 1863.

A BOOKWORM

Although Arthur remained close to his father, the family's problems were obvious to him. He wrote later that Charles's "thoughts were always in the clouds and he had no appreciation of the realities of life." In another attempt to escape her humdrum life, Mary joined the Philosophical Institution, a literary and debating society and could often be found in its library. She was a voracious reader and was never far from a book, even when knitting. Arthur later described her as:

[the] quaintest mixture of the housewife and the woman of letters ... Always a lady, whether she was bargaining with the butcher, or breaking-in a skittish charwoman, or stirring the porridge, which I can see her doing with the porridge-stick in one hand, and the other holding her Revue des deux Mondes *within two inches of her dear nose.*

The *Revue,* a bi-weekly French language literary and cultural affairs magazine was important to Arthur, and he often read from it to his mother, bringing him into contact with the latest literary and cultural developments of the time.

DR. JOHN BROWN

Mary Doyle through her membership of the Philosophical Institution made the acquaintance of a number of literary-minded people, principal among whom was Dr. John Brown (1810 – 82). Born in Biggar, South Lanarkshire, Scotland, Brown came from a long line of eminent Presbyterian clergymen. He was educated at Edinburgh High School, graduating as a medical doctor from Edinburgh University in 1833. He became an apprentice of the pioneering Scottish surgeon James Syme (1799 – 1870) before taking on a very large medical practice in Edinburgh. It was a time when the lack of sanitation and healthcare led to infectious disease and illness among the population.

Dr. Brown was a friend of many well-known literary and cultural figures, among whom were William Makepeace Thackeray and the American author and humorist Mark Twain (1835 – 1910). He wrote about classical, artistic subjects, medicine, the Jacobite Rebellion, and rural life. He is known particularly for two volumes of essays and his short story about a huge mastiff dog, "Rab and his Friends."

Another of Dr. Brown's friends was the American author Oliver Wendell Holmes (1809 – 94). A pioneering doctor himself, Holmes's surname was the name Arthur would later use for his great detective.

FRIENDSHIP WITH MARY BURTON

Mary Doyle befriended Mary Burton, an acquaintance of Dr. Brown and a campaigner for women's rights. Her next child, a girl baptized Caroline Mary, but known as Lottie, was born at Mary Burton's house on February 22, 1866. It has been suggested that the closeness of the two women might have been a consequence of Mary Burton giving shelter to Mary Doyle on one of her temporary separations from her drunken husband. Associating with Mary Burton exposed the young Arthur to the mind of her brother, the economist and historian John Hill Burton (1809 – 81). He was a regular contributor to *Blackwood's Edinburgh Magazine* for which many of the best authors of the day wrote. Arthur also had the use of the fine library at Hill Burton's house and his son William became a close friend to Arthur.

BEGINNING TO WEAVE DREAMS

Arthur's major influence, however, remained his mother. She was a fine storyteller and undoubtedly awoke in him his own storytelling instincts. He later wrote of his mother:

> *[She possessed the] art of sinking her voice to a horror-stricken whisper when she came to a crisis in her narrative ... I am sure, looking back, that it was in attempting to emulate these stories of my childhood that I first began weaving dreams myself.*

It was around this time that Arthur began to write. His first story written at the age of about six, was a badly punctuated tale of the killing of a man by a Bengal tiger. In writing that story, he realized one very important truth about fiction, later admitting "It is very easy to get people into scrapes, and very hard to get them out again."

SCHOOLDAYS

Mary's mother Catherine had left Ireland after a family argument and it was perhaps to heal the rift that Mary took Arthur to Ireland in 1866. But, soon it was time for the Doyles to move yet again, this time to 3 Sciennes Hill Place, Newington, Edinburgh, a house that Arthur always described as dirty and rough although it was nowhere near as bad as he claimed.

But that was not all that was changing for the boy. In the fall of 1866, after he and his mother returned from Ireland, he was sent to

Newington Academy, just a few streets from Sciennes Hill Place. There he encountered a headmaster, Patrick Wilson, who was not reluctant to employ corporal punishment by means of the "tawse." A stiff leather belt with lethal split ends, the tawse was used by schoolteachers to inflict painful blows across the open palm of the outstretched hand. After punishing and disciplining many generations of Scottish schoolchildren the tawse was finally banned by the European Court of Human Rights in 1982.

In August 1868, however, Arthur was taken out of Newington Academy and enrolled at Stonyhurst, a Jesuit-run Roman Catholic boarding school near Clitheroe in Lancashire, England.

Arthur at age 7 in 1866.

OLIVER WENDELL HOLMES

American physician, poet, author, professor and lecturer, Oliver Wendell Holmes was acclaimed as one of the best writers of his time. He was born in Cambridge, Massachusetts, in 1809, the son of a clergyman. He was a precocious child, sent by his father to Phillips Academy in Andover, Massachusetts, at the age of nine in the hope that he would follow him into the ministry. But the young Holmes had no inclination in that direction. At sixteen, he was accepted by Harvard University where he admitted he did not study as hard as he should have. Intending to go into law, he studied at Harvard Law School but by 1830 he had lost interest.

Around this time, he began writing poems, a number of which were published in a periodical produced by friends at Harvard. That same year, he wrote the famous patriotic poem, "Old Ironsides," in protest at the scrapping of the eighteenth century frigate USS *Constitution,* which brought him national acclaim. But instead of becoming a writer, he opted to study medicine. After graduating in 1836, he practiced medicine for the next ten years and then became an academic, holding the post of dean of Harvard Medical School until 1882.

Meanwhile, he continued writing, producing in 1858 one of his most popular works, *The Autocrat of the Breakfast-Table.* He went on to publish *The Professor at the Breakfast-Table* (1860), *The Poet at the Breakfast-Table* (1872) and *Over the Teacups* (1891). Among Holmes's other major works are the poems "The Chambered Nautilus" (1858) and "The Deacon's Masterpiece, or The Wonderful One-Hoss Shay" (1858). Holmes died in 1894, at age eighty-five.

THE DEVELOPMENT OF EDINBURGH

In the Middle Ages a hill fort was established at Edinburgh and from the tenth century it was a royal residence for the Scottish monarch. The town that began to grow around the fort was granted a royal charter in the twelfth century and by the middle of the fourteenth century Edinburgh was the capital of Scotland.

By the eighteenth century, although home to a number of Scotland's great institutions, the city of Edinburgh was dirty, insanitary and overcrowded. Proposals were put forward, therefore, to build a New Town to the north of the Old Town. Gradually, Edinburgh's professionals and businessmen decamped from the dingy and crowded Old Town to the New Town with its wide thoroughfares and squares, changing Edinburgh's character forever.

At the same time, the city gained an international reputation as a place where new ideas in philosophy, history, science, economics, and medicine flourished, attracting students from all over Britain and as far away as the North American colonies. Leading thinkers based in the city included philosopher David Hume (1711 – 76), economist Adam Smith (1723 – 90), chemist Joseph Black (1728 – 99), and historian and philosopher Adam Ferguson (1723 – 1816). This period became known as the Scottish Enlightenment, a remarkable time during which there was a wealth of intellectual and scientific accomplishments.

Edinburgh's traditional industries of brewing, printing, and distilling continued to flourish in the nineteenth century but there was little industrialization of the kind experienced by other British cities. Partly because of the arrival of the railways, linking the city with Glasgow and other parts of the country, Edinburgh's city center became a shopping and commercial area and most of the original Georgian architecture was lost. Meanwhile, the Old Town had turned into an area of dilapidated, overpopulated slums. In 1865 major improvements were undertaken in the Old Town, creating the largely Victorian Old Town that we see today.

Steel engraving of Edinburgh in the 1800s.

CHAPTER 3

IN THE CARE OF THE JESUITS

John Doyle died in January 1868 at the age of seventy. He had visited Charles and his family in Edinburgh shortly before his demise. This led Charles to blame the visit and himself for his father's passing and a deep depression affected him once again as a result. To make matters worse, Mary gave birth around this time to the couple's sixth child, Constance Amelia Monica.

But Mary was becoming concerned about her son's future, believing he had little chance of making anything of himself in this crowded household with a seriously ailing father. She discussed the matter with Charles's brothers who promised to pay the fees if Arthur went to boarding school. They chose Stonyhurst College, the world's oldest Jesuit school, where Henry Doyle's father-in-law had been educated. Although dubious about the whole business, Mary was convinced by Michael Conan who impressed upon her the good education the Jesuits provided. He did counsel against Arthur remaining there too long as the Jesuits had a reputation for convincing their more impressionable students that they had a vocation.

The school was set up so that pupils made progress as the years passed through seven classes, known as "playrooms." These were Elements, Figures, Rudiments, Grammar, Syntax, Poetry and Rhetoric. There was constant learning, even at mealtimes when pupils would be read to or there would be debates. Each level of the school would stage an entertainment regularly during term-time. Standing in the thirty acres of rolling countryside that Thomas Weld had donated as well as the college buildings, Stonyhurst provided an entirely different type of life for Arthur, the tranquil life of the spirit rather than the one with which he had become familiar in bustling, mercantile Edinburgh.

JUNIOR SCHOOL

Arthur began his scholastic career at Stonyhurst in the college's junior school, known as Hodder. He was put into the care of a twenty-three-year-old priest named Father Francis Cassidy (1845 – 1915) who later became headmaster of the junior school, a position which he held for thirty-three years. The young father was of considerable help to Arthur, telling him stories that Arthur took in "as a sponge absorbs water, until I was so saturated with them that I could still repeat them."

He settled into the routine but was shocked in November 1868 to learn that he was going to have to spend the Christmas holidays at Stonyhurst. Arthur was told that he lived too great a distance from the school, but the reality was that Charles Doyle's condition was getting worse. At home, it was thought that it would be harmful for the boy to be around his father.

Arthur made his first confession in early 1869 and in May he took his first communion, expressing his pleasure in the event to his mother in a letter:

> *Oh mama, I cannot express the joy that I felt on the happy day to receive my creator into my breast. I shall never though I live a hundred years, I shall never forget that day.*

MORE REAL THAN REALITY

As ever, Arthur read voraciously, escaping from the everyday by devouring the books he found in the Hodder library, by favorite authors such as R.M. Ballantyne (1825 – 94), writer of *The Coral Island* and Captain Mayne Reid (1818 – 83) who had published *The Headless Horseman* a couple of years before Arthur arrived at Stonyhurst. He later wrote about the vicarious pleasures of such exciting tales:

Your very heart and soul are out on the prairies and the oceans with your hero. It is you who act and suffer and enjoy. You carry the long small-bore Kentucky rifle with which such egregious things are done, and you lie out upon the topsail yard, and get jerked by the flap of the sail into the Pacific, where you cling on to the leg of an albatross, and so keep afloat until the comic boatswain turns up with his crew of volunteers to handspike you to safety. What a magic it is, this stirring of the boyish heart and mind! Long ere I came to my teens I had traversed every sea and knew the Rockies like my back garden ... It was all more real than reality.

UPPER SCHOOL

At the start of the fall term of 1870, when Arthur moved out of Hodder and into the upper school, everything changed. The Head of Stonyhurst, Father Edward Ignatius Purbrick (1830 – 1914), was hugely conservative as was the Prefect of (Lower) Studies, Father George Kingdon. Father Kingdon—known as "The Padre"—had studied at St. Bartholomew's Hospital in London but had rejected conventional medicine which showed where his views lay.

Arthur had encountered the "tawse" at Newington School in Edinburgh. Now he was confronted with the "tolley," a thick rubber slab that was used to discipline the pupils of the upper school. Arthur admitted that he did not respond well to such punishment, but he took it when subjected to it. Of course, all kinds of other religious torments were also threatened in cases of wrongdoing.

Despite the anti-secular, anti-materialistic nature of the teaching and in spite of Father Kingdon's rejection of orthodox medicine, the sciences were still taught at Stonyhurst College and Arthur opted for medicine.

STONYHURST COLLEGE

The story of the school that would become Stonyhurst College began in 1593 at St. Omer in the Spanish Netherlands. (St. Omer is now in north-west France.) Father Robert Persons S.J. (1546 – 1610), under the patronage of Philip II of Spain, established a school for English boys who could not receive a Catholic education in Protestant England. Persons became a major figure in establishing the sixteenth-century "English Mission" of the Society of Jesus. In 1762, however, the Jesuits had to flee to Bruges where they re-established their school. In 1773, it moved to Liège and twenty-one years later relocated to Stonyhurst in the north-west of England. Stonyhurst was donated to the Jesuits by Thomas Weld (1750 – 1810) of Lulworth. Weld, a former pupil of the school when it was located in Liège, had inherited Stonyhurst from Mary, Duchess of Norfolk (1692 – 1754) who was the last of the Shireburn family that had owned the hall since around 1372. Stonyhurst College is now the only Jesuit public school in England.

Stonyhurst College in 1875.

Life was far from luxurious. Breakfast consisted of a basin of milk and a couple of pieces of dry bread; lunch meant meat and twice a week the students were given pudding; in the afternoon break a brownish liquid called "beer" was handed out, and supper consisted of hot milk, bread, potatoes and a small sliver of butter.

NO STAR PUPIL

Arthur Doyle, as he was known then, was no star pupil at this point in his education. In 1870 his report card described him as "slovenly," and in 1871 he was "uncouth," "noisy," and "scatterbrain." Of course, excuses could always be made for Arthur. He must have been worried about what was going on back at home in Edinburgh. Charles was managing to hold down his job but things were difficult. So it fell to Arthur to behave like the grown-up while pretending that everything was wonderful at Stonyhurst.

He even lied to his father that he enjoyed spending Christmas at the school instead of at home with his family. On the whole, though, his feelings about his family and his concerns for his mother's welfare were suppressed in his communications. A poem called "A Student's Dream" that he wrote in October 1870 may have been a far better indicator of his feelings at the time:

The student he lay on his narrow bed
He dreamt not of the morrow
Confused thoughts they filled his head
And he Dreamt of his home with sorrow ...
He thought of the birch's stinging stroke
And he thought with fear on the morrow
He wriggled and tumbled and nearly awoke
And again he sighed with sorrow.

A DISTANT WAR

Around this time, the Franco-Prussian War broke out with Arthur, naturally, given the

Classroom photograph at Stonyhurst College. Arthur is the tallest boy in the back row, third from the left, behind the Jesuit teacher.

24

Francophile leanings of his mother and many of his family, rooting for the French. He had family there, too, which gave him a vested interest in the outcome of the conflict. Michael Conan and his wife had escaped to Dieppe to avoid the war, but his sister Annette had gone to be educated by nuns at the Institute St. Clotilde in Les Andelys, a town to the south-east of Rouen. Les Andelys was captured by the Prussians and Annette was the only "English"—as she put it—person there. Surprisingly, Mary and Charles allowed the newspaper *The Scotsman* to publish her letters at home, although they were published under a pseudonym.

CRICKET AND FISHING

Although Arthur did make friendships at Stonyhurst, it was not encouraged. Priests never allowed boys to be alone together. Thus sport was seen as a way of releasing pent-up energy and Arthur threw himself into cricket. Unfortunately, however, he was not very good at the game. Like his father he loved fishing and he caught trout and salmon in the countryside around the school.

A MATTER OF NAMES

Arthur was confirmed on July 21, 1872, in his father's name which pleased Charles considerably. Then, in November, he was admitted into the religious fraternity of the Blessed Virgin Mary. Back home, his mother seemed to be returning to her faith but his godfather Michael Conan (also his grand-uncle) was turning anti-clerical and was certainly wary of the Jesuits, as he had been when recommending that Arthur should go to Stonyhurst. But it was for the education of the Jesuits that he wanted his godson to go there, not for the religion. Michael was dismayed to learn that Arthur was not using the "Conan" part of his name but Arthur pleased him by writing and signing off as "A.C. Doyle." He was perhaps very aware that this was guaranteed to please the man who was providing financial help with his education.

LITERARY LEANINGS

Arthur's reading tastes were changing, from adventure stories to historical novels. He loved Charles Reade's *The Cloister and the Hearth*, the story of the romance of the Dutch scholar and humanist Erasmus's parents in Holland in the Middle Ages. He even described it at one point as the greatest English novel. He also enjoyed reading to his schoolmates, often in exchange for cakes.

Arthur at age 14 in 1873, ready to play cricket.

Eventually, nearing the end of his time in Stonyhurst, he founded a magazine with a few classmates. It was named *Wasp* and Arthur contributed at least one cartoon, although that is all that is left of the periodical. He then started another magazine—the *Stonyhurst Figaro*—that failed to make it beyond the pages of an exercise book. By this time, at the age of fourteen, he was reading novels in French, liking, in particular, the works of Jules Verne (1828–1905).

A BROTHER FOR ARTHUR

After a succession of girls, Mary at last gave birth to another boy. John Francis Innes Hay Doyle (known as Innes) was born on March 31, 1873. And at a time when it was almost impossible for women to get into university, Arthur's sister Annette received a bursary of £30 from the Edinburgh Ladies' Educational Association to study English literature, mathematics and chemistry. Edinburgh University had agreed to allow women to gain a "certificate in the arts" if they attended the Association's classes and passed. Arthur was delighted with all the news from home and it showed in his schoolwork as he entered what was known as the "upper line," for his last two years at Stonyhurst in 1874.

A LONDON VISIT

Back in Edinburgh, the Doyles were again on the move, the relocation forced upon them by the news that Mary Doyle was once more pregnant. She, Charles, and their growing brood moved a few streets away to 2 Argyle Park Terrace. Arthur would not be spending Christmas 1874 there, however. It was suggested, instead, that he should go to London to visit the Doyle family there. After seemingly reconciled to the life of a bachelor, James Doyle had surprised everyone by marrying and had moved out of Clifton Gardens. Dicky, too, had relocated, to Earls Court in west London, where he shared a house with Ann Martha who was still a nun but served as his housekeeper. Henry

had taken up his position as Director of the National Gallery of Ireland in Dublin and was living there.

Arthur's first visit to London lasted three weeks and he crammed a lot in. He went to the theater twice with his Uncle James, on one occasion seeing the young Henry Irving in *Hamlet*. He also visited all the sights—Westminster Abbey, Crystal Palace, London Zoo, Madame Tussauds, and the Tower of London.

Three months later there was yet another arrival in the Doyle household when Arthur's mother, Mary, gave birth to Jane Adelaide Rose who would be known as Ida. But Arthur was otherwise occupied. He was taking exams, the results of which would determine what he would do with his life. Fortunately, he passed.

FELDKIRCH

It was difficult to know what Arthur would do next because, of course, there were no finances in place to take him onto a further stage of his education. He could have remained at Stonyhurst—the school allowed for a small group of older students known as "Gentlemen Philosophers" to complete a two-year course of university standard. But, at sixteen, he was thought by Father Purbrick to be too young for this. He suggested that Arthur should go to Stella Matutina, a Jesuit secondary school at Feldkirch in the Austrian Alps. Arthur was delighted with the idea of some time in Feldkirch and at the very least, it would be an opportunity to improve his German.

Despite the bitter cold weather, worse than anything he had ever encountered, even in windy Edinburgh, Arthur enjoyed being in the Alps. There were ample opportunities to walk and the beer was wonderful. He learned how to toboggan and tried other winter sports as well as football. He even joined the school band, learning to play the bombardon, a tuba-like instrument. He also enjoyed learning about German history and culture.

There is no doubt Arthur was beginning to mature. He was strong and intelligent, seemed older than his years and was liked by others. He was a man's man, a natural leader and spokesman but, like many boys who had attended a public school, he was unused to the company of women and girls and was awkward with them.

MEETING MICHAEL CONAN AT LAST

After his time at Feldkirch, Arthur headed back toward Britain, and on the way, managed to find time to stop in Paris and at last meet his fabled "Uncle Michael." However, having spent his allowance on a lavish meal in Strasbourg, he could not afford the cab fare to Michael's house. He left his luggage at the train station and walked through the streets of Paris to the house, writing of the visit:

So, for some penurious weeks, I was in Paris with this dear old volcanic Irishman, who spent the summer in his shirt-sleeves, with a little dicky-bird of a wife waiting upon him. I am built rather on his lines of body and mind than any of the Doyles. We made a true friendship.

It seems that Michael Conan had a decisive and enduring influence on Arthur's reading habits and Arthur himself. He began to adopt Conan as part of his surname and returned from Paris entranced by the stories of mystery and imagination of Edgar Allan Poe, the American inventor of detective fiction—the genre that Arthur Conan Doyle would one day make his own.

JULES VERNE

Jules Verne was born in Nantes, France, in 1828, the son of a lawyer who sent him to Paris to study law. While there, he started writing plays and found a job as secretary of the *Théâtre Lyrique*. He published short stories and essays on scientific subjects and worked for several years as a stockbroker.

Around this time he was devising a new kind of story that merged science fact with fiction. The first of Verne's *Voyages Extraordinaires* (Extraordinary Journeys)—*Cinq Semaines en Ballon* (Five Weeks in a Balloon) was serialized firstly in a magazine in 1863 before becoming an international bestseller when it was published as a novel. Resigning from the stock market, he became a highly successful author, writing science fiction, as the new genre was called, including *Around the World in Eighty Days* and *20,000 Leagues Under the Sea*.

His books were translated into more than 140 languages, making him one of the most translated authors in history and many of his works have been filmed.

Jules Verne. Photographed by Felix Nadar in 1878.

EDGAR ALLAN POE

Edgar Allan Poe is generally considered as the inventor of detective fiction. He was born in Boston on January 19, 1809, the son of two actors, David and Eliza Poe. When Edgar was only two years old, his mother died and he was adopted by Mr. and Mrs. John Allan. A well-to-do merchant, Allan gave Edgar a good upbringing although their relationship later deteriorated.

In New York City Edgar struggled to make his way as a writer. In 1835, he landed a job as a newspaper editor in Richmond, Virginia and soon after married the love of his life, his cousin Virginia. He was twenty-seven and she was thirteen. Before long, he was unemployed again, moving back to New York where he continued to write. His first book of short stories, *Tales of the Grotesque and Arabesque* was published in 1839. It made no money, however.

He edited *Graham's Magazine* for two years and in 1841 published "The Murders in the Rue Morgue"—recognized as the first-ever detective story. He resigned from *Graham's* to launch his own magazine *The Stylus*. Unfortunately, it failed and he returned to New York. His 1843 story, "The Gold Bug" sold 300,000 copies but once again Edgar made very little from its sale.

In January 1845 Poe published his famous poem "The Raven." Noted for its musicality, stylized language, and supernatural atmosphere its publication and the writer's subsequent public performances of the poem made Poe a legend in his own lifetime, but somehow financial success still eluded him.

His wife Virginia died of tuberculosis in 1847, leaving Edgar desolate and ill, having been drinking heavily for a number of years. He died in Baltimore on October 7, 1849, at age forty, in mysterious circumstances. The cause of his death is unknown but may have been related to his alcoholism.

WILKIE COLLINS

English novelist, playwright and short story writer, Wilkie Collins, born in London in 1824, is sometimes referred to as the "grandfather of English detective fiction." His book *The Moonstone* (1868), is described by T.S. Eliot as "the first and greatest of English detective novels."

He recorded a catalog of firsts in writing the first detective story "A Stolen Letter" in 1854. His 1852 story "A Terribly Strange Bed" featured the first appearance of a police officer and the first woman detective appeared in "The Diary of Anne Rodway" of 1856. He wrote the first humorous detective story—"The Biter Bit"—in 1858. He can be said to have also been the first to use many of the features that would characterize the detective—the "inside job;" a famous, but eccentric detective; the country house murder; bungling police officers; procedural detail; false suspects; the "locked room murder;" reconstruction of a crime; and a final, surprising twist in the plot.

Collins was undoubtedly a great influence on Arthur Conan Doyle who borrowed several elements from Collins's characters for Sherlock Holmes. His best known works are *The Woman in White* (1859), *No Name* (1862), and *Armadale* (1866). He died in 1889, at age sixty-five.

CHAPTER 4

A MAN OF MEDICINE

On his return to Scotland, it was decided that Arthur would go to Edinburgh University to study medicine. It was as much as the family could afford. The experience of this particular university was altogether different to what university attendance entails today. At Edinburgh there were no colleges, no one lived in and there were no extracurricular activities. One simply attended the classes and passed the examinations. The fees were paid directly to the lecturers and if the exams were failed, there was no comeback; the money was lost.

It must have seemed like a sound decision to Mary and Charles. As a doctor, their son would always make a living and Arthur agreed with this pragmatic approach to his life. Edinburgh had an excellent reputation for medicine and its teachers were highly regarded. Arthur's sister Annette, now living in Portugal, helped with the fees, sending money home and another two of the children would soon be of an age when they would be able to bring money into the house. For his part, Arthur applied for numerous scholarships in an effort to ease the financial burden and it seemed that he had won one until he was told that only arts students were eligible for the £20 a year on offer. He eventually won a scholarship for just £7 a year. This meant that he had to find a job to be able to afford the university fees.

OUT INTO THE WORLD

In his first year he took courses in natural history, botany, chemistry, anatomy, and physiology but to earn some money and to get some medical experience, he took time off in 1878 to work in general practices in Sheffield and Shropshire. Later in his university career he also worked in Birmingham. Not only did it pay more, he also gained invaluable experience of treating the poorer inhabitants of the city and learned a little of the seedier side of life. Great background knowledge when it came to writing the Sherlock Holmes stories.

A WEARY GRIND

University was tough. It was a huge amount of work and the teaching he was receiving was not always to his satisfaction. He later summed up his five years of studying medicine:

I entered as a student in October 1876, and I emerged as a Bachelor of Medicine in August 1881. Between these two points lies one long weary grind at botany, chemistry, anatomy, physiology and a whole list of compulsory subjects, many of which have a very indirect bearing upon the art of curing.

However, while at Edinburgh University, Arthur encountered a wonderful array of bizarre characters among his teachers. There was Alexander Crum Brown (1838 – 1922), who taught chemistry. To the amusement of his students his experiments often turned out to be failures. Charles Wyville Thomson (1830 – 82) taught zoology, having just returned from his groundbreaking Challenger expedition that cataloged more than 4,000 new species. There was also the self-educated anatomist William Turner (1832 – 1916) who became principal of the university from 1903 until his death.

These men, in one form or another would all feature in the Sherlock Holmes stories but the most extraordinary character of all was Dr. Joseph Bell, who was the inspiration for Sherlock Holmes himself.

DR. JOSEPH BELL

Joseph Bell (1837 – 1911) was a lecturer at Edinburgh University but is probably better known as the inspiration for Sherlock Holmes. Bell was the grandson of a famous forensic surgeon Benjamin Bell (1749 – 1806), considered to be the first Scottish scientific surgeon and regarded as the father of the important Edinburgh school of surgery. Benjamin Bell emphasized close observation when making a diagnosis. His grandson, Joseph, followed his example, developing his observational skills to an astonishing degree. He was able, for example, to establish the departure point of sailors by observing their tattoos; from an examination of a hand, he could name the owner's profession; and he could immediately tell from a man's face whether or not he was a drinker.

Bell was a wonderful teacher, but was also a poet, cricketer, boxer, and tennis player. He had knowledge of nature, dialects, and handwriting and could shoot and ice-skate. He took part in numerous police investigations, including the case of Jack the Ripper. He is said to have provided copious notes on the case and even named the culprit. Unfortunately, however, the notes have been lost.

Arthur Conan Doyle was deeply impressed by Bell. He gave Sherlock Holmes Bell's manner of thinking and even his physique. They shared the same dynamic walk, narrow nose, gray eyes, angled chin, and high forehead. Even the clothes of Sherlock Holmes were borrowed from Bell—the long coat and the deerstalker hat. In congratulating Conan Doyle on his first Sherlock Holmes novel, *A Study in Scarlet*, the writer of *The Jungle Book*, Rudyard Kipling immediately deduced that Holmes was based on Bell, saying: "Isn't he my old friend, Dr. Joe?"

Bell was aware of his influence on Holmes and, indeed, was extremely proud of it.

A VITAL INFLUENCE

Joseph Bell certainly changed Arthur Conan Doyle's life, and made a huge impression on him. He later described Bell in full flow:

For some reason which I have never understood he singled me out from the drove of students who frequented his wards and made me his out-patient clerk, which meant that I had to array his out-patients, make simple notes of their cases, and then show them in, one by one, to the large room in which Bell sat in state surrounded by his Dressers and students. Then I had ample chance of studying his methods and of noticing that he often learned more of the patient by a few quick glances than I had done by my questions. Occasionally the results were very dramatic, though there were times when he blundered. In one of his best cases he said to a civilian patient:

"Well, my man, you've served in the army."
"Aye, sir."
"Not long discharged?"
"No, sir."
"A Highland regiment?"
"Aye, sir."
"A non-com officer?"
"Aye, sir."
"Stationed at Barbados?"
"Aye, sir."

"You see gentlemen," he would explain, "the man was a respectful man but did not remove his hat. They do not in the army, but he would have learned civilian ways had he been long discharged. He has an air of authority and he is obviously Scottish. As to Barbados, his complaint is elephantiasis, which is West Indian and not British ..."

It is no wonder that after the study of such a character I used and amplified his methods when in later life I tried to build up a scientific detective who solved cases on his own merits and not through the folly of the criminal.

But Bell was not the only person that Arthur turned into a major character. There was also Professor William Rutherford (1839 – 99), teacher of physiology and anatomy, whom he used as the model for one of his other fictional characters, Professor Challenger.

COPING WITH CHARLES

In 1879, Charles Doyle entered a nursing home for what would be the first of a number of times. His condition had deteriorated in recent years and often he did not get out of bed. Not only did he have a serious drink problem, he was also epileptic. He was unhappy in Scotland, had turned against his Catholic religion and was devastated by what he considered his own failure. Mary could no longer cope, admitting that he needed professional help.

A man named Bryan Waller (1853 – 1932) had come on the scene in 1876. He was a doctor from a well-off Yorkshire family in his final year of medical studies. Waller's family contained some literary figures and he had published a book of romantic poems, *The Twilight Land*. This captivated the impressionable Mary and when the Doyles wanted a lodger, Waller moved in. In April 1876, a difficult situation arose. Arthur was coming home from school in June of that year, but was disappointed to learn that his mother would not be there to welcome him. Instead, she would be at Masongill, the Waller mansion in Thornton in Lonsdale which was, in fact, only thirty miles from Stonyhurst. Arthur was too naive to suspect anything but Waller and his mother had evidently become very close.

A SAILOR'S LIFE

Thus, when Charles went into the nursing home, Mary headed for Masongill, leaving nineteen-year-old Arthur in charge in Edinburgh. At the beginning of the following year, however, Arthur made an extraordinary decision. One of his friends had to give up the position of surgeon on the whaling ship, the *Hope,* that was sailing from Peterhead to the Arctic. Arthur decided to interrupt his university course and take his place. Life on a whaler in those days was perilous and there was constant danger of serious injury or death. But Arthur could not resist the temptation to travel in search of adventure. His family and friends were, needless to say, horrified.

He had a wonderful experience, traveling with a crew of fifty hardened sailors who liked nothing more than to share their tales of adventure with the young surgeon. He wrote beguilingly of this time in his autobiography:

The perpetual light, the glare of the white ice, the deep blue of the water, these are the things which one remembers most clearly, and the dry, crisp, exhilarating air, which makes mere life the keenest of pleasures. And then there are the innumerable sea-birds, whose call is for ever ringing in your ears—the gulls, the fulmars, the snow-birds, the burgomasters, the looms and the rotjes. These fill the air, and below, the waters are for ever giving you a peep of some strange new creature. The commercial whale may not often come your way, but his less valuable brethren abound on every side ... I went on board the whaler a big straggling youth, I came off it a powerful, well-grown man. I have no doubt that my physical health during my whole life has been affected by that splendid air, and that the inexhaustible store of energy which I have enjoyed is to some extent drawn from the same source.

FIRST PUBLICATION

By this time, Arthur was writing in whatever free time he could grab. He was not immediately eager to publish nor was he

Arthur on the deck of the whaler *Eira* on July 12, 1880. From left to right: David Gray at the helm (Captain of the *Eclipse*), Benjamin Leigh-Smith (Captain/owner of the *Eira*), Arthur Conan Doyle (Surgeon of the *Hope*), John Gray (Captain of the *Hope*), Dr. Walker, Dr. Neale, with William Lofley (ice master of the *Eira*) behind.

keen for his name to be appended to the stories if they were published. To this end, he submitted a few articles to magazines but asked for them to be published anonymously. The stories were quickly snapped up, the Edinburgh weekly *Chambers' Journal* giving Arthur three guineas as payment for "The Mystery of the Sarassa Valley," a story set in Africa. "The American's Tale" was published by the *London Society Magazine*. The young writer was, naturally, delighted and extremely surprised. But he had to continue with his studies in the meantime.

Arthur Conan Doyle (age 22) graduating from Edinburgh University, 1881.

THE WONDERFUL POISE OF THE UNIVERSE

Crucially, at this time Arthur was re-assessing his faith and came to the conclusion that the Roman Catholic Church had it all wrong. He became agnostic but was not prepared to become atheist, as he wrote:

I had a very keen perception of the wonderful poise of the universe and the tremendous power of conception and sustenance which it implied.

Arthur called himself Unitarian at the time. Unitarianism was a liberal theological movement that believed in the unitary nature of God but rejected the doctrines of the Trinity, original sin, predestination, and the fact that the Bible is without error in all its teaching. But Unitarianism was no more than a stopping-off point in his moral search. He believed that death was no more than a passage to something far greater. The crew of the *Hope* had shared some spiritual experiences they had had with him and when he returned he was ready for his spiritualist journey.

DR. CONAN DOYLE, I PRESUME

Back in Edinburgh, Arthur Conan Doyle was awarded his medical degree and visited his family and friends whom he had not seen for so long. But almost immediately he surprised everyone by signing up for another voyage, this time on the cargo ship, SS *Mayumba*, leaving Liverpool for Madeira on October 22, 1881 with thirty passengers on board. Conan Doyle suffered from terrible seasickness on the first part of this voyage, much more so than on the *Hope* but he still had to earn the twelve pounds a month he was being paid to look after the passengers and crew.

The vessel arrived in Freetown in Sierra Leone on November 9, 1881 before traveling on to Liberia where Conan Doyle spent three days with the United States Ambassador and the black abolitionist Henry Highland Garnet (1815 – 82). On the coast of Africa, Conan Doyle hunted alligators, swam in shark-infested waters and hiked in the jungle. When he reached Lagos in Nigeria on November 18, he was ill with a fever, probably malaria. It was a serious condition and a frightening experience, as he vividly described later:

I remember staggering to my bunk and then all was blotted out. As I was myself doctor there was no one to look after me and I lay for several days fighting it out with Death in a very small ring and without a second. It speaks well for my constitution that I came out a victor. I remember no psychic experience, no vision, no fears, nothing save a nightmare fog from which I emerged as weak as a child. It must have been a close call, and I had scarcely sat up before I heard that another victim who got it at the same time was dead.

Africa was a dangerous and sometimes frightening place to be but Conan Doyle often encountered the missionaries who were trying to convert the local people. Although he was

not convinced they would save many souls, he did at least think, in the characteristic Victorian way, that they would "civilize" people. He was only twenty-two years old but was experiencing far more than the average man of his generation.

He arrived back in Liverpool in the middle of January 1882 and returned home boldly announcing to his mother that he was renouncing Roman Catholicism. She accepted it stoically and also helped him make up his mind what to do next. He realized that the time had come to settle down.

Doctor Conan Doyle in 1882.

PART TWO

★ ★ ★

THE ARRIVAL OF
MR. SHERLOCK
HOLMES

★ ★ ★

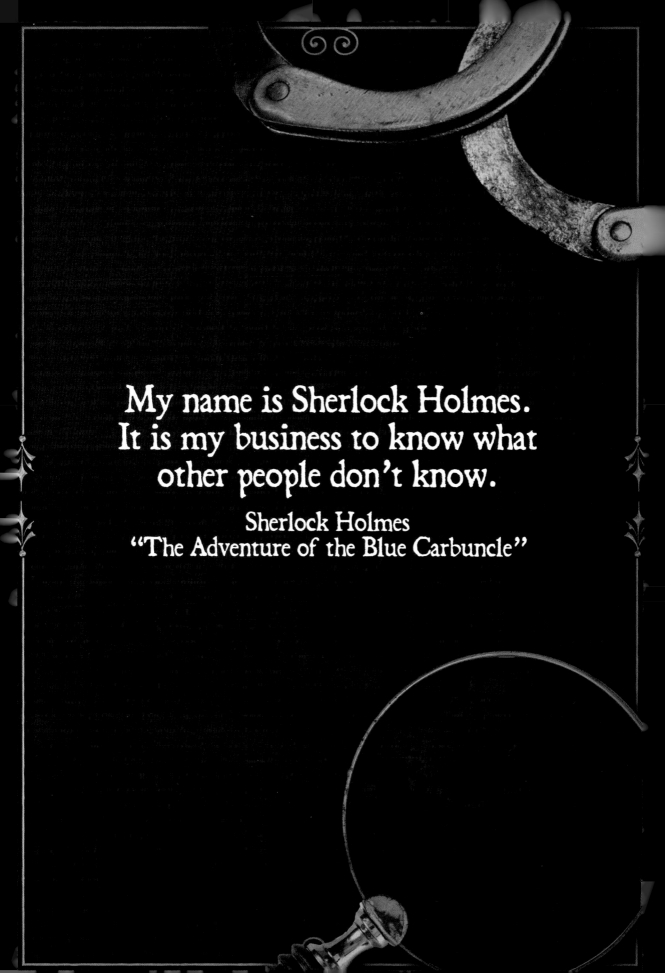

My name is Sherlock Holmes.
It is my business to know what
other people don't know.

Sherlock Holmes
"The Adventure of the Blue Carbuncle"

CHAPTER 5

IF THE SPIRIT IS WILLING

A job appeared out of nowhere in May 1882. George Turnavine Budd had been an acquaintance of Arthur Conan Doyle's in Edinburgh. They had played rugby together, when he found Budd to be "rather handicapped by the Berserk fury with which he would play." Budd was a very bright and ambitious man but was not one of the most reliable. A former bankrupt, he had created something of a stir by eloping with an under-age girl who was a ward of court. Budd wrote explaining that his doctor's surgery was doing very well in Plymouth and suggested that Conan Doyle come and join him. Everyone advised against going and Conan Doyle himself was unsure. His mother, Mary, advised her son to write asking for some financial figures, but this received an angry reply from Budd:

Your letter to hand. Why not call me a liar at once? I tell you that I have seen thirty thousand patients in the last year. My actual takings have been more than four thousand pounds. All patients come to me. We would not cross the street to see Queen Victoria. You can have all visiting, all surgery, all midwifery. Will guarantee three hundred pounds the first year.

Budd was an extraordinary character. He made his money from medicine by providing free consultations but charging for the drugs he prescribed. And he prescribed a lot, distributing it, Conan Doyle later said, in a "heroic and indiscriminate manner." He also admitted that his description of Dr. Cullingworth in his 1895 epistolary novel, *The Stark Munro Letters* was an accurate description of George Budd's outlandish bedside manner:

One poor old lady he greeted with a perfect scream. "You've been drinking too much tea!" he cried. "You are suffering from tea poisoning!" Then, without allowing her to get a word in, he clutched her by her crackling black mantle, dragged her up to the table, and held out a copy of Taylor's Medical Jurisprudence which was lying there. "Put your hand on the book," he thundered, "and swear that for fourteen days you will drink nothing but cocoa." She swore with upturned eyes, and was instantly whirled off with her label in her hand, to the dispensary.

So, against everyone's advice, Conan Doyle traveled to Plymouth. Although he wanted to believe what Budd was saying, he soon witnessed Budd's half-mad performances, alternately friendly and then callous toward him. Conan Doyle recalled a day in Budd's surgery in his memoirs:

Dropsy had disappeared before a severe dose of croton oil in a way that set all the gossips talking. People flocked into the town from 20 and 30 miles around, and not only his waiting rooms, but his stairs and his passages were crammed. His behavior to them was extraordinary. He roared and shouted, scolded them, joked them, pushed them about, and pursued them sometimes into the street, or addressed them collectively from the landing. A morning with him when practice was in full blast was as funny as any pantomime and I was exhausted with laughter.

Mary was now writing letters to her son advising him to escape the clutches of Budd as soon as he could. But when Budd accidentally got his hands on one of these letters he threw

Conan Doyle out anyway, telling him to set up his own practice. They argued and, eventually calming down, Budd suggested it was probably best that they separate and offered Conan Doyle a pound a week to go and establish himself in another town.

MOVING TO PORTSMOUTH

Accepting the offer, Conan Doyle decided to move to Portsmouth. Budd, of course, was true to type and the pound a week soon dried up, leaving Conan Doyle with only around ten pounds to his name, hardly enough to launch a new practice. His mother helped him out and, for forty pounds a year, Conan Doyle rented a house named Bush Villa in Southsea, just outside Portsmouth. It was tough and he made a living only through selling the drugs that he managed to buy wholesale. It was highly competitive in Portsmouth, but Conan Doyle refused to make money out of his patients in the way Budd did. His weight plummeted and he often went hungry. He only obtained butter-milk and tea by providing free treatment to a local grocer suffering from epilepsy. He was even forced to pawn his watch.

Gradually, however, business got better and although he really could not afford it, he hired a housekeeper. He also joined sports clubs, played football, and captained Portsmouth cricket club. He did all this partly to get himself known and it paid off. More affluent people began to attend his surgery. But he would have probably played sport whatever the circumstances. He was a man with a considerable amount of energy that needed an outlet.

PUBLISHING ANONYMOUSLY

He was also reading and writing. He devoured books, on any subject—even reference books—and also delivered lectures on his favorite authors at the Portsmouth Literary and Scientific Society. His story, "J. Habakuk Jephson's Statement," was printed in the prestigious *Cornhill Magazine*. Conan Doyle and his mother were both astonished that his work was being published, but they were even more delighted by the fee of twenty-nine guineas.

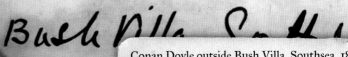

Conan Doyle outside Bush Villa, Southsea, 1882.

The story was released anonymously in 1884 and one reviewer reckoned it was the work of Robert Louis Stevenson (1850 – 94) while others believed Edgar Allan Poe must have written it.

He also began a novel around this time, *The Firm of Girdlestone*, which was eventually published in 1890.

Other essays and stories appeared in *Boy's Own Paper* and the weekly literary magazine *All the Year Round*. He sent off one novel, *The Narrative of John Smith*, but it was lost in the post and he did not have another copy. Of course, not every piece of work he sent off was accepted and, after "J. Habakuk Jephson's Statement," the *Cornhill Magazine* had rejected a few pieces he had sent them. Undeterred, he carried on writing, including letters to the national newspapers and medical journals such as *The Lancet* and *The Medical Times*.

TWO YEARS WITH INNES

Meanwhile, although improving, his medical work was still far from satisfactory. In his first year he earned one hundred and fifty-four pounds, in his second two hundred and fifty and in his third three hundred pounds. This was far below the one thousand pounds a year he claimed he was earning in his letters home. The arrival of his younger brother Innes lightened the mood. Conan Doyle dressed the ten-year-old boy in a page's uniform and he opened the door for patients and performed other tasks around the surgery. They enjoyed each other's company immensely and Innes remained in Portsmouth until he went to boarding school in Yorkshire two years later in 1885. Needless to say, Conan Doyle was very sad to see him go and missed him hugely.

"TOUIE"

A dashing young doctor and sportsman, Conan Doyle was regarded as quite a catch, and local mothers were keen for their unmarried daughters to get to know him better. One girl to whom he took a liking was Louisa Hawkins. He had been asked by another doctor to take over the case of a boy, Jack Hawkins, suffering from cerebral meningitis. Conan Doyle did everything he could to make the boy comfortable, even caring for him in his own home, but there was little to be done and the boy died. Jack's mother and sister were very appreciative of what he had done and soon Conan Doyle and Jack's sister, Louisa, became romantically involved. Louisa was a pleasant-looking, quiet, reserved girl whose nickname was "Touie." She could sing, play piano and was a skilful artist. The two got on very well and, although Mary Doyle was not convinced that Louisa was the best choice for her son, they were married on August 6, 1885.

Louisa brought with her an allowance of one hundred pounds a year from her family which certainly eased her husband's financial situation. However, it was a hurried marriage and, although Conan Doyle was genuinely fond of Louisa, he undoubtedly later regretted rushing into it.

VOICES FROM BEYOND

Conan Doyle's interest in spiritualism was beginning to increase. He had heard an American medium talking in 1880 and now decided to investigate it further. The Portsmouth spiritualist leader, J. Horstead, had acquired a reputation for being the conduit of the words of John Wesley, founder of Methodism. He also received the voices of a number of dead Liberal politicians. There were many charlatans, of course, in this field, but Horstead avoided some of the excesses of the others whose meetings were dramatic events with smoke and screams.

After Horstead's death, the main figure in Portsmouth spiritualist circles was retired army officer, Major-General Alfred W. Drayson (1827 – 1901), who was also a writer. Some of Drayson's stories had been published in the same magazines as Conan Doyle, and the two men hit it off. Drayson got Conan Doyle interested in mesmerism, and hypnotism went on to feature in Conan Doyle's story of the supernatural, "John

Barrington Cowles," published in *Cassell's Saturday Journal* in April 1884.

Just before he married Louisa, Conan Doyle's story, "The Great Keinplatz Experiment" was published in *Belgravia Magazine*. The plot also dealt with mesmerism, detailing the case of a professor who managed through hypnotism to move his spirit into the body of another man and vice-versa.

COMING UNDER THE SPELL

Conan Doyle took part in a séance but it was fairly inconclusive, leaving him undecided as to its veracity, even though the table had moved and messages were delivered. It was Major-General Drayson who convinced him that there was truth in spiritualism. Falling under the spell of this intelligent and reliable man, Conan Doyle began to regard him as something of a genius—"a very distinguished thinker," as he described him.

He became a regular at séances and read the spiritualist journal, *Light*. Some of the séances, however, were very obviously fraudulent. Ropes and pulleys were visible and the voices were very clearly coming from cupboards. When Conan Doyle brought this up, Drayson argued that because a few spiritualists were fraudulent did not mean that the entire concept was. Drayson went on to introduce Conan Doyle to Buddhism and its core concepts of re-incarnation and karma as well as Madame Blavatsky's Theosophical Society.

THE RELIGIOUS FRAME OF MIND

In an effort to prove to himself that there was some truth in spiritualism, Conan Doyle decided to hold a séance in his own house. Unfortunately, the sittings he held proved inconclusive, as he later wrote:

I have no psychical powers myself, and those who worked with me had little more. Among us we could just muster enough of the magnetic force, or whatever you will call it, to get the table movements with their

suspicious and often stupid messages. I still have notes of those sittings and copies of some, at least, of the messages. They were not always absolutely stupid. For example, I find that on one occasion, on my asking some test question, such as how many coins I had in my pocket, the table spelt out: "We are here to educate and to elevate, not to guess riddles." And then: "The religious frame of mind, not the critical, is what we wish to inculcate." Now, no one can say that that was a puerile message. On the other hand, I was always haunted by the fear of involuntary pressure from the hands of sitters.

Drayson passed on Conan Doyle's tutelage in matters spiritual to a man named Henry Ball and soon Conan Doyle was so convinced about spiritualism that he wrote a very important letter to *Light* in which he expressed his conviction that this phenomenon was real:

I could no more doubt the existence of the phenomena than I could doubt the existence of lions in Africa, though I have been to that continent and have never chanced to see one.

He went on to describe a séance he had recently attended, describing the medium, an elderly gentleman, writing a message to each of the attendees. To Conan Doyle he wrote:

This gentleman is a healer. Tell him from me not to read Leigh Hunt's book.

Conan Doyle had earlier mentioned in the letter that he had considered buying that author's *Comic Dramatists of the Restoration* a few days before the séance. He described the message as "inexplicable."

So gradually Conan Doyle was convinced and emerged as a full-blown believer in spiritualism. It showed great courage to do so because, although not devalued to the extent that it is today, it was still a marginal, fringe belief. It was all the more serious, of course, because Conan Doyle was a doctor and the medical profession did not take kindly to one of its own harboring such beliefs.

SPIRITUALISM IN VICTORIAN BRITAIN

In 1848, a new quasi-religious movement emerged from upstate New York. Two girls, the Fox sisters—Margaret (1833 – 93) and Kate (1837 – 92)—claimed that they had contacted the spirit of a murdered man in their house who communicated with them by means of loud knocks. Although the sisters confessed in 1888 that it was a hoax, they created a sensation and the spiritualist movement was born.

The normal routine was for spirits to communicate at séances using mediums who were normally women as the female sex was deemed to possess more sensitive nervous systems than men. Male mediums were often abused and despised. Although expressly forbidden in the Bible, communicating with spirits became hugely popular and was seen as a dissenting belief.

Spiritualism became even more popular in 1852 when the American medium Mrs. Hayden arrived in Britain and conducted séances with many celebrated names of London society. It spread and became popular in the north of England where there was already a dissenting tradition. Bizarrely, many scientists also embraced spiritualism and in 1892, the Society for Psychical Research was founded, its objective to investigate mesmerism, spiritualism, and ghost stories. It melded the latest developments in the physical and psychological sciences in order to find proof of the existence of life after death.

In the 1880s, London was home to many mystical societies and there was a revival of magic. Madame Helena Blavatsky (1831 – 91), medium for messages from the Mahatmas, made her home there and founded her Theosophical Society— described by her as "the synthesis of science, religion, and philosophy." The Hermetic Order of the Golden Dawn provided a focus for those who sought Hermetic secrets. Among its members were the Irish poet William Butler Yeats (1865 – 1939), Welsh fantasy and horror writer Arthur Machen (1863 – 1947), and occultist Aleister Crowley (1875 – 1947).

The Fox sisters in 1852. From left to right: Margaret Fox, Kate Fox, and Leah Fox Fish.

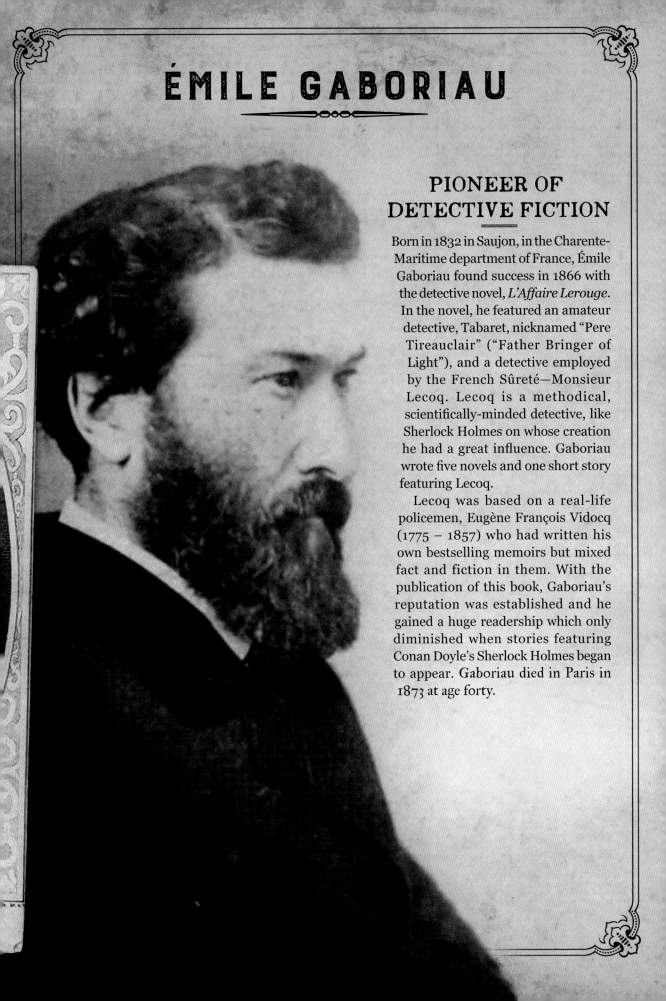

ÉMILE GABORIAU

PIONEER OF DETECTIVE FICTION

Born in 1832 in Saujon, in the Charente-Maritime department of France, Émile Gaboriau found success in 1866 with the detective novel, *L'Affaire Lerouge*. In the novel, he featured an amateur detective, Tabaret, nicknamed "Pere Tireauclair" ("Father Bringer of Light"), and a detective employed by the French Sûreté—Monsieur Lecoq. Lecoq is a methodical, scientifically-minded detective, like Sherlock Holmes on whose creation he had a great influence. Gaboriau wrote five novels and one short story featuring Lecoq.

Lecoq was based on a real-life policemen, Eugène François Vidocq (1775 – 1857) who had written his own bestselling memoirs but mixed fact and fiction in them. With the publication of this book, Gaboriau's reputation was established and he gained a huge readership which only diminished when stories featuring Conan Doyle's Sherlock Holmes began to appear. Gaboriau died in Paris in 1873 at age forty.

CHAPTER 6

A STUDY IN SCARLET

Arthur Conan Doyle was, as ever, reading avidly and among the books by his bedside were a number of detective novels. They were, on the whole, poor, with formulaic plots and weak characters. What irritated him most, however, was how the unraveling of the mysteries left the reader dissatisfied. Coincidence, simple confession and mistakes made by the criminals were the usual means by which the crimes were solved. Of course, there were some that were a cut above the rest:

Gaboriau had rather attracted me by the neat dovetailing of his plots, and Poe's masterful detective, M. Dupin, has from boyhood been one of my heroes. But could I bring an addition of my own?

Thus, Conan Doyle's decision to write detective stories was a commercial one. He had spotted a gap in the market for intelligent stories with intelligent plots, convincing characters and solutions to the mysteries based on logic and reasoning.

Of course, he needed a name for his detective. The name he first decided on was "Sherringford Holmes." He even devised the name of the first story in which he would feature—"The Tangled Skein." Then he had second thoughts, deciding that the name was a little complicated.

Soon, he had come up with "Sherlock" as the Christian name for his hero. Patrick Sherlock had been a fellow pupil of Conan Doyle's at Stonyhurst, and Sherlock was also the maiden name of his Aunt Jane (the wife of Henry Doyle). As for the title of that first story? It would be *A Study in Scarlet*.

Conan Doyle polished off *A Study in Scarlet* and sent it to James Payn (1830 – 98), experienced editor of the *Cornhill Magazine* where he had already enjoyed some success. But Payn rejected the story, apparently

because of its length. It was too short to be serialized and too long to go into the magazine as a stand-alone piece.

Undeterred (Conan Doyle was never upset by criticism), he sent the book out to a couple of other publishers and after more rejections it was finally accepted by Ward, Lock & Co. To his chagrin, he was offered only twenty-five pounds. He had little option but to accept it. His funds were low and he was eager for publication. Unfortunately, it took a while to appear. The publisher wrote to him explaining the delay:

We could not publish it this year ... the market is flooded at present with cheap fiction.

GOOD REVIEWS

A Study in Scarlet, the first of the four Sherlock Holmes novels, appeared in *Beeton's Christmas Annual* of 1887, illustrated by D.H. Friston (1820 – 1906). In July 1888, Ward, Lock & Co. published it in book form with illustrations by Conan Doyle's father, Charles. The *Glasgow Herald* gave it a good review after it appeared in *Beeton's*:

The piece de resistance is a story by A. Conan Doyle entitled "A Study in Scarlet." It is the story of a murderer, and of the preternatural sagacity of a scientific detective, to whom Edgar Allan Poe's Dupin was a trifler, and Gaboriau's Lecoq a child. He is a wonderful man is Mr. Sherlock Holmes, but one gets so wonderfully interested in his cleverness and in the mysterious murder which he unravels that one cannot lay down the narrative until the end is reached.

PRICE ONE SHILLING.

BEETON'S CHRISTMAS ANNUAL

A STUDY IN SCARLET

By A. CONAN DOYLE

Containing also
Two Original
DRAWING ROOM PLAYS.

I.

FOOD FOR POWDER
By R. ANDRE

2

THE FOUR LEAVED SHAMROCK
By C. J. HAMILTON

WITH ENGRAVINGS
BY D. H. FRISTON
MATT STRETCH.

Beeton's Christmas Annual, 1887, with *A Study in Scarlet* on the front cover. The magazine featured the very first appearance of Sherlock Holmes.

A STUDY IN SCARLET

PART I: THE REMINISCENCES OF JOHN H. WATSON, M.D.

One morning, Dr. Watson reads a newspaper article about deduction and dismisses it as "ineffable twaddle." Sherlock Holmes announces that he, in fact, wrote the article and explains to Watson that he has "a turn both for observation and for deduction." He confesses he is a "consulting detective" and the regular visitors he receives are his clients:

Well, I have a trade of my own. I suppose I am the only one in the world. I'm a consulting detective, if you can understand what that is. Here in London we have lots of Government detectives and lots of private ones. When these fellows are at fault they come to me, and I manage to put them on the right scent. They lay all the evidence before me, and I am generally able, by the help of my knowledge of the history of crime, to set them straight.

Holmes is working on a case and takes Watson to an abandoned house near Brixton Road. Approaching the building, Holmes carefully examines the pavement and garden. They meet Police Inspectors Gregson and Lestrade and examine the crime scene, Holmes using a magnifying glass and a tape measure. A man, named Enoch Drebber, who has been in London with his secretary, Joseph Stangerson, has been killed there. There is blood but the corpse has no wound on it. Written on a wall in blood is the word *"RACHE"* which Holmes points out is German for "revenge." He deduces that the victim has been poisoned and that the perpetrator is six feet tall, has small feet, a florid complexion, wears square-toed boots and smokes a Trichinopoly cigar. The fingernails of his right hand are long and he arrived at the house in a cab whose horse had three old shoes and one new one. The writing of the word

"RACHE" on the wall, he insists, is deliberately designed to fool the police. The body is moved and a woman's gold wedding ring is discovered. They learn that a drunk man had been seen in the street outside the house by the policeman who discovered the body.

Holmes sends some telegrams and takes an advertisement in the newspaper announcing that the ring had been found. He suspects that the murderer will respond in an effort to retrieve the ring. Sure enough, an old woman turns up claiming the ring is her daughter's. Holmes gives her a duplicate of the ring he has had made and follows her on the back of her cab but she vanishes. Holmes says that she was the murderer in disguise.

An arrest is made. It is the older brother of a girl who lived at the boarding house where Drebber and Stangerson had stayed prior to the murder. Drebber had tried to kiss the girl and the two men had been evicted. The brother had chased Drebber with a cudgel, but is claiming that he had lost him.

Lestrade arrives with news that Stangerson has been murdered, stabbed in the heart in his hotel and again *"RACHE"* has been scrawled in blood on the wall. At the scene a novel, a pipe, and a small box containing two pills are found. One of the pills contains poison.

A boy named Wiggins arrives at the door. He is the leader of the Baker Street Irregulars, a group of homeless children that Holmes employs to help him occasionally. He announces that he has found the cab that Holmes had requested. Holmes asks him to send up the cab-driver, pretending to have luggage to be carried downstairs. When the cabby arrives and bends to pick up Holmes's trunk, the detective suddenly handcuffs the man. Holmes announces that the man is Jefferson Hope, killer of Drebber and Stangerson.

PART II: THE COUNTRY OF THE SAINTS

The next section of the tale takes us to Salt Lake Valley in Utah where John Ferrier and a girl named Lucy, sole survivors of a band of pioneers, are rescued in the desert by a group of Mormons. Led by Brigham Young, President of the Church of Jesus Christ of the Latter-Day Saints, the Mormons allow Ferrier and Lucy to live with them as long as they embrace the Mormon faith. Years later, Lucy becomes engaged to marry Jefferson Hope, a young non-Mormon man who is working away from the valley.

Brigham Young tells Ferrier that Lucy should not be permitted to marry a man outside their faith. Instead, she should marry either Joseph Stangerson or Enoch Drebber, sons of two Mormon leaders. Lucy is given a month to decide. Ferrier sends a message to Hope, but each night the number of days remaining for Lucy to make a decision is painted threateningly somewhere on the farm.

Hope finally arrives the night before the last day and succeeds in getting Lucy and Ferrier away but while he is hunting for food Ferrier is murdered and Lucy taken away and married to Drebber. A month later she dies of a broken heart. Hope swears revenge but a heart problem forces him to leave Salt Lake City.

Several years later, when he returns, Hope learns that Drebber and Stangerson have left town after a conflict among the Mormon community, fleeing to Cleveland and then to Europe. The cab driver whom Holmes has handcuffed is, in fact, Jefferson Hope. He had tracked the two men down to Euston Station where they were due to take a train to Liverpool but Drebber had insisted on returning to the boarding house and the girl but was accosted by her brother. He had instructed Stangerson, meanwhile, to take the train and await him at their hotel.

Drebber had summoned a cab driven by the disguised Hope who had taken him to the house near Brixton Road, where he made him choose a pill from the two in a box he had in his pocket. Drebber chose the poisoned pill and as he lay dying, Hope had shown him

Lucy's wedding ring. His heart condition, plus the excitement of the moment gave Hope a nosebleed and he used the blood to write on the wall. As he left the building, he remembered he had left the wedding ring behind but it was too late because police was already on the scene.

He made his way to Stangerson's hotel, climbed in the window and stabbed him when Stangerson attacked him. Hope dies of a heart attack caused by his condition the night before he is due to appear in court, but when found he has a smile on his face.

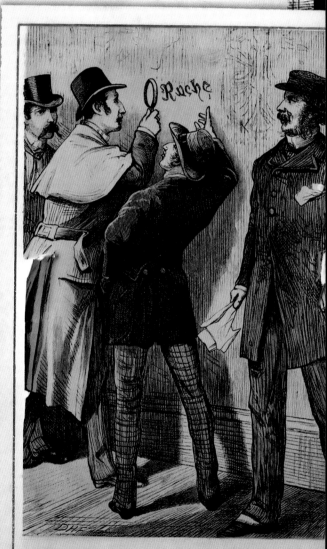

"He examined with his glass the word upon the wall, going over every letter of it with the most minute exactness." (Page 25.)

He examined with his glass the word upon the wall, going over every letter of it with the most minute exactness. The first characterization of Sherlock Holmes by D.H. Friston, from *Beeton's Christmas Annual*, 1887.

47

THE LONDON OF SHERLOCK HOLMES

In the time of Sherlock Holmes, London was the largest city in the world, attracting people of every nationality. Sir Arthur Conan Doyle exploited the cosmopolitan city life in his stories, introducing exotic poisons and snakes from South America, rare jewels from India, and military spies from Germany. John O'Connor's painting of 1884 captures the mysterious, menacing atmosphere of Pentonville Road, with the gothic spires of the St. Pancras railway station in the background.

CHAPTER 7

THE SIGN OF THE FOUR

At this point in his literary career, Conan Doyle was determined to establish himself not as a writer of detective stories, but as a historical novelist. In the middle of 1887, he began work on a novel, *Micah Clarke*, set in the seventeenth century. Published two years later, the book was not received enthusiastically. James Payn angrily rejected it, writing to Conan Doyle:

How can you, how can you waste your time and your wits writing historical novels!

Other publishers also rejected it for its lack of commercial potential. They were right. It did not sell well when finally published by Longman, only performing better after the Sherlock Holmes stories boosted the reputation of its author.

Interestingly, *A Study in Scarlet* sold well in the United States, although Conan Doyle did not benefit financially from the success. In 1889 he was approached by Lippincott's, the magazine and book publisher in Philadelphia, who wanted another Sherlock Holmes story.

DINING WITH OSCAR WILDE

Although Conan Doyle was not taken seriously by the literary world in general, he found one fan at a dinner in London thrown by Lippincott's. The great Irish writer Oscar Wilde (1854 – 1900) had read *Micah Clarke* and Conan Doyle spent a memorable evening in his company. Wilde had also agreed to write for Lippincott's and the work he produced for them was *The Picture of Dorian Gray*. Conan Doyle signed a contract with the publisher to deliver a 40,000-word novel to them for one hundred pounds. The book he planned to write was *The Sign of the Four* which appeared in the February 1890 edition of *Lippincott's Magazine*.

The Sign of the Four featured on the front cover of *Lippincott's Monthly Magazine* in February 1890.

BECOMING A WORKAHOLIC

The Sign of the Four was, on the whole, well-reviewed and Conan Doyle resolving to capitalize on its success, created for himself a daily schedule that was both daunting and demanding. He was invariably late to bed and up early next morning, at work by about 7:30 a.m. He had experimented to ascertain how much sleep he could get by with at night, sometimes allowing himself only four hours. But it was very difficult and not always possible to maintain, especially if work was going badly. In fact, when he was unable to write or was misfiring, he was more likely to become tired but he tended to smoke a lot more and eat badly or not at all when he was working hard. Nonetheless, he displayed great willpower and strength of spirit to work the way he did.

THE WHITE COMPANY AND DISAPPOINTMENT

In 1890, Conan Doyle published the historical novel, *The White Company*, set in England, France, and Spain during the Hundred Years' War. He researched it extensively, reading around a hundred books. The novel—a companion work to the later *Sir Nigel*—was serialized in the *Cornhill Magazine* during 1891. Now little read, *The White Company* sold well for forty years but was poorly reviewed. Nonetheless, Conan Doyle was very proud of these two books:

> *I have no hesitation in saying that the two of them taken together did thoroughly achieve my purpose, that they made an accurate picture of that great age ... They form the most complete, satisfying and ambitious thing that I have ever done. All things find their level, but I believe that if I had never touched Holmes, who has tended to obscure my higher work, my position in literature would at the present be a more commanding one.*

A BABY AND A TRIP TO BERLIN

In 1890, Conan Doyle's sister Annette died, but a few months before her death he and Louisa had a baby daughter, Mary Louise. Although the thirty-one-year-old doctor seemed to have everything, he was dissatisfied. He longed to travel, and yearned for adventure. He decided almost on a whim to indulge his passion for adventure by traveling to Berlin. There, Dr. Robert Koch (1843 – 1910) was using a process called lymphinoculation as a method for curing tuberculosis which was the scourge of Europe at the time.

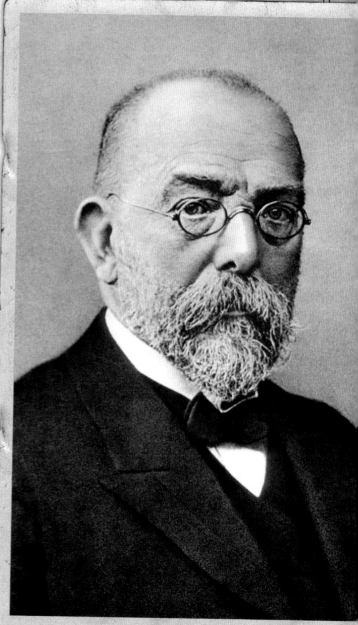

Dr. Robert Koch, age 57, in 1900.

THE SIGN OF THE FOUR

The Sign of the Four introduces for the first time Dr. Watson's future wife, Mary Morstan.

In 1878, Mary's father, who had returned from military service in India, had sent a telegram, asking her to meet him at the Langham Hotel in London. When she arrived at the hotel, however, she was informed that her father had gone out the previous night and had failed to return. Mary had contacted her father's only friend, Major John Sholto, who had been in the same regiment as him but had retired to England. He claimed not even to have known that her father was back in England.

Every year since 1882, an anonymous person has been sending Mary a pearl in the post. The last pearl she had received was accompanied by a letter saying that she had been wronged and requesting a meeting.

Having accepted the case, Holmes quickly discovers that Major Sholto had died in 1882 and it was shortly after his death that the pearls began to arrive, implying a connection between the two. Mary provides Holmes with a map of a fortress that was found in her father's desk along with the names Jonathan Small, Mahomet Singh, Abdullah Khan and Dost Akbar.

The pearls had been sent by Major Sholto's son, Thaddeus who confirms to Holmes, Watson and Mary that his father had seen Mary's father the night he disappeared. They met to discuss a priceless artifact that the major had brought back from India. The two men had quarreled and Captain Morstan had a heart attack and died.

Sholto was concerned that it might look as if he had killed Morstan, especially as he struck his head on a table when he fell. He was also reluctant to draw attention to the artifact he had brought home from India. Therefore he had disposed of the body and hidden the object. But Major Sholto is dying and his health deteriorated after receipt of a letter from India in 1882. He confessed on his death-bed to his two sons but just as he was about to tell them where the object was, he suddenly shouted: "Keep him out!" and died. Sholto's sons saw a face at the window but when they rushed outside they found only a single footprint.

On going back inside they discovered a note on their father's body saying: "The Sign of the Four." The sons argued over whether Mary Morstan should be given anything from their father's estate but Thaddeus took a string of pearls and began sending them, one each year, to Mary. When his brother Bartholomew discovered the treasure, Thaddeus had written to Mary.

Soon after, however, Bartholomew was found dead, killed by a poison dart, and the

Solving a Problem. Illustration of Sherlock Holmes by Frederic Dorr Steele, 1903.

treasure was nowhere to be found. Thaddeus was arrested for the murder of his brother, but Holmes surmises that two people had been involved in the murder. One is a one-legged man, Jonathan Small, and the other is a small accomplice. The detail of Holmes's description of Jonathan Small to the police is remarkable:

> *His name, I have every reason to believe, is Jonathan Small. He is a poorly-educated man, small, active, with his right leg off, and wearing a wooden stump which is worn away upon the inner side. His left boot has a coarse, square-toed sole, with an iron band around the heel. He is a middle-aged man, much sunburned, and has been a convict. These few indications may be of some assistance to you, coupled with the fact that there is a good deal of skin missing from the palm of his hand.*

Small has hired a steam launch which Holmes traces with the help of a small dog named Toby, the Baker Street Irregulars and a disguise. When their police launch catches up with Small's vessel, the *Aurora*, Jonathan Small's companion is killed trying to murder Holmes with a poison dart fired from a blow-pipe. Small is arrested but there is nothing in the treasure box. Small claims to have emptied it over the side of the *Aurora*.

Small confesses all. He had served in India where he had lost his right leg to a crocodile while swimming. In 1857, he was on guard duty one night at the fortress in Agra when he was attacked by two Sikh troopers who gave him a stark choice. He could either die or help them steal a fortune in precious stones from the servant of a rajah who was taking it to the British for safekeeping. He chose the latter, the robbery took place and although his involvement was discovered, the valuables vanished.

Small served penal servitude on the Andaman Islands but twenty years later heard that John Sholto had incurred serious gambling debts. Small brokered a deal with Sholto and Morstan whereby Sholto would recover the treasure and then send a boat to the Andaman Islands to free him and the Sikhs. The boat never arrived, however, and Small escaped from captivity with an islander named Tonga.

News of Small's escape caused Sholto to become ill. Small arrived too late to hear of the location of the treasure but left the note which signified the agreement between him and his three Sikh accomplices. Small protests that he had not intended to kill Bartholomew who had found the treasure. It was the result of a misunderstanding with Tonga.

Mary Morstan will not have the treasure, but she will receive the rest of the pearl necklace that Thaddeus had been sending to her. Dr. Watson has by this time fallen in love with her and at the end of the story we learn that the two are to be married.

"*In the light of the lantern I read, with a thrill of horror, 'the sign of the four.'*"
Page 86

In the light of the lantern I read, with a thrill of horror, the sign of the four. Charles Kerr's illustration for the first edition of *The Sign of the Four* published by Spencer Blackett, London, 1890.

TREATING TUBERCULOSIS

Conan Doyle would almost certainly have treated many people suffering with the disease, but it was not a particular specialization of his. Nonetheless, he decided he had to go to Berlin to see lymphinoculation being practiced. In all likelihood, he went because he was bored with the routine of family life and work. Remarkably, he departed for Germany just a few hours after making his mind up to go.

There was an element of work involved as he had persuaded the magazine *Review of Reviews* to let him write a piece on Koch. But it was not easy to get an audience with this man who had become something of a media sensation. As well as patients who flocked to his clinic in search of a cure from across Europe, there were countless journalists and other doctors vying with each other to get close to the great man. For his part, Conan Doyle was horrified by the whole circus and argued with Koch's assistants and supporters that people were being given false hope of being cured. On November 17, he wrote a letter to the *Daily Telegraph* which appeared three days later:

Great as is Koch's discovery, there can be no question that our knowledge of it is still very incomplete, and that it leaves large issues open to question. The sooner that this is recognized the less chance will there be of serious disappointment among those who are looking to Berlin for a panacea for their own or their friends' ill health.

ONWARD TO VIENNA

Arthur Conan Doyle made another rushed decision after meeting a fellow doctor on the train to Berlin. Malcolm Morris was a Harley Street skin specialist and he advised Conan Doyle that he should leave Portsmouth and set up in London. He recommended that the younger man should go to Vienna to study to be an eye specialist as there was a need for them in London. On his return to Britain, Conan Doyle consulted, as ever, with

his mother and she agreed to look after his daughter while he and Louisa went to Vienna. They arrived in Vienna on January 5, 1891.

Arthur Conan Doyle had a habit, throughout his life, of making spur-of-the-moment decisions and this was certainly one of those. Louisa had little say in the matter and although he spoke some German learned at Stonyhurst and Feldkirch, he was going to be studying in a German-speaking country and had no German medical vocabulary. He funded the venture by writing a play, *The Doings of Raffles Haw*. It was not a very good piece of work, but he was able to sell it easily because of his growing literary reputation. For four months he and Louisa lived in a modest guesthouse while he attended lectures at the hospital. He quickly realized the rashness of his decision to go to Vienna:

... [I] could certainly have learned far more in London ... No doubt "has studied in Vienna" sounds well in a specialist's record, but it is usually taken for granted that he has exhausted his own country before going abroad, which was by no means the case with me. Therefore, so far as my eye work goes, my winter was wasted, nor can I trace any particular spiritual or intellectual advance. On the other hand I saw a little of gay Viennese society.

MONTAGUE PLACE

Conan Doyle and Louisa returned to London and moved into rooms at 23 Montague Place, just behind the British Museum and rented space at 2 Upper Wimpole Street for a surgery. Many wondered why he persevered as a doctor, but he was determined to see it through. Soon, however, this practice was faring as badly as his others and, even though he was now treating London's wealthy elite, he often struggled to pay the rent. He was unhappy and bored.

By this time, he had started work on a new Sherlock Holmes story, "A Scandal in Bohemia," which he delivered to his agent, Alexander Pollock Watt, on April 3, 1891, marking the beginning of a remarkably prolific period. By the end of April, he had added "A Case of Identity," "The Adventure of the Red-Headed League" and "The Boscombe Valley Mystery" to the growing Sherlock Holmes canon.

A BOUT OF FLU

This especially productive spell would have continued but for the fact that Conan Doyle was laid low by a serious bout of flu in the first week of May. It was so serious, in fact, that Louisa feared for his life. Soon, however, he was back at work, even writing in bed as he recuperated. "The Five Orange Pips" was finished on May 18 and in August he completed "The Man with the Twisted Lip." In the midst of all this, the Conan Doyles also relocated to a house at 12 Tennison Road in South Norwood. He was now living entirely on what he earned from writing:

There we settled down, and there I made my first effort to live entirely by my pen. It soon became evident that I had been playing the game well within my powers and that I should have no difficulty in providing a sufficient income. It seemed to me that I had settled into a life which might be continuous.

LITERARY PIONEER

There was no doubt that Conan Doyle was a literary pioneer. In fact, he had created a popular new literary genre—a series of stand-alone tales featuring the same main characters. The stories were written for *The Strand Magazine* and by the time he had started the next set of six little masterpieces, he was less worried about his finances and able to devote more time to them. He had completed five of the next batch of stories by November 1891, but was threatening to kill Sherlock Holmes off in the sixth.

He wrote to his mother about his plans but she succeeded in persuading him to keep the detective alive, even helping him with the twelfth story, "The Adventure of the Copper Beeches" (published June 1892). The others in this grouping were "The Adventure of the Blue Carbuncle" (published January 1892), "The Adventure of the Speckled Band" (published February 1892), "The Adventure of the Engineer's Thumb" (published March 1892), "The Adventure of the Noble Bachelor" (published April 1892), and "The Adventure of the Beryl Coronet" (published May 1892).

THE GREATEST SINCE POE

The much respected editor of *The Strand Magazine*, Herbert Greenhough Smith (1855 – 1935), later described his reaction to the first two Sherlock Holmes stories submitted by Conan Doyle:

I at once realized that here was the greatest short story writer since Edgar Allan Poe.

And, indeed, the Sherlock Holmes stories were good for *The Strand Magazine*, boosting subscriptions, emboldening Conan Doyle to ask for more money. He was paid thirty guineas for each story in this initial run of twelve. In October 1892, the twelve stories were collected in book form as *The Adventures of Sherlock Holmes*, published by George Newnes, publisher of *The Strand Magazine*. The few reviews that were written were generally good. Joseph Bell wrote in the December 1892 issue of *The Bookman*:

He had the wit to devise excellent plots, interesting complications. He tells them in honest Saxon-English with directness and pith; and above all his other merits, his stories are absolutely free from padding.

The initial British print run was for 10,000 copies with a further 4,500 being printed in the United States where it was published by Harper Brothers.

GEORGE NEWNES

George Newnes (1851 – 1910) began his career as a publisher and editor by launching the weekly magazine, *Tit-Bits*, in 1881. It consisted of competitions and extracts from books and other publications. Moving from Manchester to London, Newnes began to work with the editor and journalist W.T. Stead (1849 – 1912) and the two men founded *Review of Reviews* in 1890. *Tit-Bits* can be said to have pioneered popular journalism as both Alfred Harmsworth who founded the *Daily Mail* and Arthur Pearson who started the *Daily Express* worked for the magazine. In 1891, Newnes founded *The Strand Magazine* and went on to found numerous other titles.

In 1885, Newnes was elected Liberal Member of Parliament for Newmarket, holding his seat for ten years and in 1895, he was created a baronet. In 1900, he re-entered Parliament as MP for Swansea but lost his seat in 1910. George Newnes died in June of that year, at age fifty-nine. His publishing company continued until 1963 when it became part of IPC Media, but books under the Newnes imprint continue to be published to this day by Elsevier.

SIDNEY PAGET

Sidney Paget is best known for his illustrations of Conan Doyle's Sherlock Holmes stories. Born in 1860, he entered the Royal Academy Schools in 1881 and there met Alfred Morris Butler, a student of architecture who may have been the model for Paget's depiction of Dr. Watson. Between 1879 and 1905, Paget exhibited eighteen paintings at the Royal Academy exhibitions. He began drawing for magazines and his work appeared in a number of publications including *The Sphere*, *The Illustrated London News* and the *Pall Mall Magazine*.

His work on the Sherlock Holmes stories was the result of an accident when *The Strand Magazine* sent a commissioning letter to him instead of to his younger brother, Walter. In 1893, Paget provided the illustrations for *The Memoirs of Sherlock Holmes* which were published in *The Strand* as an extension of the "Adventures." When Conan Doyle brought Sherlock Holmes back with *The Hound of the Baskervilles*, serialized in *The Strand* in 1901 – 02, he specifically asked for Paget to be the illustrator. In 1903 – 04, Paget also illustrated *The Return of Sherlock Holmes*. He was responsible, in total, for the illustrations in one Sherlock Holmes novel and 37 of the short stories—356 published drawings—and there is little doubt that his style influenced the perception of the detective in fiction, drama and film. His work had a dark, shadowy quality that undoubtedly had a bearing on the later film noir movies of Hollywood.

The deerstalker hat and characteristic Inverness cape came from Paget's imagination because Conan

Doyle did not include them in his depiction of Holmes. They first appeared in the illustrations for the 1891 story, "The Boscombe Valley Mystery" and can be seen again in his work for the 1892 story "The Adventure of Silver Blaze."

Paget died in 1908, at age forty-eight, but his work lives on every time anyone adapts a Sherlock Holmes story.

THE STRAND MAGAZINE

George Newnes founded *The Strand Magazine* in 1891 and between then and March 1950, 711 issues were published. Containing short fiction and topical articles, it was immediately popular, its first issue selling almost 300,000 copies. Within a short time sales had climbed to 500,000 and remained at that level until the 1930s.

When the Sherlock Holmes stories were first published in *The Strand*, they were brilliantly illustrated by Sidney Paget who also illustrated *The Hound of the Baskervilles*. Its serialization between August 1901 and April 1902, boosted sales and readers waited in line outside the magazine's offices to get their hands on the next installment.

The magazine published many great writers during its existence, including H.G. Wells, Agatha Christie, E. Nesbit, Rudyard Kipling, Dorothy L. Sayers, Georges Simenon, Edgar Wallace, P.G. Wodehouse, and Winston Churchill.

The Strand changed to a smaller size in 1941 but this could not prevent its demise due to falling circulation nine years later. It was revived in 1998 in Birmingham, Michigan, as a quarterly and has since published many well-known authors among whom are Ray Bradbury, Alexander McCall Smith, Ruth Rendell, and John Mortimer.

The cover of the December 1913 edition of *The Strand Magazine*.

CHAPTER 8

THE ADVENTURES OF SHERLOCK HOLMES

Stories published 1891 – 92 in *The Strand*

"A Scandal in Bohemia" .... July 1891

"The Adventure of the Red-Headed League" .... August 1891

"A Case of Identity" .... September 1891

"The Boscombe Valley Mystery".................. October 1891

"The Five Orange Pips" .... November 1891

"The Man with the Twisted Lip" .... December 1891

"The Adventure of the Blue Carbuncle" .... January 1892

"The Adventure of the Speckled Band" .... February 1892

"The Adventure of the Engineer's Thumb".......... March 1892

"The Adventure of the Noble Bachelor" .... April 1892

"The Adventure of the Beryl Coronet" .... May 1892

"The Adventure of the Copper Beeches" .... June 1892

"A SCANDAL IN BOHEMIA"

Dr. Watson is now married to Mary Morstan and no longer living at 221B Baker Street. One day, while he is paying Holmes a visit, a caller arrives at the door, Count Von Kramm, who describes himself as an agent for a wealthy client. Very quickly, however, Holmes deduces that the man is actually the hereditary King of Bohemia. When he realizes that Holmes knows his real identity, the king removes the mask he has been wearing.

The king is to marry Clotilde Lothman von Saxe-Meiningen, a Scandinavian princess.

" THIS PHOTOGRAPH ! "

Five years ago, however, he had enjoyed a liaison with Irene Adler, an American opera singer, while she was principal singer at the Imperial Opera of Warsaw. Miss Adler has now retired to London but he is concerned that the family of his fiancée will find out about his relationship and call the marriage off. He is anxious, therefore, to recover letters he had sent Adler and a photograph of him with her. His men have tried to obtain the photo by every means, including burglary and the theft of her luggage, but without success. She has refused payment for the material and, reluctant to allow him to marry any other woman, is threatening to send them to his prospective in-laws. The king gives Holmes the large sum of one-thousand pounds to cover expenses.

Disguised as a drunken, unemployed groom, Holmes learns that Adler has a gentleman friend, a lawyer named Godfrey Norton who visits her every day. Holmes follows Norton to the Church of St. Monica on Edgware Road in London. Shortly after Adler drives to the same church. Holmes is surprised to be dragged into the church to act as a witness at the wedding of Adler and Norton. But, after the ceremony, they each go their separate ways.

Holmes solicits the help of Watson before donning another disguise, this time that of a clergyman. As they arrive at Irene Adler's house, they see a group of unemployed men on the street and when Adler's coach stops outside her house, they quarrel over who can help her down from the coach. Holmes is apparently injured by one of the men when he rushes in to separate them. Grateful, Adler invites him into her sitting room. He asks her to open the window, and when he raises his arm in a pre-arranged signal, Watson throws a plumber's smoke rocket into the room, screaming *"Fire!"*

This photograph! Illustration by Sidney Paget from "A Scandal in Bohemia," 1891.

As Holmes had expected, on the shout of "fire," Adler had gone for her most valuable possession—the photograph which was kept behind a sliding panel in the wall. He was not able to steal it in the confusion because he was being carefully observed by the coachman. As he explains all this to Watson outside the house, a youth whose voice sounds familiar bids them goodnight before disappearing into the crowd gathered outside the house.

The following morning, when Holmes, Watson, and the king arrive at Irene Adler's house, they learn that she has hurriedly left for Charing Cross railway station. Holmes rushes to the secret compartment where he discovers a picture of Irene Adler in an evening dress and a letter to him in which Adler congratulates him on finding where the photograph was hidden and on fooling her with his disguises. She informs him that it had been her, disguised as the youth, who had bid him goodnight and that she and Norton have fled England. She tells him she has the photograph but will not use it against the king.

The king offers Holmes an emerald snake ring as a reward for his work, but Holmes surprises him by asking instead for the photograph of Irene Adler, a souvenir of the cleverness of Irene Adler and of the time when he was beaten by an intelligent woman:

> To Sherlock Holmes she is always the woman ... In his eyes she eclipses and predominates the whole of her sex ... there was but one woman to him, and that woman was the late Irene Adler, of dubious and questionable memory.

"THE ADVENTURE OF THE RED-HEADED LEAGUE"

A pawnbroker named Jabez Wilson visits 221B Baker Street with a puzzle. Holmes and Watson notice his red hair, which has a distinct flame-like hue. To supplement the falling income from his failing business, Wilson had been persuaded by a recently employed young assistant, Vincent Spaulding, to reply to a newspaper advertisement offering employment to a man with red hair. Wilson gets the job, being able to do it in the afternoons because his pawnbroker's business is quiet then. Bizarrely, the work consists of making a copy of the *Encyclopedia Britannica* for an organization called the Red-Headed League. One day, however, when he turned up for work, he found a notice on the door telling him that the Red-Headed League had been dissolved. When Holmes visits Vincent Spaulding, he notices that his trouser knees are dirty. He then taps the floor outside Wilson's pawnbroker shop with his cane. Holmes deduces that Spaulding is part of a conspiracy to get Wilson out of his shop so that he and an associate can tunnel from the basement of the pawnbroker's shop into the bank vault next door.

Irene Adler, illustrated by Charles Dana Gibson, 1891.

"A CASE OF IDENTITY"

Miss Mary Sutherland, a woman who enjoys a substantial income from a fund that has been set up for her, is engaged to marry Hosmer Angel, a quiet man from London who has mysteriously disappeared. All Miss Sutherland knows about her fiancé is that he works in an office in Leadenhall Street in the City of London. The letters he has written to her have all been typed—even his signature—and he told her that when she wrote back to him the letter had to go to his local Post Office where he would collect it.

Angel disappeared on the morning of his wedding to Miss Sutherland. Holmes is aware that Angel had only met Miss Sutherland when her young stepfather, James Windibank, who disapproved of the relationship, was out of the country. He concludes that the person responsible can only be James Windibank. But he does not tell his client, explaining to Watson: "If I tell her she will not believe me. You may remember the old Persian saying, 'There is danger for him who taketh the tiger cub, and danger also for whoso snatches a delusion from a woman.'" He merely advises his client to forget Hosmer Angel. Refusing to accept his advice, Miss Sutherland says she will remain faithful to Mr. Angel for at least ten years, by which time she is certain he will have returned.

Glancing about him like a rat in a trap. Illustration by Sidney Paget from "A Case of Identity," 1891.

"THE BOSCOMBE VALLEY MYSTERY"

Holmes is asked to investigate a case in which James McCarthy has been accused of murdering his father, Charles. The evidence against him is overwhelming, but Holmes secures his freedom using a footprint from the murder scene, an envelope of cigar ash and a misplaced rock. This complex tale takes in Australian bushrangers, stolen gold, closely guarded secrets and blackmail but ends in marriage for the young couple in the middle of it all.

"THE FIVE ORANGE PIPS"

Holmes is consulted by John Openshaw whose uncle, Colonel Elias Openshaw, has been found dead after receiving a letter from Pondicherry in India containing five orange pips and the initials *KKK*. John's father who has inherited Elias's estate also dies after receiving a letter from Dundee in Scotland with the letters *KKK*. The letters, Holmes works out, refer to the secret American organization, the Ku Klux Klan that had been disbanded in 1869. Elias had stolen papers that contributed to the organization's demise and now someone was taking revenge. Holmes deduces that the letters have been posted by someone working on a ship. Using shipping records he locates that ship as the *Lone Star*. John Openshaw is murdered a week after the ship has docked in London. Holmes alerts the police at the ship's next destination but it perishes in a storm at sea.

"THE MAN WITH THE TWISTED LIP"

Neville St. Clair, a businessman, discovers he can earn more from begging than from business but he fails to tell his wife about the source of his income. Matters become complicated, however, when it appears that St. Clair has been murdered, but while disguised as a beggar he is arrested. Holmes washes the dirt from the beggar's face to uncover Neville St. Clair. He promises to cease begging if Holmes does not tell his wife.

He broke into a scream. Illustration by Sidney Paget from "The Man with the Twisted Lip," 1891.

"THE ADVENTURE OF THE BLUE CARBUNCLE"

When the priceless jewel, the "Blue Carbuncle" is stolen from the Countess of Morcar's hotel suite, a plumber with a criminal record, John Horner, is arrested. The jewel is not found, however, until Peterson, an acquaintance of Holmes discovers it in the throat of a goose that he found in the street after it had been dropped by a man in a scuffle with some ruffians. The goose bears a tag on which is written the name "Henry Baker" and Peterson asks Holmes if he can locate the man. But it is impossible and Peterson takes the goose home to cook it.

He rushes in shortly after, however, having found the "Blue Carbuncle." Eager now to locate Henry Baker, Holmes studies a hat that had also been dropped in the scuffle. He is able to deduce much about the man from the hat but cannot say whether he knew he was carrying the precious stone when he was waylaid.

Holmes places a newspaper advertisement and Baker sees it and arrives at 221B Baker Street. He accepts a replacement bird proffered by Holmes and rejects the offer of taking the original bird's entrails which persuades the detective that he knows nothing of the "Blue Carbuncle."

The bird was bought by Baker at the Alpha Inn, a pub in the vicinity of the British Museum. Holmes and Watson quiz the owner of the pub about the bird and discover that it was purchased from a dealer in the Covent Garden area. When they visit the dealer, however, a salesman named Breckenridge becomes angry with Holmes, complaining that he has been pestered recently about birds he had sold to the owner of the Alpha Inn. Holmes manages to trick Breckenridge into letting slip that the bird had been supplied by a Mrs. Oakshott of Brixton.

As Holmes and Watson are about to set off for Brixton, James Ryder, who works at the hotel where the theft occurred appears, once again harassing Breckenridge as to the whereabouts of the goose. Holmes and Watson ask Ryder to accompany them to Baker Street, telling him that they know that he is searching for a goose with a black bar on its tail. But, when Holmes discloses to Ryder that the goose "laid an egg after it was dead—the bonniest, brightest little blue egg that was ever seen," Ryder, terrified of

He burst into convulsive sobbing. Illustration by Sidney Paget from "The Adventure of the Blue Carbuncle," 1892.

being turned over to the police, explains that he and Catherine Cusack, the Countess's maid, conspired to frame Horner for the theft, believing that Horner's record would convince the police that he was the culprit. However, he was terrified of being caught and while visiting his sister, Mrs. Oakshott, had fed the jewel to a goose that she had promised him. Unfortunately, when Ryder dropped the bird, he picked up another thinking it was his and by the time he worked out what had happened, Mrs. Oakshott had sold the other goose to the owner of the Alpha Inn.

Ryder flees to Europe and without his testimony John Horner is released. As it is Christmas, Holmes takes pity on Ryder:

"After all, Watson," said Holmes, reaching up his hand for his clay pipe, "I am not retained by the police to supply their deficiencies."

"THE ADVENTURE OF THE SPECKLED BAND"

A woman named Helen Stoner is worried that her stepfather, Dr. Grimesby Roylott may be trying to kill her when he tries to get her to move into the bedroom her sister had occupied when she died two years earlier, shortly before she was due to be married. Her sister asked the night she died if she had heard anyone whistle in the dead of night, but Helen had not. There was also a metallic sound, she added. Her sister died that night and her last words had been: "The speckled band!"

Dr. Roylott had lived in India where he married Helen's mother. But he was a violent man. Now Helen is engaged to be married but has started to hear strange noises—including whistles at about three in the morning—and witness strange activities at Stoke Moran, the impoverished estate where she lives with her stepfather. Dr. Roylott is friendly with the gypsies who live on the estate and keeps a cheetah and a baboon as pets.

Holmes decides to visit the estate but before he can leave he is surprised by a visit from Dr. Roylott. He has a "large face, seared with a thousand wrinkles, burned yellow with the sun, and marked with every evil passion ..." Roylott threatens Holmes: "Don't you dare to meddle with my affairs. I know that Miss Stoner has been here. I traced her! I am a dangerous man to fall foul of! See here." He stepped forward, seized the poker, and bent it into a curve with his huge brown hands.

Holmes is undeterred, however. He examines Helen's late mother's will before proceeding to Stoke Moran. Once there, he inspects the premises carefully, finding some strange things such as a bed that is anchored to the floor, a bell cord that does not work and a ventilator hole between Helen's dead sister's room and Dr. Roylott's.

Good-bye and be brave. Illustration by Sidney Paget from "The Adventure of the Speckled Band," 1892.

Holmes and Watson decide to spend the night in Helen's room waiting until they hear a metallic noise. A dim light can be seen through the ventilator hole. Holmes grabs a candle and discovers a venomous snake on the bell cord—the "speckled band" referred to by Helen's sister. He hits the snake with a stick and it slithers back through the ventilation hole where it attacks Roylott.

He had been trying to ensure that he did not lose control of his wife's fortune when the two girls married. The whistle was the sound Roylott made to make the snake return to him and the metallic noise was the closing of the box in which he kept it. It was almost a perfect crime, the poison undetectable and the puncture marks on the skin minute.

"THE ADVENTURE OF THE ENGINEER'S THUMB"

Victor Hatherley turns up at Dr. Watson's surgery, having had his thumb cut off by a cleaver. Watson takes him to 221B Baker Street where Hatherley explains to Holmes that he is a hydraulic engineer engaged to look at a hydraulic stamping machine by a man named Lysander Stark who spoke with a German accent. On arrival at Stark's house Hatherley is warned by a beautiful woman to "get away from here before it is too late!"

The machine he was to examine is located in a small chamber with a piston that came down and stamped material. When Hatherley began examining a metal deposit on the floor, Stark sets the machine in motion and the piston threatens to squash Hatherley. He is rescued by the beautiful woman but is pursued by Stark who chops off his thumb as he hangs from a window ledge.

When Holmes and Watson go to the house the next day, they find it alight from an oil lamp Hatherley had dropped the previous night. Stark and the woman have fled and Holmes works out that they had been counterfeiting coins with the machine.

"THE ADVENTURE OF THE NOBLE BACHELOR"

Hatty Doran has disappeared after her wedding to Lord Robert St. Simon who approaches Holmes to help find out what has happened to her.

Hatty had been seen in whispered conversation with her maid and ten minutes into the wedding breakfast, had suddenly retired to her room. Inspector Lestrade arrives to inform Holmes that Hatty's wedding dress and wedding ring have been washed up on the shore of the Serpentine lake in Hyde Park, London, after Hatty had been seen entering the park with a man.

It does not take Holmes long to solve the mystery. He finds Hatty at a hotel with a mysterious "common-looking" man who had sat in the front pew at the wedding and had picked up her bouquet when she dropped it after the ceremony. The man is Hatty's husband, Francis H. Moulton, whom she thought had died in an Apache raid in the United States but he had been taken prisoner and escaped. He had only succeeded in contacting Hatty by placing a note in her bouquet when he had picked it up. Holmes convinces the couple that they should tell Lord St. Simon the truth but, needless to say, his Lordship is very upset by the news.

"THE ADVENTURE OF THE BERYL CORONET"

A banker, Alexander Holder of Streatham, asks Holmes to investigate the damaging of a "Beryl Coronet" at his home. He had loaned fifty thousand pounds to a client and had been given the valuable coronet as security. Holder took it home as he thought it would be safer there than at the bank. He had been awakened by noise and had discovered his wayward son, Arthur, trying to bend the damaged coronet back into shape. Holder's niece Mary walks in and faints at the sight. Three beryls—precious stones—are missing from the coronet and Arthur refuses to explain himself, neither denying nor admitting guilt in the matter.

When Holmes investigates, he realizes that Arthur is not strong enough to have bent the coronet. He discovers footsteps in the snow outside the house and deduces that the banker's niece, in concert with a notorious criminal named Sir George Burnwell, had tried to steal the coronet. Arthur had caught Burnwell in the act and in the ensuing struggle the coronet had been damaged. He was in love with his cousin and was unwilling to incriminate her in the crime. Holmes recovers the jewels missing from the coronet but Mary flees with Sir George.

"THE ADVENTURE OF THE COPPER BEECHES"

Holmes is visited at 221B Baker Street by Violet Hunter, a governess who tells him that she has been offered a job in Hampshire which is subject to a number of unusual conditions, one of which is to have her long hair cut short. The pay is extraordinarily high and she decides that she will accept the position.

Not long after, she sends Holmes a telegram asking him to meet her in Winchester. She tells him that her employer, Mr. Rucastle required her to occasionally wear a particular electric blue dress and sit reading in the front room of the house with her back to the window.

She has discovered that there was a man outside looking toward the house. At one point she discovered a bundle of cut hair in a drawer that is identical to hers, even down to the unusual color.

An entire wing of the house is sealed off and Holmes discovers that someone has been kept prisoner in the wing but as he, Watson, and Violet find when they enter it, it is now unoccupied. The prisoner was Alice, the daughter of Mr. Rucastle who

accuses them of freeing her. He sets his dog on them but it turns on him instead forcing Watson to shoot it.

It is revealed that when Alice came of age she would receive an annuity from her late mother's will. Rucastle had attempted to persuade Alice to sign control of the money over to him which had made her ill, and in a distressed state she had cut off all her hair.

Rucastle had locked Alice in the closed wing to keep her away from her fiancé and employed Violet to unwittingly impersonate her to give the impression that Alice was no longer interested in him. Alice had managed to escape and the couple married soon afterward.

I clapped a pistol to his head. Illustration by Sidney Paget from "The Adventure of the Beryl Coronet," 1892.

DR. JOHN H. WATSON

"You have a grand gift for silence, Watson. It makes you quite invaluable as a companion."

Sherlock Holmes, "The Man with the Twisted Lip"

Conan Doyle decided that his hero needed an associate/assistant who would provide a means of telling the stories of Sherlock Holmes's cases. The initial name he came up with for this narrator was "Ormond Sacker," but he decided that it was too clumsy, preferring the much less flamboyant "John Watson," possibly based on a colleague, James Watson.

A Study in Scarlet introduces us to Watson and his storytelling, in the subtitle of the novel— *Being a reprint from the Reminiscences of John H. Watson, M.D., Late of the Army Medical Department.* The "H" of his middle name is never revealed.

Born in 1852, two years before Holmes, Watson received his medical degree from St. Bartholomew's Hospital and the London School of Medicine and Dentistry at the University of London in 1878. He joined the army and trained as an assistant surgeon at the Royal Victoria Military Hospital at Netley. He went to India attached to the 5th Northumberland Fusiliers before seeing active service in the Second Anglo-Afghan War with the 66th (Berkshire) Regiment of Foot. He was wounded at the Battle of Maiwand in July 1880, suffered enteric fever, and was sent back to England where he was invalided out of the army on a monthly pension of eleven shillings and nine pence.

Looking for accommodation in the winter of 1881, Watson is introduced by a mutual friend, Stamford, to Sherlock Holmes who was looking for someone to share rooms at 221B Baker Street. Stamford takes Watson to meet Holmes at St. Bartholomew's Hospital, warning him that his friend is a little eccentric.

In a laboratory at the hospital, they find Holmes conducting an experiment. Stamford introduces Watson and Holmes immediately deduces, to Watson's astonishment, that he has been in Afghanistan. The two men discuss the prospect of sharing an apartment and, after deciding they would be able to live together, they view the Baker Street premises and move in.

Watson moves out of 221B Baker Street when he marries Mary Morstan, but in later stories it appears that Mary has died and Watson moves in again. In "The Adventure of the Blanched Soldier" Holmes mentions that "Watson had at that time deserted me for a wife." So, it appears that Watson remarried but Conan Doyle never divulges Watson's second wife's name.

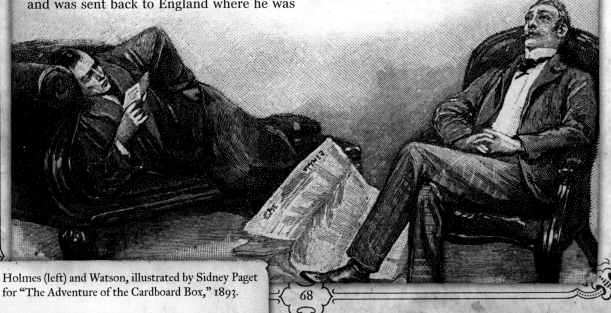

Holmes (left) and Watson, illustrated by Sidney Paget for "The Adventure of the Cardboard Box," 1893.

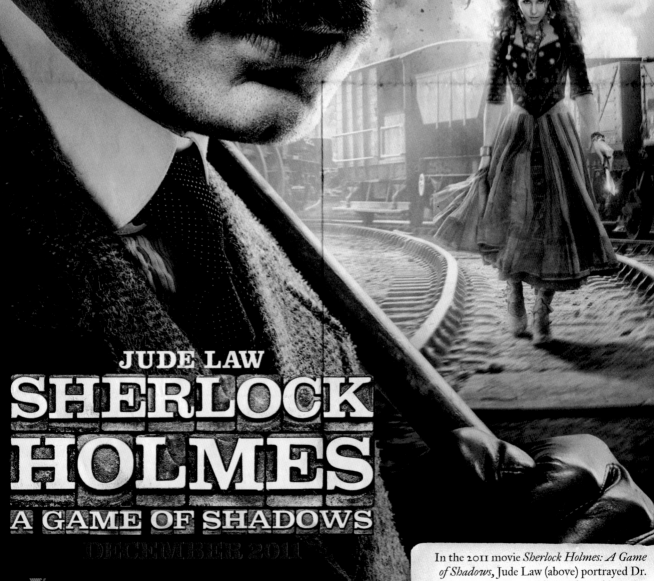

JUDE LAW

SHERLOCK HOLMES

A GAME OF SHADOWS

DECEMBER 2011

In the 2011 movie *Sherlock Holmes: A Game of Shadows*, Jude Law (above) portrayed Dr. Watson as a tough ex-soldier and gambler, who is good with a gun and has an eye for the ladies.

VILLAGE ROADSHOW PICTURES

www.SherlockHolmes2.com

PART THREE

★ ★ ★

THE END IS ONLY THE BEGINNING

★ ★ ★

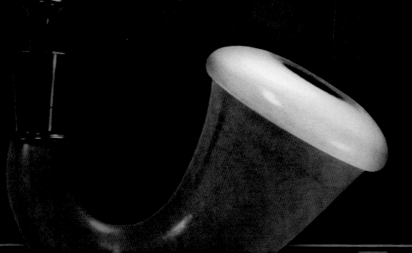

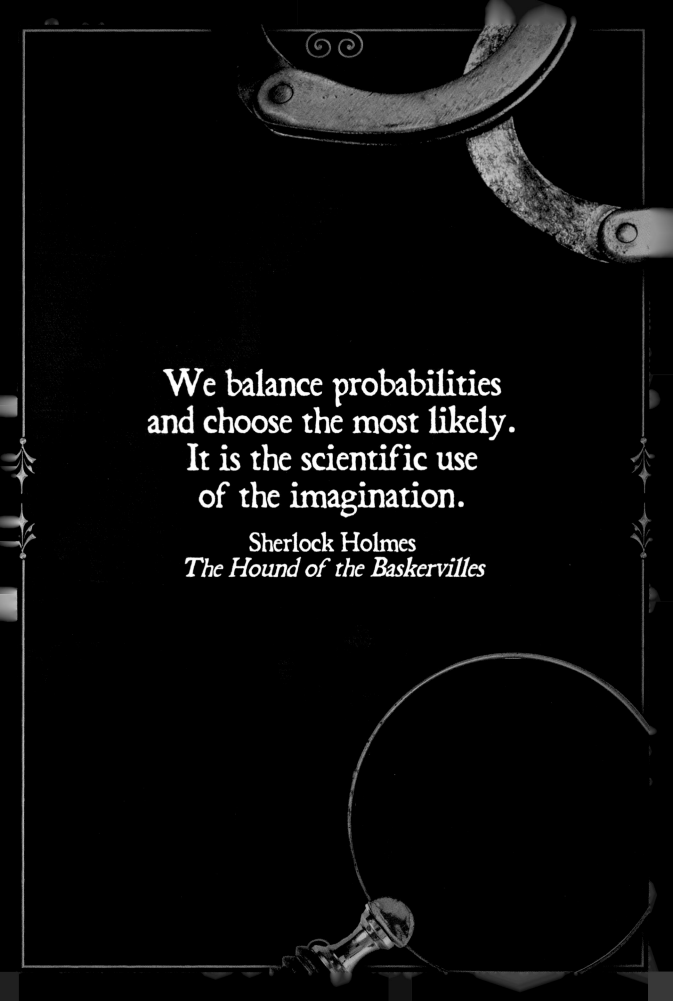

We balance probabilities
and choose the most likely.
It is the scientific use
of the imagination.

Sherlock Holmes
The Hound of the Baskervilles

CHAPTER 9

BURYING SHERLOCK HOLMES

The Conan Doyles were now blessed with a son—Alleyne Kingsley—born in 1892. Conan Doyle was thirty-four and a long way from where he expected to be, living a life he could not have dreamed of when he was a child in Edinburgh. He enjoyed a certain amount of fame and associated with some of the finest literary figures of his time. He went to Norway with the writer of *Three Men in a Boat*, Jerome K. Jerome (1859 – 1927) and skied for the first time. His work was loved by publishers and magazine editors because it turned a good profit for them. All was well.

PRODIGIOUS OUTPUT

Conan Doyle was working hard. He earned one hundred pounds by selling a play about the Battle of Waterloo to the great actor Henry Irving in 1892. There was an operetta (*Jane Annie*) written with his good friend J. M. Barrie. His production was prodigious. He was actually producing so many stories and essays that *The Strand* could not keep up. He sold some to Jerome K. Jerome's literary and humorous magazine *The Idler* and to other magazines.

A CHANGE IN THE AIR

Just when everything was going so well, Conan Doyle's fortunes changed. In 1893, his father Charles finally gave up the fight. Admittedly, Charles had not been a good father when Conan Doyle was young, but the two had got on much better later in Charles's life. Then, following a holiday in Switzerland, his wife Louisa developed a persistent and painful cough. When he summoned a doctor, the news was as bad as it could be. The doctor told him:

... the lungs were very gravely affected, that there was every sign of rapid consumption and that he thought the case a most serious one with little hope, considering her record and her family history, of a permanent cure.

It was dreadful news. Conan Doyle had two children to think of—a four-year-old and one-year-old. The solution was to abandon everything, sell all their furniture and move at once to Davos in the Swiss Alps. They were well aware, of course, that there was usually just one outcome to an illness such as Louisa's but they faced the situation with considerable courage.

CARING FOR TOUIE

They moved into the Kurhaus Hotel in Davos and tried to maintain their happy family life. Conan Doyle was irrepressibly cheery, reading to Louisa and comforting her when necessary. His friends and associates in London wrote to him, sending their thoughts and prayers while he tried to maintain the brave front in the hope that she would pull through. In fact, Louisa responded well to the trip and although she was never completely well again and often took to her bed, she lived for another thirteen years.

KILLING THE GOOSE THAT LAID THE GOLDEN EGG

Surrounded by these devastating incidents, Conan Doyle made a big decision. He was going to write one more Sherlock Holmes story but at the end of it he would kill off his great character. He broke the news in a letter to his mother in April 1893: "I am in the middle of the last Holmes story, after which the gentleman vanishes, never to reappear. I am weary of his name." He still felt that his popular character was somehow beneath him, expressing this view later in his memoirs:

I saw that I was in danger of having my hand forced, and of being entirely identified with what I regarded as a lower stratum of literary achievement. Therefore, as a sign of my resolution I determined to end the life of my hero. The idea was in my mind when I went with my wife for a short holiday in Switzerland, in the course of which we saw the wonderful falls of Reichenbach, a terrible place, and one that I thought would make a worthy tomb for poor Sherlock.

There might, of course, be financial implications in killing the goose that had laid the golden eggs for the last few years, but Conan Doyle was determined to see the back of Holmes. At the time, he was writing another series of Holmes stories, *The Memoirs of Sherlock Holmes*, that consisted of a dozen tales:

"The Adventure of Silver Blaze"
"The Adventure of the Cardboard Box"
"The Adventure of the Yellow Face"
"The Adventure of the Stockbroker's Clerk"
"The Adventure of the Gloria Scott"
"The Adventure of the Musgrave Ritual"
"The Adventure of the Reigate Squire"
"The Adventure of the Crooked Man"
"The Adventure of the Resident Patient"
"The Adventure of the Greek Interpreter"
"The Adventure of the Naval Treaty" and
"The Adventure of the Final Problem."

BURYING SHERLOCK HOLMES

The new set of stories was notable for the introduction of another Holmes—Sherlock's brother, Mycroft. But the most sensational of the twelve was the last one, "The Adventure of the Final Problem." It appeared in *The Strand Magazine* in December 1893 and was intended by Conan Doyle to free him from his Holmesian shackles. He wrote to his mother:

I must save my mind for better things, even if it means I must bury my pocketbook with him.

THE WORLD MOURNS HOLMES

There was a massive reaction around the world to the apparent demise of the great detective. In London, young men wore bands of black silk around their hats as a sign of mourning, and letters were written to newspapers and to MPs. The Prince of Wales even received letters of complaint. Protestors gathered outside magazine offices and marched down Fleet Street, the home of the newspaper industry in central London, and a rumor spread that it was all a hoax and that Holmes was not really dead. Threatening letters were sent to a bemused Conan Doyle who was, of course, in the midst of his own mourning for his father.

First edition of *The Memoirs of Sherlock Holmes*, published by George Newnes in 1894.

CHAPTER 10

THE MEMOIRS OF SHERLOCK HOLMES

Stories published 1892 – 93 in *The Strand*

"The Adventure of Silver Blaze" . . . . December 1892

"The Adventure of the Cardboard Box" . . . . January 1893

"The Adventure of the Yellow Face" . . . . February 1893

"The Adventure of the Stockbroker's Clerk" . . . . March 1893

"The Adventure of the Gloria Scott" . . . . April 1893

"The Adventure of the Musgrave Ritual" . . . . May 1893

"The Adventure of the Reigate Squire" . . . . June 1893

"The Adventure of the Crooked Man" . . . . July 1893

"The Adventure of the Resident Patient" . . . . August 1893

"The Adventure of the Greek Interpreter" . . . . September 1893

"The Adventure of the Naval Treaty" . . . . October – November 1893

"The Adventure of the Final Problem" . . . . December 1893

"THE ADVENTURE OF SILVER BLAZE"

One of the most popular Sherlock Holmes stories, "The Adventure of Silver Blaze" is famous for the exchange:

> *Detective Gregory of Scotland Yard: "Is there any other point to which you wish to draw my attention?"*
>
> *Holmes: "To the curious incident of the dog in the night-time."*
>
> *Gregory: "The dog did nothing in the night-time."*
>
> *Holmes: "That was the curious incident."*

Holmes and Watson travel to King's Pyland on Dartmoor to investigate the disappearance of Silver Blaze, a famous racehorse that had been favorite for the Wessex Cup, and the murder of the horse's trainer, John Straker. They have been invited by Inspector Gregory of Scotland Yard and the horse's owner, Colonel Ross. A young man, Fitzroy Simpson has been arrested in connection with the crime.

One night the horse was being guarded as usual by a stable lad, Ned Hunter, when the maid bringing his supper encountered a man, "a person of gentlemanly bearing," who gave her a note for the stable boy. Afraid, she ran to the stable to explain to Hunter. The man followed and asked the lad which of the stable's two entrants for the big race was likely to win—Silver Blaze or Bayard—offering him money for the information. Angered, Hunter tried to set his dog loose on the man but he had disappeared. Hunter told Straker, the trainer, what had happened and returned to the stables. In the morning, when his wife went looking for him, Hunter was sleeping, apparently drugged, the stable was empty and there was no sign of the horse or the trainer. Straker was soon found on the moor, killed by a blow to the head but also wounded on the thigh by a sharp implement. He had put up a fight before his death and in his hand was the red and black silk cravat the stranger had been wearing the previous night. Hunter presumed the stranger had managed to drug his food.

Suspicion rested on Fitzroy Simpson, a well-educated man of good background who had lost a fortune gambling and was now a small-time bookmaker. He admitted that he had visited the stables the previous night but insisted that he had only sought information. However, he was unable to account for the cravat being in the hand of the dead trainer.

Silver Blaze. Illustration by Sidney Paget from "The Adventure of Silver Blaze," 1892.

But Holmes is not satisfied that Simpson is the culprit. Why would he have taken the horse out onto the moor to kill or maim him? That could have been done in the stall. Why would he have stolen the thoroughbred? It would have been no use to him. And why has the horse not been found?

Holmes soon finds Silver Blaze, having followed his tracks which are accompanied by those of a man. They go to the nearby Mapleton stables where Holmes confronts the owner, Silas Brown, who claims to have found the horse wandering on the moor. It so happened that Silver Blaze was the horse most likely to beat Brown's own horse in the Wessex Cup and he had presumably planned

to keep him captive until the race was run.

Holmes and Watson travel to Winchester four days later for the Wessex Cup. Silver Blaze has not been returned, but the betting shows his price has shortened. When the horse appears, the colonel claims that it is not Silver Blaze which has a distinctive white forehead and "mottled off-foreleg." This horse has no white at all on his body.

Silver Blaze wins by six lengths and Holmes takes the bemused colonel to look at the horse. Holmes explains that it is, indeed, the colonel's horse, but its white and mottled parts have been dyed. When the colonel expresses his hope that Holmes apprehends John Straker's murderer, Holmes tells him that the murderer is, in fact, the horse. On the train journey back to London Holmes explains what has actually occurred.

Simpson could not have put an opiate in the stable boy's food on the night in question which means that it had to be placed there by Straker and his wife. Furthermore, there was a dog in the stable but it had not barked that night, implying that it knew the person who entered. John Straker, Holmes explains, took the horse from the stable out onto the moor to make a cut in its tendons to render it lame and then return it to the stable. He stood to gain a great deal of money if Silver Blaze did not win the Wessex Cup. But Silver Blaze had kicked out at him and struck his forehead. As he fell, his knife had gashed his own thigh. The horse had bolted and was taken in by the colonel's neighbor. Straker had taken the cravat, dropped by Simpson, to make a sling for the horse's leg in order to cut it.

They found the dead body of the unfortunate trainer. Illustration by Sidney Paget from "The Adventure of Silver Blaze," 1892.

"THE ADVENTURE OF THE CARDBOARD BOX"

Holmes is called upon to investigate one of the most gruesome cases of his career. Miss Susan Cushing of Croydon receives a cardboard box in the post that contains two severed human ears carefully preserved in salt. Scotland Yard deems it a prank perpetrated by medical students that Miss Cushing has hosted as lodgers in the past. Holmes is certain, however, that there is something more sinister behind the delivery of the ears. He thoroughly examines the box and its contents and sends a cable to Liverpool before paying a visit to Miss Cushing's sister, Sara. Holmes believes that she is the person for whom the box was intended. Holmes deduces that the ears actually belong to Susan Cushing's youngest sister, Mary, and her extramarital lover who, he believes, have been murdered. The murderer is Mary's husband, Jim Browner.

"THE ADVENTURE OF THE YELLOW FACE"

Holmes and Watson miss a visitor when they are out for a stroll which irritates Holmes who has not undertaken an investigation for several months. The man, Grant Munro, returns and explains that he has been deceived by his wife, Effie, who had asked him for one hundred pounds but requested that he did not ask what she needed it for. She is caught having secret liaisons with the occupants of a cottage near their home, one of whom appears to be a mysterious yellow-faced person.

When Holmes, Watson, and Munro enter the cottage they discover the yellow face is a mask concealing the features of a young half-black girl. She is Effie's daughter. In America she had married a black man who had died and she had thought her daughter had also died but discovered that she was, in fact, alive. The one hundred pounds was to bring her to

England. The story is remarkable because, for once, Holmes's deduction is wrong. He had believed the yellow-faced figure to belong to Effie's first husband. According to Dr. Watson:

> ... *where he failed it happened too often that no one else succeeded ... Now and again, however, it chanced that even when he erred the truth was still discovered.*

"THE ADVENTURE OF THE STOCKBROKER'S CLERK"

Dr. Watson is delighted when Sherlock Holmes turns up on his doorstep one day with a client by the name of Hall Pycroft. Pycroft's story is so unusual that Watson drops everything to accompany the two men to Birmingham. Pycroft has concerns about the company by whom he has been employed. He is further concerned when he is asked by his new employers not to resign his old post. The plan of his new employers is to impersonate Pycroft at his old business in order to steal valuable securities but the plan is foiled.

"THE ADVENTURE OF THE GLORIA SCOTT"

Unusually, this is a story narrated by Sherlock Holmes and is his first professional case. While still at university, Holmes visits the Norfolk home of the only friend he has made at college, Victor Trevor. While there, he stuns Trevor's father, Trevor Senior, with some facts he has deduced about him. The man is so stunned that he faints. This is because Holmes refers to painful events in the past that Trevor Senior believed were dead and buried.

The night before Holmes is due to leave, an old man named Hudson who had been a shipmate of Trevor Senior thirty years previously, appears at the door. Trevor Senior promises to find him work and gets drunk. Some weeks later, Holmes is summoned back to Norfolk because Trevor Senior is dying, having suffered a stroke after receiving a letter. By the time Holmes arrives, the old man is dead. Holmes is told that Hudson, had become troublesome. He was often drunk and the other members of staff hated him. But Trevor Senior let him get away with it.

Shortly after Hudson left, to visit another old shipmate named Beddoes, Trevor Senior received a letter that read:

> *The supply of game for London is going steadily up. Head-keeper Hudson, we believe, has been now told to receive all orders for fly-paper and for preservation of your hen pheasant's life.*

Holmes deciphers this coded letter by taking every third word. It reads, therefore: "The game is up. Hudson has told all. Fly for your life." Holmes deduces that blackmail is involved, Hudson holding some power over Trevor Senior. The truth turns up when a document is found.

In the document, Trevor Senior confesses that long ago he had been arrested and sentenced to transportation to Australia for embezzling money from a bank where he was working. On the ship bound for Australia— the *Gloria Scott*—he learned of a plan to take over the ship. The takeover happened but the transported men argued over what to do with the surviving crew members.

Trevor Senior and others who did not want to be part of cold-blooded murder were cast adrift in a boat, but shortly after leaving the vessel it blew up, the gunpowder having been accidentally ignited. There was only one survivor—Hudson. The next day Trevor Senior and his colleagues were rescued. The old man had lived quietly until Hudson showed up and threatened to expose everything. Holmes believed that the other man, Beddoes, had probably killed Hudson and escaped.

"THE ADVENTURE OF THE MUSGRAVE RITUAL"

In this early Sherlock Holmes case, an old university friend, Reginald Musgrave asks Holmes to help him solve the mystery of his butler and maid who have gone missing. Holmes considers the riddle of the Musgrave Ritual and solves it, finding it leads to a stone slab in the cellar of Musgrave's house. When they lift it they find an empty rotten chest and the body of the butler, Brunton.

Holmes explains that Brunton must have deciphered the meaning of the Musgrave Ritual, surmising that it would lead to something valuable. In order to lift the stone slab he was forced to seek the help of the maid. She hated Brunton and may have kicked away the supports of the slab or it may have been an accident. The maid had been hysterical and had then disappeared but her footprints had been found leading to a lake. A bag was found there containing the valuables to which the Musgrave Ritual led.

"THE ADVENTURE OF THE REIGATE SQUIRE"

Holmes falls ill after a strenuous case in France. Watson insists on taking his associate on holiday to the estate of a friend near Reigate in Surrey. Inevitably, Holmes becomes embroiled in an investigation. An ordinary burglary is not what it seems and the murder of a coachman is linked to a disputed legal claim between the Acton and Cunningham families. The main clue in the murder is a scrap of paper found in the coachman's hand. It is obvious to Holmes that it has been written by two men, one young, the other older, each writing alternate words. Holmes finds the remainder of the note after some subterfuge. The coachman had seen the two Cunningham men sneaking into the estate of the Actons where they unsuccessfully tried to find some papers relating to the dispute.

He blackmails them and Alec Cunningham kills him, making it look like a burglary gone wrong.

"THE ADVENTURE OF THE CROOKED MAN"

Sherlock Holmes arrives at Watson's house to ask him to take part in an unusual case. Two days previously, he had been called upon to investigate the murder of Colonel James Barclay who seems to have been killed by a blow to the head. His wife, Nancy, is suspected of being the murderer. Holmes has quickly deduced, however, from footprints that a third person and a strange animal companion had also been in the room and this man had taken away the key to the room.

Nancy's friend, Miss Morrison, reveals a chance meeting with a deformed man on the night of the murder who Nancy seems to have known. Holmes soon finds the man, Henry Wood, and solicits his story from him. Wood had been in the army and had once vied with the colonel for Nancy's attentions. But the colonel had sent him deliberately into an ambush which led to his capture and torture resulting in his present condition.

That fateful night he had followed Nancy home and heard an argument. When he entered the room where the colonel and Nancy were arguing, the colonel had a fit on seeing him and died, banging his head on a table as he fell. Mrs. Barclay fainted. Wood had fled with the key, having taken it from Nancy intending to get help but realizing it would look as if he had killed the colonel. He picked up the mongoose that he used in conjuring tricks and fled. An inquest exonerates Nancy, finding the colonel was dead before his head hit the table.

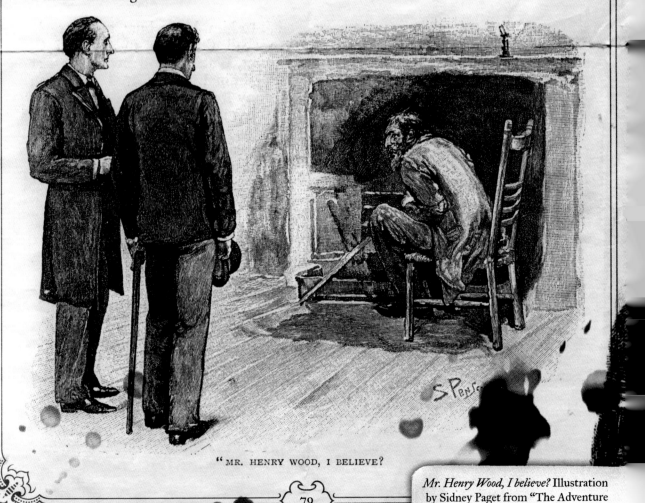

"MR. HENRY WOOD, I BELIEVE?

Mr. Henry Wood, I believe? Illustration by Sidney Paget from "The Adventure of the Crooked Man," 1893.

"THE ADVENTURE OF THE RESIDENT PATIENT"

Sherlock Holmes is consulted by Dr. Percy Trevelyan who is in a business arrangement with a man named Blessington who has set him up in practice in return for three-quarters of his earnings. Blessington is also ill. Therefore, he always has a doctor on hand. Blessington has become very agitated after reading of a burglary.

One evening a Russian nobleman and his son arrive for a consultation. They suddenly disappear but return the following evening. After they left Blessington was very agitated, claiming someone had been in his room, that there were footprints. It must have been the son of the nobleman, but nothing has been taken. At the surgery, Blessington admits that he keeps all his money in a box in his bedroom but Holmes believes there is more to it. He tells Watson that Blessington knows who the two men are.

Next morning they learn that Blessington has hanged himself. Holmes deduces, however, that it was not suicide. The two men must have been let in by the surgery's newly employed page. It is discovered that all four men had been members of a gang of bank robbers. Blessington had informed on them but they had been released early from prison, causing Blessington's terror. One of their number had been hanged and they chose this means of punishing Blessington.

"THE ADVENTURE OF THE GREEK INTERPRETER"

This story begins with Dr. Watson musing upon the character and origins of his friend:

During my long and intimate acquaintance with Mr. Sherlock Holmes I had never heard him refer to his relations, and hardly ever to his own early life. This reticence upon his part had increased the somewhat inhuman effect which he produced upon me, until sometimes I found myself regarding him as an isolated phenomenon, a brain without a heart, as deficient in human sympathy as he was pre-eminent in intelligence.

Mycroft Holmes, as we learn has every bit the intellect of his brother but lacks his energy. Therefore, his first instinct when he is approached by a Greek interpreter named Melas, is to hand the case over to Sherlock.

"Come in," said he, blandly. Illustration by Sidney Paget from "The Adventure of the Greek Interpreter," 1893.

Melas has been engaged by a man named Harold Latimer to do some translating for him, but Melas works out quickly that the job is not entirely legal. He is threatened to keep silent about it.

Latimer and his henchman, Wilson Kemp, take him into a room and another, emaciated man is brought in who has sticking plaster on his face with a large piece covering his mouth. Melas is asked to translate instructions to this man to sign some papers. The man tells Melas in writing that his name is Kratides and he has been taken captive. Latimer was trying to get him to sign over property but suddenly a woman called Sophy who is involved rushes in and recognizes Kratides. Melas is taken home again and had gone to Mycroft for help.

Holmes and Watson find out where the woman Sophy lives and make their way there, learning that Melas has now been taken prisoner by Latimer. The house is abandoned when they get there but they find Melas and Kratides tied up in a closet. Kratides is the woman's brother and her friends had summoned him from Greece to help her against Latimer. We learn that Latimer and Kemp later kill each other in a fight in Hungary although Holmes is convinced that it is Sophy who has stabbed them to death in revenge for the treatment she and her brother received.

"THE ADVENTURE OF THE NAVAL TREATY"

Watson's old schoolmate, Percy Phelps, has endured some problems that could lead to a scandal and disgrace. He had been working late one night, copying a top-secret naval treaty but after briefly leaving the room, had discovered that the treaty had been stolen from his desk. Immediately after, he had become ill and had not worked for several months. Asked to look into the matter, Sherlock Holmes discovers the culprit to be the brother of Phelps's fiancée.

"THE ADVENTURE OF THE FINAL PROBLEM"

It is 1891 and Holmes arrives at Dr. Watson's house in a panic with grazed and bleeding knuckles. They are the results of several attempts on his life that day by his nemesis, Professor Moriarty. Dr. Watson begins this tale in a sombre tone:

> *It is with a heavy heart that I take up my pen to write these last words in which I shall ever record the singular gifts by which my friend Mr. Sherlock Holmes was distinguished.*

Moriarty's first attempt on Holmes's life had involved a speeding carriage that the detective had only just managed to avoid. Next a brick had fallen from a house, narrowly missing him. Then, as he had been making his way toward Watson's residence, he was attacked by a thug wielding a "bludgeon." Holmes succeeded in overcoming his assailant and handed him over to the police but he was unable to prove the attacker was in the employ of Moriarty.

Holmes explains that he is on the verge of bringing Moriarty and his gang to justice, but Moriarty is aware of this and the criminal genius had visited Holmes at 221B Baker Street to try to warn him off, telling him:

> *You stand in the way not merely of an individual, but of a mighty organization, the full extent of which you, with all your cleverness, have been unable to realize. You must stand clear, Mr. Holmes, or be trodden underfoot.*

Holmes explains to Watson that he is essential to a conviction of Moriarty and suggests that the two of them disappear to Europe for a few days.

When Watson arrives in his designated train carriage at Victoria station the following morning, there is no sign of Holmes. He finally turns up, disguised as an aged Italian priest. As the train leaves, they see Moriarty arrive on the platform too late to board the train. Holmes explains that the previous night Moriarty's henchmen had set fire to their rooms at 221B Baker Street. He also warns Watson that Moriarty will catch up with them later.

They change their plans, getting off the train at Canterbury and making for the sea ferry at Newhaven to cross to Dieppe in France. From there they will travel to Switzerland. As they wait on the platform, a special train flies past, undoubtedly chartered by the criminal mastermind. The two cross the English Channel and on Monday, Holmes telephones London to learn that the gang has been arrested, but Moriarty has escaped. Holmes realizes that with his gang gone, Moriarty will have just one objective—revenge.

Holmes and Watson make their way to Meiringen in Switzerland but Holmes is uneasy during the journey. He looks forward to "the day that I crown my career by the capture or extinction of the most dangerous and capable criminal in Europe."

On May 3, they arrive at the Englischer Hof in the village of Meiringen and the following day they set out to spend the night at the hamlet of Rosenlaui. They make a small detour en route to visit the spectacular falls of Reichenbach of which Watson gives a vivid description:

It is indeed, a fearful place. The torrent, swollen by the melting snow, plunges into a tremendous abyss, from which the spray rolls up like the smoke from a burning house. The shaft into which the river hurls itself is an immense chasm, lined by glistening coal-black rock, and narrowing into a creaming, boiling pit of incalculable depth, which brims over and shoots the stream onward over its jagged lip. The long sweep of green water roaring forever down, and the thick flickering curtain of spray hissing forever upward, turn a man giddy with their constant whirl and clamor. We stood near the edge peering down at the gleam of breaking water far below us against the black rocks, and listening to the half-human shout which came booming up with the spray out of the abyss.

Suddenly, a boy arrives bearing a letter from the landlord of the Englischer Hof explaining that a doctor is required at the hotel. Watson is forced to return to Meiringen, the detective continuing with the boy as his guide.

As I turned away I saw Holmes, with his back against a rock and his arms folded, gazing down at the rush of the waters. It was the last that I was ever destined to see of him in this world.

As Watson nears the bottom of the hill, he looks up and sees the black figure of a man walking very fast up above him. On arriving at the village, however, he discovers that the letter is a hoax. The landlord informs him that a tall Englishman who had arrived after they had left must be responsible. Watson rushes off in the direction of the falls, fearing the worst.

On arriving at the spot where he had left Holmes, he discovers the detective's Alpine stock. Two lines of footprints on the soft ground lead away from this spot, but none return. There are signs of a struggle. Watson lies down and looks over the edge of the falls, shouting, but there is no sign of anyone. Then, on the rocks, he spies Holmes's silver cigarette case. As he picks it up, a small square of paper flutters from it to the ground. It is a final letter to Watson from Holmes that Moriarty has allowed him to write.

Watson and experts who have subsequently examined the scene, have little doubt that the two men have fallen over the falls while "locked in each other's arms" and have died "deep down in that dreadful cauldron of swirling water and seething foam."

Watson concludes by describing Sherlock Holmes as "the best and the wisest man whom I have ever known."

THE DEATH OF SHERLOCK HOLMES
ILLUSTRATED BY SIDNEY PAGET
FROM "THE ADVENTURE OF
THE FINAL PROBLEM"

As the Sherlock Holmes stories grew in popularity, *The Strand Magazine* became one of the most prestigious publications of the time, and Sidney Paget's illustrations began to play a bigger part. Starting with "The Adventure of the Final Problem" in 1893, almost every Holmes story featured a full-page illustration as well as many small pictures within the text.

Paget's work has been a great influence on portrayals of Holmes ever since. In the 2011 movie *Sherlock Holmes: A Game of Shadows*, Holmes, played by Robert Downey Jr., uses the two-handed clasp shown in the illustration when fighting Moriarty, although Conan Doyle never actually describes the fight in the story.

JOHN BARRYMORE IN

Sherlock Holmes, played by John Barrymore (right) confronts Professor Moriarty (Gustav von Seyffertitz) in a poster from the 1922 silent movie *Sherlock Holmes*. This classic film was considered lost for decades, but rolls of jumbled and out of order negatives were rediscovered in the mid-1970s. A full restoration was finally completed in 2001 and released as a DVD in 2009.

PROFESSOR JAMES MORIARTY
THE NAPOLEON OF CRIME

Although frequently mentioned, Professor Moriarty appears in only one Sherlock Holmes story, "The Adventure of the Final Problem." In this tale, Holmes, on the verge of bringing down Moriarty's criminal empire, flees to Europe with Dr. Watson to avoid assassination attempts by Moriarty's henchmen.

An underworld overlord, Moriarty protects all the criminals in England in return for their obedience and a share of their ill-gotten gains. Holmes depicts him as a powerful mastermind who is ruthless, cunning, and manipulative, remarking several times that Moriarty is at least as intelligent as him. Holmes implies that Moriarty is consistently capable of second guessing him and describes his nemesis as:

... extremely tall and thin, his forehead domes out in a white curve, and his two eyes are deeply sunken in his head ... his face protrudes forward, and is forever slowly oscillating from side to side in a curiously reptilian fashion ... He is the Napoleon of crime, Watson. He is the organizer of half that is evil and of nearly all that is undetected in this great city ... He sits motionless, like a spider in the center of its web, but that web has a thousand radiations, and he knows well every quiver of each of them.

CHAPTER 11

THE ECHOES OF WAR

CROSSING THE OCEAN

In 1894, Conan Doyle had the opportunity to visit North America for the first time, taking his brother Innes with him. They were met when their ship docked, by Major J.B. Pond (1838 – 1903), a lecture manager and Civil War hero who won the Medal of Honor while fighting in the Union army. Pond had organized Conan Doyle's tour as he had for Charles Dickens, Mark Twain and others. Conan Doyle was a different prospect, however. There were none of the theatrics that Dickens employed during his speaking engagements. Conan Doyle was sometimes under-prepared and untidily dressed. Several newspapers expressed the disappointment in the performances of the author of Sherlock Holmes that was also felt by many among his audiences, although the tour of Chicago, Indianapolis, Cincinnati, Toledo, Detroit and Milwaukee was not entirely unsuccessful. In Toronto, Canada, he spoke to 1,500 people and undoubtedly felt more comfortable. He visited Niagara Falls and expressed regret to his wife that he had not chosen that natural phenomenon instead of the Reichenbach Falls for the denouement of "The Final Problem."

IN THE SHADOW OF THE PYRAMIDS

The U.S. tour was a commercial success introducing Sherlock Holmes to thousands of new readers but Conan Doyle was still restless. Returning to England, he almost immediately departed for Egypt but not before he bought a parcel of land in the affluent town of Hindhead in Surrey. He engaged an architect to design a house on the land before setting off for Egypt. They checked into the Mena Hotel, close to the Pyramids and spent the winter there. He climbed the Great Pyramid, played golf and rode, at one point climbing onto a horse that bolted and threw him off, resulting in a wound above the eye that required five stitches.

A NEW DOYLE CHARACTER: BRIGADIER GERARD

Following his travels, Conan Doyle returned to writing and in 1896 *The Exploits of Brigadier Gerard* was published. The stories in the book first appeared in *The Strand Magazine* between December 1894 and December 1895 and included eight tales told by the French brigadier now retired and living in Paris. Conan Doyle modeled the brigadier on a real-life character, Baron Jean Baptiste Antoine Marcellin de Marbot, who was a French light cavalry officer during the Napoleonic Wars. De Marbot was a slightly pompous and vain individual, but had shown considerable courage in battle. For Conan Doyle, although these stories fitted nicely into his historical fiction oeuvre, they were not as serious as some of his other works and were written almost as recreation. In fact, *Brigadier Gerard* has stood the test of time far better than his other historical works and the brigadier himself comes across as a convincing character with whom the reader sympathizes which cannot be said of many of Conan Doyle's other creations.

A LOVE OF BOXING

Conan Doyle published another book in 1896. *Rodney Stone* was a Gothic mystery featuring prizefighting. It is narrated by Rodney, a boy from the Sussex countryside, who is taken to London by his well-to-do uncle, Sir Charles Tregellis. Tregellis is a highly respected man-about-town, an arbiter of fashion and a member of the social elite. The novel tells the coming-of-age story of Rodney and his friend Boy Jim's efforts to become a boxer.

Conan Doyle loved *Rodney Stone*, and it was one of the most profitable of all his works. The publisher Smith, Elder & Co. paid him four thousand pounds and serial rights went to *The Strand Magazine* for a further one thousand five hundred pounds. Conan Doyle was a fan of boxing, a sport in which he had participated at school and he had also boxed a little on the ships on which he had worked as a doctor. He had boxed in Southsea and he had also attended boxing matches and supported initiatives to launch boxing clubs for the sons of the poor of Glasgow and London's East End. He wrote:

> *I had always a weakness for the old fighting men and for the lore of the prize-ring, and I indulged it in this novel.*

FAITHFUL TO TOUIE

Meanwhile, Louisa remained an invalid, spending much of her life incapacitated in bed. This, of course, meant a loss of intimacy between the pair, but there is no evidence that Conan Doyle remained anything but faithful to his ailing wife. He spent long hours at her bedside reading his latest writing to her, sharing reviews with her and gossiping about their acquaintances. He fed her and helped her to drink and ensured that she was never alone.

ENTER JEAN LECKIE

Everything changed on March 15, 1897. Conan Doyle was attending a party in London when he was introduced to a young woman by the name of Jean Leckie who was from a wealthy family from Blackheath in south London. She was a good singer, a very competent horsewoman and was fourteen years younger than Conan Doyle. She was also fulsome in her praise of his work, lavishing blandishments on his medieval novels and describing his Sherlock Holmes stories as works of genius. Conan Doyle fell

deeply in love as he had never done before, not even with Louisa in happier times before she had so tragically fallen ill. He informed his mother and she was sanguine about it. Some of his friends encouraged him while others were disparaging of the relationship. He promised himself, however, that he would remain faithful to and care for Louisa until she finally succumbed to her illness but would also love and care for Jean.

Jean Leckie (1874 – 1940).

WAR BREAKS OUT

Around this time, the Conan Doyle family moved into the house he had built in Hindhead, Surrey, about 40 miles south-west of London. It was named "Undershaw." An impressive residence designed by Conan Doyle, it had a two-story entrance hall, eleven bedrooms and a dining room that could comfortably seat thirty diners. The house even had its own power plant to provide electricity. The location in the countryside surrounding London was chosen to help Louisa's tuberculosis. Doctors of the era recommended healthy air, for which Surrey was known.

It was a difficult time, however. Conan Doyle was moody and restless and reacted badly when friends suggested that as a measure of relief from the trials and tribulations of his personal life, he should perhaps return to Sherlock Holmes. But he was busy, writing short stories and delivering lectures. It was not enough, however, and when the Boer War broke out in 1899, he offered himself to the army. By this time he was forty years old and considerably overweight. He was rejected as not fit enough which hurt him greatly. The war would not last long, they told him and there were sufficient troops. He was also annoyed by the fact that colonial troops were being employed to fight the Boers. Why not British men? With indignation he wrote to *The Times*:

The suggestion comes from many quarters that more colonials should be sent to the seat of war. But how can we in honor permit our colonial fellow-civilians to fill the gap when none of our own civilians have gone to the front? Great Britain is full of men who can ride and shoot. Might I suggest that lists should at least be opened and the names of those taken who are ready to go if required—preference might be given to those men who can find their own horses? There are thousands of men riding after foxes or shooting pheasants who would gladly be useful to their country if it were made possible for them. This war has at least taught the lesson that it only needs a brave man and a modern rifle to make a soldier.

A MEDICAL VOLUNTEER

Disturbed by the casualty figures, Conan Doyle offered himself next as a volunteer in the medical unit of his friend, the philanthropist John Langman (1846 – 1928). It was odd because he had been on the side of the Boers who he saw as purely fighting for

Arthur Conan Doyle (back row, second from left) with the staff of Langman Hospital, Bloemfontein, South Africa, 1900.

their homes and their families. He conducted interviews for people to work at the hospital and then traveled to the Cape of Africa where he found even worse conditions than he had foreseen.

It was April 1900 and the town of Bloemfontein was ravaged by fever, the water supply having been cut off by the Boers. The troops and people in the town had no option but to drink contaminated water, leading to as many troops dying of fever as in the fighting. It was a dreadful place, as he described it:

The outbreak was a terrible one. It was softened down for public consumption and the press messages were heavily censored, but we lived in the midst of death—and death in its vilest, filthiest form. Our accommodation was for fifty patients, but a hundred and twenty were precipitated upon us, and the floor was littered between the beds with sick and often dying men. Our linen and utensils were never calculated for such a number, and as the nature of the disease causes constant pollution, and this pollution of the most dangerous character and with the vilest effluvia, one can imagine how dreadful was the situation. The worst surgical ward after a battle would be a clean place compared to that pavilion ... In the

very worst of it two nursing sisters appeared among us, and never shall I forget what angels of light they appeared, or how they nursed those poor boys, swaddling them like babies and meeting every want with gentle courage. Thank God, they both came through safe.

THE CHAOS OF WARFARE

Conan Doyle was horrified by the chaos, far removed from the chivalric warfare he had written about and not at all what he had expected. However, he was remembered by troops around him in those dreadful scenes as compassionate and unselfish. He saw many things that would never leave him, witnessed the worst of people—looting, silly arguments, bitterness and anger. But he also saw acts of great and selfless individual courage.

As ever he was turning his imagination to how the war could be better prosecuted, inventing a way, for instance, of turning a rifle into a howitzer. His plans were duly delivered to the War Office but received an insulting and patronizing response. Meanwhile, the war continued for another two years and evidence of British atrocities began to emerge. Concentration camps did little to help the image of the British around the world and Conan Doyle was exasperated by this.

PAMPHLET WARFARE

Conan Doyle vented his anger in a pamphlet *The War in South Africa: Its Cause and Conduct* which, costing sixpence, sold 300,000 copies in Britain within eight weeks of publication. He donated almost all of the proceeds from the pamphlet to relevant charities such as the Chelsea Pensioners and even to Boers who were suffering hardships. He also established a scholarship for South African students at Edinburgh University.

In his pamphlet, however, he did defend the use of concentration camps. The Boers fought a guerrilla-style war, shooting British troops and then disappearing into the population. Therefore, if the women and

SHERLOCK HOLMES'S KNIGHTHOOD

In 1902, the same year that Arthur Conan Doyle received a knighthood for his writing in support of the Boer War, Sherlock Holmes turned down a knighthood. Watson tiptoes around the matter somewhat in "The Adventure of the Three Garridebs:"

I remember the date very well, for it was in the same month that Holmes refused a knighthood for services which may perhaps some day be described. I only refer to the matter in passing, for in my position of partner and confidant I am obliged to be particularly careful to avoid any indiscretion.

We are not told in this story what these services were, but one may surmise that Holmes had undertaken work for the government, possibly under the auspices of his brother Mycroft.

children in certain towns were kept isolated in a camp there was no opportunity for the Boer fighters to disappear into normal life again. He argued that the poor conditions in the camps—a lack of adequate food and water—only reflected the conditions faced by British troops in South Africa. However, Conan Doyle also denied the reports of other atrocities and abuses, such as rape, torture and looting. He repudiated the claims that the British had used dum-dum bullets, particularly nasty ammunition with a soft nose that exploded on impact, blasting a massive wound in its target. He was wrong. The dum-dum bullet was indeed employed by British troops although they had been ordered not to and risked serious punishment if any were found.

People congratulated Conan Doyle in the street for his writing on the war and he was feted as something of a national hero.

HOW TO FIGHT A WAR

Conan Doyle decided to make some recommendations to the army. He believed the cavalry that he had seen in use in South

Arthur Conan Doyle in Waterfall prisoner's tunnel, South Africa, 1900.

Africa to be outdated and utterly useless against the modern fighting man. He championed the use of part-time reserve soldiers, like the modern territorials. This would make it quicker to train men in the event of war. This time the army was forced to pay a little more attention. He had become a figure of national repute regarding the Boer War, after all. Unfortunately, the army ultimately did not incorporate any of his ideas at the time although eventually they did become part of British Army practice.

Conan Doyle was somewhat preoccupied by this time, however. In April 1902, he was offered a knighthood. Initially, he refused the honor, suggesting he was not worthy of such a distinction, as the mere writer of Sherlock Holmes, but he was reassured that the knighthood was for his service to Britain in the Boer War—mainly his pamphlet. His mother instructed him to accept it and he became Sir Arthur Conan Doyle.

THE GREAT HIATUS 1891 – 94

Dr. Watson tells us in the story "The Final Problem" how Sherlock Holmes had died in 1891 in a titanic struggle with his nemesis Professor Moriarty at the Reichenbach Falls.

Holmes, of course, did not die, but faked his death in order to fool his enemies, of whom at least three were intent on killing him. He reckoned that if he was apparently off the scene, these men would "take liberties" and, thus, open themselves to the wiles of Sherlock Holmes who would destroy them. He embarked upon the three year period known to Holmes scholars as "the Great Hiatus."

A week after his "death," he was in Florence, with only one person, his brother Mycroft aware that he was alive. When he reveals that he is alive to Dr. Watson, he apologizes. He had reckoned that Watson would not have written so convincing an account of his friend's death had he known that it was a ruse. Mycroft, on the other hand, had to be informed so that Holmes would have the means to stay out of sight.

So, what did Holmes occupy himself with during the three years he was missing? Firstly he traveled to Tibet where he spent two years, visiting Lhasa and passing several days with the head lama. There had been reports in the newspapers of the "remarkable explorations" of a Norwegian named Sigerson who was actually Sherlock Holmes in disguise. (This name has led several Sherlockian scholars to speculate that Holmes's father may have been named "Siger," but there is nothing in the canon to confirm this).

Holmes next traveled through Persia and visited Mecca, no doubt in disguise like the great explorer Richard Burton (1821 – 90). At the time, Europeans were forbidden access to the Holy City on pain of death.

In another perilous venture, he visited the Khalifa at Khartoum, relaying back to the Foreign Office discussions with the Muslim religious leader who had succeeded the Mahdi, the man whose forces had taken Khartoum and killed General Gordon just a few years before Holmes's visit.

Holmes's next port-of-call was a laboratory at Montpellier in the south of France where he "spent some months in a research into the coal-tar ..." It was never explained what aspect of coal-tar derivatives so exercised the mind of the great detective although several theories have been put forward. One had it that Holmes was trying to isolate carcinogens from coal-tar; another said that he was active in the development of radiation technology; and several sources have suggested that synthetic dyes were the object of his attention during these experiments. At this time, England was losing its pre-eminence in the production of dyes and it has been suggested that Holmes was patriotically attempting to breathe life back into the dye industry.

It was news of the murder of Ronald Adair in the case that Watson called "The Adventure of the Empty House" that persuaded Holmes to return to the fray.

CHAPTER 12

THE HOUND OF THE BASKERVILLES

Sir Arthur Conan Doyle's efforts during and after the Boer War earned him still greater recognition than he had enjoyed previously. Even those who had little interest in Sherlock Holmes knew his name. Politics seemed to beckon and the main political parties sought his support while newspapers suggested that a career in politics lay ahead. But he despised the leader of the Liberal Party, Henry Campbell-Bannerman (1836–1908) and was eager to stand as an independent candidate against him but that did not happen and, instead, he fought the 1900 General Election as a Unionist in Edinburgh. Known as the "khaki election" because the Boer War was still going on, this election resulted in a majority of 130 for the Conservatives and the Liberal Unionists. Although he performed better than could be expected in a difficult constituency, Conan Doyle lost.

A JOINT PRODUCTION?

There was still a clamor for more Sherlock Holmes stories but Conan Doyle was unwilling to bring back the great detective from the dead. Why not, therefore, satisfy the demand with a story from before his demise? In March 1901, Conan Doyle spent a happy golfing holiday in Cromer on England's east coast, with the editor of the *Daily News*, Bertram Fletcher Robinson (1870–1907) whom he had met in July 1900 aboard a ship from Cape Town to Southampton. They met again in Devon and Robinson recounted to Conan Doyle stories of ghostly hounds and traveled with him around Dartmoor, showing him the sights. Conan Doyle wrote to his mother that "Robinson and I are exploring the moor together over our Sherlock Holmes book." Robinson told

him the supernatural tale of Squire Richard Cabell III.

It has been said that Baskerville Hall is based on a house situated in mid-Wales that was built in 1839 by a man named Thomas Mynors Baskerville. Originally named Clyro Court, it was renamed Baskerville Hall toward the end of the nineteenth century. Conan Doyle was a family friend and often stayed there and he is certain to have learned of a local legend of the hounds of the Baskervilles. It is suggested, however, that he relocated his story to Devon so that tourists would not be put off coming to the hotel.

This was the genesis of what, for many, is the very best Sherlock Holmes novel— *The Hound of the Baskervilles*. Conan Doyle was not terribly generous about Robinson's contribution to the story, however, dismissing it as merely a "remark" but it is, of course, impossible to know just how much he contributed. Robinson himself described his role as that of "assistant plot producer."

BEST HOLMES EVER

The Hound of the Baskervilles was serialized in *The Strand Magazine* between August 1901 and April 1902, each of its chapters ending on a suitable cliff-hanger. It was published in book form the following year. It has since gained legendary status, and in 1999, it was rated the best Sherlock Holmes novel with a rating from Holmes scholars of 100.

It is a rare example of Conan Doyle coming up with a story first and making Sherlock Holmes the vehicle for it. He initially described it as a straight "Victorian creeper" and the notion of Holmes emerging as the *deus ex machina* only became apparent later.

THE HOUND OF THE BASKERVILLES

A.G.J.

CONAN DOYLE

First edition cover of *The Hound of the Baskervilles*, designed by Alfred Garth Jones, 1902.

SHERLOCK HOLMES CASE FILE
THE HOUND OF THE BASKERVILLES

THE GREAT BLACK BEAST

The novel opens with Holmes and Watson wondering who is the unknown visitor who has left a cane in their rooms. Holmes amazes Watson by brilliantly deducing that the cane belongs to James Mortimer. Holmes predicts the arrival of Mr. Mortimer and he duly turns up. Mortimer unveils an eighteenth century manuscript and reads the legend of the lecherous Hugo Baskerville.

Baskerville, the manuscript says, captured and imprisoned a young country girl at his estate in Devonshire. She escaped and he pursued her across the moors with his pack of hunting hounds and his guests also take off in pursuit. The guests came across a shepherd who told them that he had seen the girl with the hounds on her trail but he had also seen Hugo on his horse, pursued by a large hound:

> *... for Hugo Baskerville passed me upon his black mare, and there ran mute behind him such a hound of hell as God forbid should ever be at my heels.*

They finally found the girl, dead from exhaustion and fright, and beside her lay Baskerville's body. Standing over him and plucking at his throat was:

> *... a foul thing, a great, black beast, shaped like a hound, yet larger than any hound that ever mortal eye has rested upon.*

The beast tore out Baskerville's throat and the riders escape into the night, terrified.

THE CURSE OF THE BASKERVILLES

Since that fateful night, Mortimer informs Holmes and Watson, the lives of the Baskerville family have been blighted by a mysterious, supernatural hound that may even be responsible for the recent, tragic death of Sir Charles Baskerville who had met his end during his nightly walk close to Baskerville Hall. Cries had been heard and although there were no marks on Sir Charles's body, his face was grossly distorted. Fears of the curse of the Baskervilles have arisen again especially as the footprints of a gigantic hound had been discovered near Sir Charles's body.

Mortimer informs Holmes and Watson that Sir Charles's heir, Sir Henry Baskerville, has arrived in London from America and would soon be taking up his role at Baskerville Hall. Holmes meets Sir Henry who shows him an anonymous note he has received made up of cut and pasted pieces of newsprint. It says: "As you value your life or your reason keep away from the moor."

Strangely, one of Sir Henry's new boots has been taken from his hotel room. They talk about the Baskerville family. Sir Charles was the oldest of three brothers. The youngest, Rodger—the black sheep of the family—is thought to have died in South Africa and Sir Henry is the son of the middle brother.

Holmes and Watson discover that while he is in London, Henry Baskerville is being followed by a mysterious, bearded stranger and they are unsure whether this man is friend or enemy. Mortimer informs them that Mr. Barrymore, a servant at Baskerville Hall, has a beard. Sir Henry's missing new boot reappears, but an older one vanishes.

"The Hound of the Baskervilles."
Illustration by Sidney Paget, 1902.

WATSON GOES TO DEVON

Holmes remains in London sending Watson to Devon instead. When Watson and Sir Henry arrive they discover that a murderer named Selden who has escaped from prison has been sighted in the area. Armed guards are patrolling in search of the man. They learn that Barrymore and his wife want to leave their employment at the estate soon but Watson hears a woman crying during the night. It is obvious that it is Mrs. Barrymore. Next morning her husband denies it.

Watson can find no evidence to prove that Barrymore was in Devon the day that he and Holmes had followed the bearded man in London. He meets a brother and sister who live near the hall—the Stapletons. Mr. Stapleton denies that a wild noise heard from the moors is related to the legendary beast. When her brother leaves them, the beautiful Miss Stapleton, believing Watson to be Sir Henry, warns him to leave. When Miss Stapleton finally meets Sir Henry, the couple fall in love, to the annoyance of Mr. Stapleton but he apologizes to Sir Henry for his anger and invites him to come to dinner a few nights later.

One night, Dr. Watson's suspicion of Barrymore is increased when he and Sir Henry discover the servant in an empty room with a candle. Barrymore refuses to answer any questions but his wife confirms that the escaped convict Selden is, in fact, her brother and her husband is signaling to him out on the moor. Dr. Watson and Sir Henry rush out and pursue Selden but he manages to escape. However, Watson, spies an eerie figure out on the moor, standing on a nearby tor.

An agreement is reached with Barrymore that his brother-in-law Selden will be allowed to leave the country. In return Barrymore tells them that Sir Charles had gone out on the fateful night to meet a woman whose initials were "L.L." He knew this from a burnt letter his wife had found in Sir Charles's study. The woman is Laura Lyons and she had written to Sir Charles to ask him to finance her divorce, but she did not keep the appointment she had made with him that night.

BLOODHOUNDS AND BASKERVILLES

Holmes appears and Watson learns that he was the figure on the tor. He informs Watson that the Stapletons are not brother and sister—they are actually married to one another. Mr. Stapleton has proposed marriage to Laura Lyons in order to ensure she cooperated with him and arranged the appointment with Sir Charles. There is a scream and Selden is found to have fallen to his death but they mistake him for Sir Henry because the dead man is wearing Sir Henry's clothes given to him by Barrymore.

Back at the hall, Holmes perceives a similarity of features between Barrymore and a portrait of the unfortunate Hugo Baskerville and reasons that the servant may, in fact, be an unknown Baskerville family member who is trying to get his hands on the Baskerville fortune by eliminating the other family members.

By this time, Holmes has summoned Inspector Lestrade of Scotland Yard and they travel to Baskerville Hall where they rescue Sir Henry from a dog that Stapleton has released on the moor. Holmes shoots it and realizes that it is a perfectly normal hound, not the fiendish one of whom everyone is terrified. It is a mix of bloodhound and mastiff that has been painted with phosphorous to lend it a terrifying appearance. Inside the house, they discover Mrs. Stapleton bound and gagged and outside her husband dies in a muddy bog as he tries to reach his hideout. They discover the missing boot that had been used to give the dog Sir Henry's scent. The new one, of course, did not have the scent.

Weeks later, Holmes apprises Watson of some more facts about the case. Stapleton was, in fact, the son of Rodger Baskerville, whose name was also Rodger. His widow is a South American woman named Beryl Garcia. Rodger had lived a life of crime for many years before discovering that if he murdered his uncle and cousin he would inherit Baskerville Hall and a substantial fortune. Selden had died when the hound had pursued the scent on Sir Henry's clothing and Mrs. Stapleton had been tied up because she no longer wanted anything to do with the plot her husband had devised.

Holmes emptied five barrels of his revolver into the creature's flank. Illustration by Sidney Paget from *The Hound of the Baskervilles,* 1902.

SHERLOCK HOLMES' MOS

PETER CUSHING
as SHERLOCK HOLMES

ANDRE MORELL
as Dr. Watson

CHRISTOPHER LEE
as Sir Henry Baskerville

MARLA LANDI

DAVID OXLEY

the Hound of th

TECHNICOLOR

Produced by ANTHONY HINDS
Directed by TERENCE FISHER
Executive Producer MICHAEL CARRERAS
Associate Producer ANTHONY NELSON KEYS
Screenplay by PETER BRYAN

Movie poster for the 1959 British gothic horror version of *The Hound of the Baskervilles*. Starring Peter Cushing as Sherlock Holmes, it was the first movie adaptation of the novel to be filmed in color.

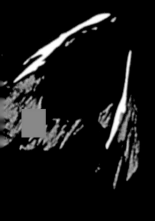

TERRIFYING ADVENTURE!

Baskervilles

•A•

Based on the novel by Sir Arthur Conan Doyle

A HAMMER FILM PRODUCTION UNITED ARTISTS

THE BAKER STREET IRREGULARS

The Baker Street Irregulars are a bunch of street urchins, led by an older boy named Wiggins, that occasionally help Sherlock Holmes in his investigations. Holmes pays them a shilling a day each plus expenses, and offers a reward of a guinea for an important clue or piece of evidence. The irregulars turn up in *A Study in Scarlet* and *The Sign of the Four* which has a chapter named after them. They are also mentioned in "The Adventure of the Crooked Man," when Holmes tells Watson:

I have one of my Baker Street boys mounting guard over him who would stick to him like a burr, go where he might.

The Baker Street Irregulars illustrated by George Hutchinson in *A Study in Scarlet*, 1887.

MORE HOLMES, PLEASE

Reaction to *The Hound of the Baskervilles* was very positive. Fans were delighted by this atmospheric story that was far more complex and sophisticated in approach. The bad news for Conan Doyle, of course, is that he was inundated with offers from both his own country and the United States.

Large sums of money were being bandied about which made them exceedingly difficult to resist. New York publisher Collier's offered him four thousand dollars, a huge sum at the time, for each of six stories. They would take more if he felt so inclined and they did not even stipulate the length. He relented and signed a contract to provide them with eight Sherlock Holmes stories with an option for another four if all went well.

The problem was, of course, how to resurrect the seemingly dead detective. It happens in the first story of the new series, "The Adventure of the Empty House." Collier's trumpeted the new Sherlock Holmes stories on September 19, 1903:

In next week's issue of Collier's, the Household Number for October, will begin the most notable series of short stories of the year—"The Return of Sherlock Holmes," by Sir Arthur Conan Doyle. Those familiar with the previous adventures of the famous detective—and are there any who are not?—will remember that the last we heard of Mr. Holmes was the report that he had been hurled headlong over a precipitous cliff. It was not believed that any man—either in fact or fiction—could survive such a shock as this, and even the detective's best friends (even those who most realized the very good reasons Holmes might have for wishing himself to be considered dead) began to give up hope of ever again hearing of his wonderful genius or of witnessing its almost infallible operation. But Holmes did not die. He survived the deadly peril through which he passed, and of this and of the ensuing adventures Sir Conan Doyle [sic] tells us in the remarkable series which he has called "The Return of Sherlock Holmes."

SHERLOCK HOLMES'S DRUG HABIT

"Which is it to-day," I asked, "morphine or cocaine?" He raised his eyes languidly ... "It is cocaine," he said, "a seven-per-cent solution. Would you care to try it?"

Sherlock Holmes, *The Sign of the Four*

The Sign of the Four introduces us to one of the more shocking habits of the ineffably complex Sherlock Holmes—his drug habit. The book opens with Dr. Watson expressing the dilemma he faced as a doctor and as a friend of the detective when confronted with Holmes's regular drug use:

Sherlock Holmes took the bottle from the corner of the mantelpiece, and his hypodermic syringe from its neat morocco case. With his long, white, nervous fingers he adjusted the delicate needle, and rolled back his left shirt-cuff. For some little time his eyes rested thoughtfully upon his sinewy forearm and wrist, all dotted and scarred with innumerable puncture-marks. Finally, he thrust the sharp point home, pressed down the tiny piston, and sank back into the velvet-lined arm-chair with a long sigh of satisfaction.

Holmes used cocaine as well as morphine, a means, he said, of escaping from what he described as "the dull routine of existence." In fact, in Victorian times the sale of these two drugs as well as others such as opium and laudanum was not against the law. Holmes takes the drug in the belief that his busy brain requires stimulation when not engaged in solving complex cases but he never takes it when working on a case. He is also, in common with most Victorians, unaware of the dangerous side-effects of such drugs. He is aware that it is not good for him, of course but he defends his use by claiming that it is "transcendentally stimulating and clarifying to the mind."

The second half of the nineteenth century saw a surge in cocaine use for recreational and health purposes as scientists and doctors waxed lyrical about the drug's miraculous properties, calling it the "divine drug." It was said to be able to help with a number of ailments including toothache, labor pains, hay fever and melancholy. The young Austrian doctor, Sigmund Freud, founder of psychoanalysis, was a huge supporter of cocaine, recommending it as treatment for various maladies.

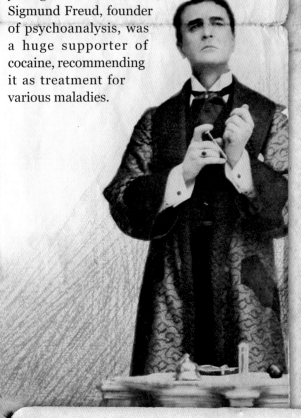

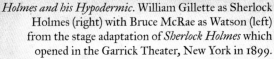

Holmes and his Hypodermic. William Gillette as Sherlock Holmes (right) with Bruce McRae as Watson (left) from the stage adaptation of *Sherlock Holmes* which opened in the Garrick Theater, New York in 1899.

THE SCIENTIFIC DEDUCTION OF SHERLOCK HOLMES

The great detective has had an influence upon criminal investigation and forensic techniques. In fact, it could be said that Sir Arthur Conan Doyle created a character whose methods were a century ahead of his time. In the fifty-six stories and four novels featuring Holmes, we see him doing things that we have come to expect from the detective stories we watch on television or at the cinema. But these were not methods being used commonly by police officers at the time Conan Doyle was writing.

Holmes was interested in blood, ballistics, and footprints. He was an advocate of the protection of a crime scene so that evidence would not be destroyed or contaminated. He made exhaustive examinations of these scenes, searching out the most minute scrap of evidence that might help to solve the crime.

FINGERPRINTING

In Victorian times, police officers lacked the knowledge and the modern aids that are so valuable today. Fingerprinting was not thought of as a means of identifying people until Dr. Henry Faulds (1843 – 1930), a Scottish physician working at the Tsukiji Hospital in Tokyo, published a letter in the British scientific journal *Nature*. It was in India, under the auspices of Sir Edward Henry (1850 – 1931), Inspector General of Police in Bengal, in 1891, that fingerprinting was first adopted. Holmes initially uses fingerprints in *The Sign of the Four*, published in 1890. Scotland Yard would not introduce fingerprinting recovery, comparison and identification until eleven years later.

Scientists were often introduced in court as experts in specific fields, but forensic science was not an integral part of a criminal investigation. The publication, in 1893, of *Handbuch für Untersuchungsrichter, Polizeibeamte, Gendarmen, u.s.w.* (*A Handbook For Examining Magistrates, Police Officials, Military Policemen, etc*) by the Austrian magistrate, Hans Gustav Adolf Gross (1847 – 1915) described methods that we take for granted today, such as crime scene photography. In 1895, at the International Union of Criminologists Congress, Gross was referred to, as "the father of Criminology."

REASONING BACKWARDS

Holmes surprised Dr. Watson as well as police officers with his innovative methods of deduction. He believed, for instance, in "reasoning backwards," as he explains to Watson in *A Study in Scarlet*:

> *In solving a problem of this sort, the grand thing is to be able to reason backwards ... Most people, if you describe a chain of events to them, will tell*

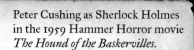

Peter Cushing as Sherlock Holmes in the 1959 Hammer Horror movie *The Hound of the Baskervilles*.

you what the result will be. They can put these events together in their minds, and argue from them that something will come to pass. There are few people, however, who if you told them a result, would be able to evolve from their own inner consciousness what the steps were that led up to that result. This power is what I mean when I talk of reasoning backwards or analytically.

CIPHERS AND CODES

In Victorian times, clues hidden in ciphers or coded messages were common. In "The Adventure of the Dancing Men" Sherlock Holmes analyzes 160 separate ciphers and uses the fact that the letter "e" is the most common letter in the English language to find a solution. In "The Adventure of the Gloria Scott" he works out that by taking the third word in each line of gibberish he can decipher the message that frightened Old Trevor. Cipher techniques such as Holmes employed, were particularly effective in time of war.

FOOTPRINTS AND HANDPRINTS

Footprints were especially informative to Holmes. From just one print he could deduce the height, weight, gait and occupation of a perpetrator. In fact, footprint evidence is used in twenty-nine of the sixty Holmes stories. They are found in mud, clay, soil, on carpets, on snow, in ash and even on curtains and doors. Holmes has written on the subject, as he tells Watson in *The Sign of the Four*:

Here is my monograph upon the tracing of footsteps, with some remarks upon the uses of plaster of Paris as a preserver of impresses.

In the same paragraph, he also mentions a work on the hand and how the trade of the owner impacts upon it:

Here, too, is a curious little work upon the influence of a profession upon the form of the hand, with lithotypes of the hands of slaters, sailors, corkcutters, compositors, weavers and diamond-polishers. That is a matter of great practical interest to the scientific detective— especially in cases of unclaimed bodies, or in discovering the antecedents of criminals.

HANDWRITING ANALYSIS

Holmes also used handwriting to work out the gender, class and age of a writer of a message or letter. He was also able to draw conclusions about the character of the writer from his or her penmanship. In "The Adventure of the Norwood Builder," the detective deduces from the timing or spacing of the imperfections in the handwriting used to create a will that it must have been written on a moving train. He presumes that an important document such as a will would never be written on a train and assumes, therefore, that the writer must have been under some form of duress when writing it. Handwriting analysis is now a scientific technique used to spot forgeries and differences that may be caused by drugs, alcohol, exhaustion or illness.

BLOODSTAINS

Of course, when Watson and Holmes first met in the chemistry lab of a London hospital, the detective was carrying out experiments into blood.

I've found it! I've found it! ... I have found a re-agent which is precipitated by hemoglobin, and by nothing else.

These are the first words uttered by Sherlock Holmes as he runs toward Dr. Watson and Stamford with a test tube in his hand in *A Study in Scarlet*. What Holmes has discovered is "an infallible test for blood stains." In reality it would be another thirteen years before a German medical researcher created a real test for "the differential diagnosis of human blood."

Conan Doyle's popularization of the forensic approach to solving crime, with the use of such methods as well as microscopic inspection, mathematical calculations, gunpowder residue analysis, typography, and photographic enlargements was undoubtedly vital to the development of forensic science, the advancement of criminal investigation as well as the art of scientific deduction.

PART FOUR

★ ★ ★

BACK FROM THE DEAD

★ ★ ★

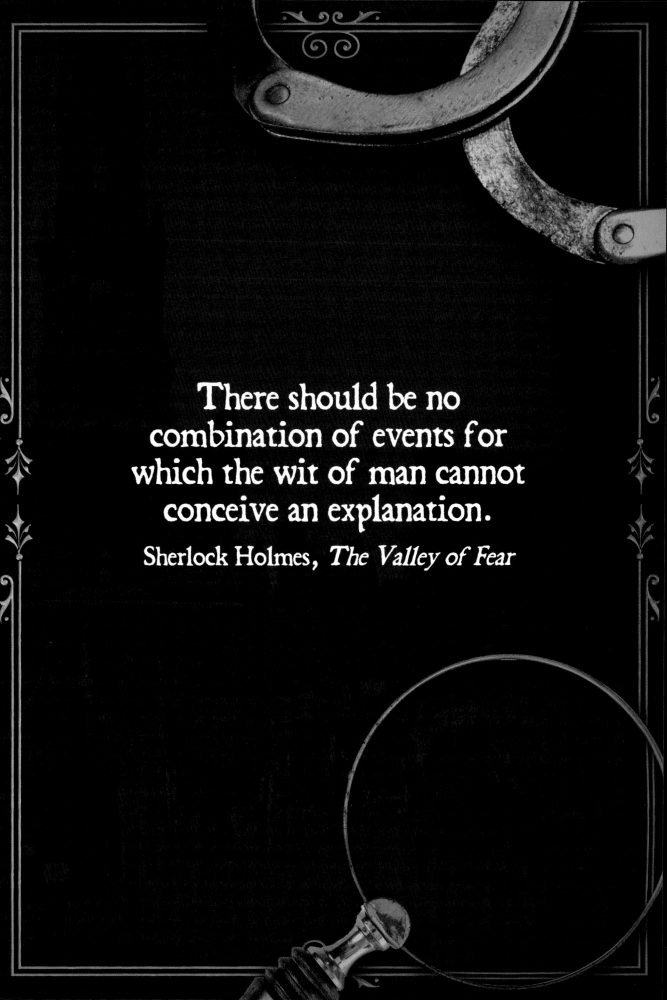

There should be no combination of events for which the wit of man cannot conceive an explanation.

Sherlock Holmes, *The Valley of Fear*

Collier's
Household Number for October

DRAWN BY FREDERIC DORR STEELE

...BER 26 1903   PRICE 10 CENTS

FREDERIC DORR STEELE

Sherlock Holmes at the Reichenbach Falls on the cover of *Collier's Magazine*, 1903, illustrated by Frederic Dorr Steele (1873 – 1944). Steele's drawings proved so popular that he illustrated Sherlock Holmes for the remainder of his career. He based his character on the American actor William Gillette who played Holmes on stage.

CHAPTER 13

THE RETURN OF SHERLOCK HOLMES

Stories published 1903 – 04 in *The Strand*

"The Adventure of the Empty House".............. October 1903

"The Adventure of the Norwood Builder" .... November 1903

"The Adventure of the Dancing Men"........... December 1903

"The Adventure of the Solitary Cyclist" .... January 1904

"The Adventure of the Priory School" .... February 1904

"The Adventure of Black Peter" .... March 1904

"The Adventure of Charles Augustus Milverton" .... April 1904

"The Adventure of the Six Napoleons"............. May 1904

"The Adventure of the Three Students" .... June 1904

"The Adventure of the Golden Pince-Nez" .... July 1904

"The Adventure of the Missing Three-Quarter"...... August 1904

"The Adventure of the Abbey Grange" .... September 1904

"The Adventure of the Second Stain"........... December 1904

"THE ADVENTURE OF THE EMPTY HOUSE"

The story opens in the spring of 1894 when London was enthralled by the inexplicable murder of the Honorable Ronald Adair. Dr. Watson is writing ten years later. He apologizes for not sharing what he knows about the case earlier but he had been sworn to secrecy by Sherlock Holmes.

He explains that following the death of his friend he had tried to employ Holmesian methods to cases but without a great deal of success. The case of Ronald Adair, he explains, would have very much appealed to Sherlock Holmes.

The Honorable Ronald Adair was the second son of the Earl of Maynooth. He was living at 427 Park Lane, London, along with his mother and sister Hilda. Adair moved in the best circles and did not appear to have any enemies.

On the night of March 30, 1894, he returned from his club at 10:00 p.m. and had gone into the front room on the second floor that he used as his sitting room. Coming home at 11:20 p.m., his mother and sister found his door locked from the inside. They could not rouse Ronald and the door was knocked down. Inside they found Adair lying on the floor, his head shattered by an expanding bullet but there was no sign of a weapon.

On the table were two ten-pound notes and seventeen pounds, ten shillings in piles of coins. On a sheet of paper were scribbled some figures and opposite them were the names of friends from his club. It was a mystery. How did the murderer escape from a room locked from the inside with a drop of two floors to the ground from the opened window?

Later, outside the house on Park Lane, Watson bumps into an elderly, deformed bookseller. He goes home and is told he has a visitor. It is the old bookseller. Then Watson gets a surprise:

"May I ask how you knew who I was?"

"Well, sir, if it isn't too great a liberty, I am a neighbor of yours, for you'll find my little bookshop at the corner of Church Street, and very happy to see you, I am sure. Maybe you collect yourself, sir. Here's British Birds, *and* Catullus, *and* The Holy War—*a bargain, every one of them. With five volumes you could just fill that gap on that second shelf. It looks untidy, does it not, sir?"*

I moved my head to look at the cabinet behind me. When I turned again, Sherlock Holmes was standing smiling at me across my study table. I rose to my feet, stared at him for some seconds in utter amazement, and then it appears that I must have fainted for the first and last time in my life.

Holmes was seized by the throat by Colonel Moran. Illustration by Sidney Paget from "The Adventure of the Empty House," 1903.

Holmes explains to Watson when he comes round that he managed to escape the clutches of Moriarty at the Reichenbach Falls and dispatched him into the chasm. By the time Watson had arrived on the scene, Holmes had climbed up the cliff-face and was high above the doctor. He had lain low to escape the murderous intentions of Moriarty's gang but has been drawn back to London by the mystery of Ronald Adair's death.

Holmes is convinced that Adair was killed by Colonel Sebastian Moran, one of Moriarty's lieutenants. He and Watson travel a circuitous route through London before entering an empty house and making their way to a front room which, Watson is surprised to find, overlooks 221B Baker Street. Across the street is Holmes's window and even more surprising, Holmes appears to be there, silhouetted against a blind. It is a waxwork likeness of the great detective that is occasionally moved by the landlady, Mrs. Hudson, to make it appear that he is moving about the room.

Moriarty's men know that Holmes is back in London and he fully expects them to make an attempt on his life that night but Watson is unaware that the police are close by. Although he has worked out every detail, Holmes makes one mistake, failing to foresee that the would-be killer would use the very house in which they stood. The killer enters with a specially designed airgun but the room is dark and he is unable to see that the man he is trying to kill is actually in the same room.

He takes aim and fires his gun, scoring a direct hit on the dummy across the street. Holmes and Watson immediately fall upon him and the police arrive, led by Inspector Lestrade. The culprit is, indeed, Colonel Moran whom Holmes instructs Lestrade to charge with the murder of Ronald Adair.

Moran's gun has been specially modified to fire revolver bullets and a forensic examination proves that it had fired the bullet that killed Ronald Adair. Holmes theorizes that Adair had caught Moran cheating at cards and threatened to expose him. As this was how Moran supported himself, his only option was to kill Adair.

"THE ADVENTURE OF THE NORWOOD BUILDER"

John Hector McFarlane, a young lawyer accused of murdering Jonas Oldacre after he had prepared Oldacre's will, asks Holmes to clear him of the murder. Holmes uses clever forensic science and a fake fire to make Oldacre who is, in fact, not dead, emerge from hiding.

Oldacre appeared from his hiding place. Illustration by Sidney Paget from "The Adventure of the Norwood Builder," 1903.

"THE ADVENTURE OF THE DANCING MEN"

Holmes and Watson force a man to stop stalking a woman and Holmes is hired by Hilton Cubitt to discover who has been sending him strange coded messages that are upsetting his wife. Holmes cracks the code and although he arrives too late to prevent the deaths of Hilton and his wife, he apprehends the culprit.

"THE ADVENTURE OF THE SOLITARY CYCLIST"

Every week Violet Smith cycles from the house in which she works as a music teacher to a railway station. She notices, however, that she is being followed on these trips by an unknown man. She has recently met two friends of her late uncle, one of whom hires her as a governess and then proposes to her. But, already engaged, Violet turns down his proposal. She finds the comments and behavior of the other man, Woodley, disturbing. Holmes works out what is happening and arrives just in time to free Violet after she is kidnapped by Woodley.

"THE ADVENTURE OF THE PRIORY SCHOOL"

Holmes and Watson are hired by the head of a boarding school to find a young heir to a fortune who has disappeared. Their investigations lead them to the boy's father, the Duke of Holdernesse and his secretary, James Wilder. They confront the duke who confesses that, in fact, James Wilder is not really his secretary but is actually his illegitimate son. Wilder had hired a man, Reuben Hayes, to help him to kidnap the duke's son and heir in order to force him into naming him as a legitimate heir. The boy is found and returned home safely.

"THE ADVENTURE OF BLACK PETER"

It is 1895 and Peter Carey, a ship's captain, is found dead, having been stabbed with a harpoon. Holmes is introduced to the case by Police Inspector Stanley Hopkins who is being mentored by the great detective. Carey had been a nasty piece of work and it is not surprising that he had enemies. Holmes, Dr. Watson, and Hopkins wait at the scene of the crime and arrest a man named John Hopley Neligan who turns up, trying to retrieve some incriminating evidence. Neligan denies any involvement in the murder and Holmes believes him. The real killer is Carey's first mate, Patrick Cains. Carey had been involved in some financial chicanery that Cains had wanted to be part of.

Holmes arrested the culprit. Illustration by Sidney Paget from "The Adventure of the Dancing Men," 1903.

"THE ADVENTURE OF CHARLES AUGUSTUS MILVERTON"

Notorious blackmailer, Charles Augustus Milverton, has ruined many and caused problems to numerous others. A lady who is being blackmailed by Milverton, approaches Holmes for help and Holmes decides to bring an end to Milverton's activities once and for all. Milverton is a very devious individual, however, and it is very difficult for the detective to pin anything on him.

To remedy this situation and to retrieve some letters belonging to their client, Holmes and Watson break into Milverton's house. But while they are there they see Milverton being murdered by an angry, unknown woman. They do not share their information with the police and the identity of Milverton's killer remains their secret.

"THE ADVENTURE OF THE SIX NAPOLEONS"

Cheap plaster casts of Napoleon Bonaparte are being smashed to pieces by an unidentified man who breaks into shops and houses and destroys them. This all seems fairly harmless until an unidentified man is found dead on the doorstep of a journalist's house and the journalist's plaster cast of Napoleon is discovered smashed to pieces in the garden of an empty house some distance away. Holmes works out that the statues have all been made by the same person, an Italian named Beppo who has hidden something inside one of the statues. Holmes catches Beppo and buys the sixth and last of the plaster Napoleons. When he smashes it open he finds the famous black pearl of the Borgias which had been sensationally stolen from a hotel room.

"THE ADVENTURE OF THE THREE STUDENTS"

Holmes is in a university town with Watson and is carrying out some research when the two men are approached by a professor who needs their help. The following day he is due to administer a Greek exam but someone has broken into his rooms and has seen and maybe

Milverton was shot by an angry, unknown woman.
Illustration by Sidney Paget from "The Adventure of Charles Augustus Milverton," 1904.

even copied the exam paper. By deduction, Holmes reduces the list of potential suspects to just three students. He then lays a trap for Gilchrist who outwardly appears the least likely of the three to be a cheat. Gilchrist confesses that he was the culprit. In order to avoid a scandal, he leaves the college for a job elsewhere.

"THE ADVENTURE OF THE GOLDEN PINCE-NEZ"

Inspector Stanley Hopkins involves Holmes and Watson in an intriguing and baffling case. A quiet young man by the name of Willoughby Smith has been murdered. Smith had been assistant to the elderly Professor Coram. Just before he died, he uttered the words: "The professor ... it was she." A golden pince-nez had been found on the body. To the astonishment of Hopkins, Holmes comes up with a description of the killer.

He says that a lady entered the chambers on the day of the murder in order to steal documents which were in a bureau. She was interrupted by Smith and stabbed him by accident. The professor is actually Russian and the killer is his wife, Anna. He had fled Russia after betraying colleagues in the revolution for a huge sum of money. The woman was trying to steal her diary and some letters to her lover, stolen from her by her husband. These would save her lover if shown to the Russian authorities. After confessing she swallows a poison capsule and dies.

"THE ADVENTURE OF THE MISSING THREE-QUARTER"

Cyril Overton is a young rugby player from Trinity College, Cambridge, who asks Holmes and Watson to find a teammate, Godfrey Staunton, who has gone missing before an important match. Apparently, a "rough-looking young man with a beard" had arrived at the team hotel and Staunton

had gone off with him. Holmes and Watson go to the home of Dr. Leslie Armstrong, an acquaintance of Staunton, but Armstrong refuses to help them.

Eventually, Holmes works out where Staunton is and deduces that he has been secretly married but his wife has recently fallen ill and died. As a friend, Dr. Armstrong had been trying to help the young couple keep their secret. Holmes and Watson depart, leaving the young rugby player to grieve for his dead wife.

They tracked him down with a scent-hound. Illustration by Sidney Paget from "The Adventure of the Missing Three-Quarter," 1904.

"THE ADVENTURE OF THE ABBEY GRANGE"

In the winter of 1897, Holmes wakes Watson one morning and tells him, "The game is afoot." They take a train to Kent and Holmes reads a note to him that has come from Inspector Stanley Hopkins who is at Abbey Grange. He asks for their help in "what promises to be a most remarkable case." A woman, Mary Fraser, who is the wife of the owner of Abbey Grange, Sir Eustace Brackenstall, has witnessed his murder. She says that a gang of men broke into the house, murdered her husband and tied her up while they stole some silver dishes.

Holmes is somewhat dubious about Mary Fraser's story and soon learns that she is lying. He confronts her with evidence that a man named Jack Crocker is involved in the case. Soon, Jack confesses to his involvement. Sir Eustace, it seems, was an abusive husband when drunk and his wife had fallen in love with Crocker.

When Crocker came to visit Mary, Sir Eustace confronted him and in a rage struck Mary across the face. In the ensuing struggle, Crocker beat him to death in self-defense with a poker. Jack Crocker, Mary Fraser and the maid conspired to make it look as if Sir Eustace had been killed during a break-in. Holmes agrees that Crocker had been justified in defending himself and does not report him to the police.

"THE ADVENTURE OF THE SECOND STAIN"

The Prime Minister of Great Britain, Lord Bellinger, and the European Secretary, Trelawney Hope, employ Holmes and Watson to recover a stolen political document which, in the wrong hands, could cause a war. They follow the document's trail to a spy named Eduardo Lucas, but he has recently been murdered by his own wife. She had been married to him under one of his many false identities.

Investigation by Holmes leads him to understand that Trelawney Hope's wife is actually in possession of the letter. Having been blackmailed, she delivered it to Lucas but had been unaware of the danger the document posed. When he was murdered, she was able to steal the letter back. The document is returned to the Prime Minister and the crisis averted.

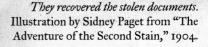
They recovered the stolen documents.
Illustration by Sidney Paget from "The Adventure of the Second Stain," 1904.

CHAPTER 14

A COMPLICATED RELATIONSHIP

Conan Doyle was now a wealthy man and could work as he pleased. At home, however, things were not getting any better. Louisa's health was deteriorating and although still remaining faithful to his wife, he was becoming ever closer to Jean Leckie. But, he continued to nurse his wife through these difficult times. She was so ill that she sometimes could not open her eyes or even talk. Meanwhile, he distracted himself by playing cricket, taking seven wickets for fifty-one runs while playing for the M.C.C. against Cambridgeshire.

Jean remained faithful to Conan Doyle through these tribulations. He told her that he would completely understand if she wanted to go off and find someone else, but she remained with him. Both knew that the end would come for Louisa soon, but such thoughts merely brought guilt and self-recrimination. Divorce was, of course, an option and Conan Doyle had championed new divorce laws, but he simply would never consider it as a solution to his own situation.

A SECOND MARRIAGE

In the summer of 1906, Louisa's health entered a period of rapid decline and she finally died at three o'clock in the morning on July 4, at age forty-nine. Conan Doyle was distraught and cried his eyes out. After she was buried at Hindhead, he was overwhelmed with letters of sympathy—some five hundred a day—but he experienced guilt and shame and felt unwell although there was really nothing medically wrong with him.

He and Jean were finally married on September 18, 1907. They moved to Windlesham Manor in Crowborough, East Sussex, from where later he would say he could hear the distant thunder of the guns on the Western Front in France. Conan Doyle would live there for the remainder of his life.

TILL DEATH US DO PART

Even if Conan Doyle could not envision divorce for himself, he wanted to make it more available for other people.

In 1906, a new society lobbying for change in the divorce laws of England was formed by Conan Doyle's new friend, the writer Thomas Hardy, who thought that the institution of marriage damaged through "overregulation" what it was actually trying to protect. He believed it was misguided of society to expect two people to take vows to love each other forever and then if they fell out of love to expect them to live unhappily together. When Hardy approached Conan Doyle to join, he accepted and became president of the society. He used his fame and his influence to try to change things, writing in his memoirs:

... I cannot understand why England should lag behind every other Protestant country in the world, and even behind Scotland, so that unions that are obviously disgusting and degrading are maintained in this country while they can be dissolved in our Colonies or abroad ... It is one of several questions which makes me not sorry to see Labour, with its larger outlook, in power for a time in this country. Our marriage laws, our land laws, the cheapening of justice and many other things have long called out for reform, and if the old parties will not do it then we must seek some new one that will.

Although Conan Doyle consistently supported women suffering in abusive relationships, he never believed that women should be given the vote. The suffragettes mounted a campaign against him, booing and jeering him at public events. He received hate mail and even had sulfuric acid poured through his letterbox.

The suffragettes never really believed he meant what he said about the divorce laws with regard to women. The Church, too, took up against him, describing him as interfering. They thought that as a man with no Christian beliefs, he could not possibly understand the morality that underpinned the existing laws. But Conan Doyle was never the most popular man with the Church of England on account of his views on spiritualism.

THE OLYMPICS THAT NEVER WERE

Other issues took Conan Doyle's attention—zoos, galleries, the need for a new international language, British roads, photography, even the Loch Ness Monster. He campaigned to improve how British sports were organized. Lord Northcliffe asked him to work on Great Britain's Olympic effort and to improve the way British athletics was run. It was something of a poisoned chalice and Conan Doyle had to act as a middle-man between various warring factions—Northcliffe, the British Olympic Committee and the press—in order to put together a team for the 1916 Olympiad to be held in Berlin. A paltry sum of money was raised for the team, but, of course, it was all rendered academic by the outbreak of the First World War in 1914, and the subsequent cancellation of the 1916 Olympics.

RETURN TO THE HUSTINGS

Undeterred by having lost one election, Conan Doyle stood as a Unionist candidate again, in the General Election of 1906. This time, the constituency was Hawick, Selkirk and Galashiels in the borders of Scotland. But once again, he lost.

That same year, Conan Doyle published another historical novel, *Sir Nigel*, set during the Hundred Years' War. It describes the life of Sir Nigel Loring, a knight in the service of King Edward III. He regarded it very highly, claiming that it "represents my high-water mark in literature" but, unfortunately, the critics failed to concur and it passed, generally speaking, unnoticed. He wrote in disappointment:

In England, versatility is looked upon with distrust. You may write ballad tunes or you may write grand opera, but it cannot be admitted that the same man may be master of the whole musical range and do either with equal success.

Sir Arthur Conan Doyle's second marriage on September 18, 1907. From left to right: Lily Loder-Symonds, Jean Leckie, Arthur Conan Doyle, Lesley Rose, Innes Doyle (brother and best man) and sitting on the floor Branford Angell.

SIR ARTHUR CONAN DOYLE AND HIS FAMILY IN 1904

Standing from left to right: Innes Doyle with young Oscar Hornung, Constance Doyle (Connie), Ernest W. Hornung, Mary and Kingsley, Sir Arthur Conan Doyle, Caroline Doyle (Lottie) and Leslie Oldham, Bryan Mary Doyle (Dodo) and Cyril Angell. Seated from left to right: Nelson Foley, Louisa Conan Doyle, Mary Doyle (The Ma'am), Ida Foley with Innes Foley. Seated on floor: Percy Foley and Branford Angell.

THE CASE OF GEORGE EDALJI

Of course, Conan Doyle's prowess with solving crimes through the auspices of Sherlock Holmes brought him into contact with numerous strange cases. He mostly ignored the letters requesting help, but one apparent miscarriage of justice caught his eye. He first read about the case of George Edalji in the publication *The Umpire* in 1906. Of Indian ethnicity, with a father who was a Church of England vicar, Edalji had been arrested in the midlands of England in 1903 for maiming cattle.

Since moving into the parish of Great Wyrley in Staffordshire, in 1875, the Reverend Shapurji Edalji had encountered some racism, but it was not particularly serious. Three years later, however, he began receiving threatening and obscene letters. A servant confessed to having written them and that seemed to be the end of it. But between 1892 and 1895 more letters arrived that were worse than the original ones.

Interestingly, the vicar's neighbors received similarly abusive missives. Offensive postcards began falling through the letterboxes of other clergymen, ostensibly signed by Reverend Edalji and graffiti appeared on the walls of his church. Edalji's son, George, was suspected of having been responsible and as soon as this suspicion became public it all ceased.

In 1903, livestock around Reverend Edalji's parish were found brutally maimed and slaughtered and after a number of letters circulated accusing George, now a lawyer in Birmingham, he was arrested. His home was searched and evidence such as four dirty razors was uncovered. Bloodstains and hair were found on his clothing and the handwriting of the letters was confirmed to be a match for George's. He was tried and sentenced to seven years in prison.

MISCARRIAGE OF JUSTICE

Newspapers had a field day, accusing Edalji of being a pagan, despite his father's position as a vicar while no one seemed to take into consideration that further mutilations occurred while George was in custody. Some believed Edalji to be innocent but a petition to the Home Office changed nothing. Suddenly, however, when he had served only half of his prison sentence, George Edalji was released. Unable to find work and vilified wherever he went, he fought to clear his name.

It seemed ludicrous that he had been convicted at all. Firstly, he had a perfectly good alibi for the evening in question, having visited his boot-maker and his father vouched for him for the remainder of the evening, although of course, people thought that he would say anything to save his son. Thirdly, mud found on his boots failed to match the mud in the field in which the animals were slaughtered and fourthly, the razors were caked in rust, not dried blood.

CONAN DOYLE CAMPAIGNS

Conan Doyle studied the original trial, met the Edalji family, visited the scene of the crimes and wrote about the case in a series

George Edalji (1876 – 1953).

of articles for the *Daily Telegraph*. These circulated widely and Conan Doyle immersed himself in the case, giving lectures about it and soliciting the support of influential friends. He toured the scene of the crime with supporters and they searched for evidence in every inch of the area. Conan Doyle reveled in being at the heart of a cause that he really believed in. And he also believed in George Edalji:

> *These wrongs would have been almost comic had they not had so tragic an upshot. If the whole land had been raked, I do not think it would have been possible to find a man who was so unlikely, and indeed so incapable, of committing such actions. He was of irreproachable character ... It was clear that the inherent improbability of such a man committing a long succession of bloody and brutal crimes was so great that it could only be met by the suggestion of insanity.*

INVESTIGATING THE PAST

Conan Doyle searched for the culprit, turning to Edalji's schooldays for answers. He had attended Walsall Grammar in the West Midlands. The key to which school had at one point been left outside Edalji's house during the trouble. The headmaster gave Conan Doyle the name of a pupil, Royden Sharp, and a few days after he received a letter that claimed the headmaster to be a liar.

Royden Sharp had worked in a butcher's shop away from the area after leaving school and had then served in the merchant navy. Interestingly, he had worked on-board a cattle ship in 1902. But, even faced with such evidence, the police refused to re-open the case.

A government committee was formed and came to the conclusion that Edalji had been convicted without any compelling evidence that he had committed the crimes. Nonetheless, they still believed Edalji to have written the letters and, therefore, contributed to his own miscarriage of justice. Thus, he was, denied compensation.

A WRETCHED DECISION

Conan Doyle was dismayed, of course, by what he described as "a wretched decision." He expressed his disappointment in public with the system he had always supported so wholeheartedly. But in 1908, the Court of Criminal Appeal in England and Wales was established and Conan Doyle and George Edalji played a part in the establishment of this vital arm of justice. As for Edalji, he was re-admitted to the Law Society which was a tacit implication that he was innocent. A fund established by the *Daily Telegraph* and Conan Doyle raised more than three hundred pounds. Edalji was even a guest at Conan Doyle's wedding to Jean Leckie on September 18, 1907.

THE CASE OF OSCAR SLATER

As a result of his success with George Edalji, Conan Doyle was inundated with letters asking for his help. One case leapt out at him. Oscar Slater (1872 – 1948) was a Jew who had been born Oscar Leschziner in Germany. He moved to London in 1893 to avoid military

Oscar Slater.

service in Germany. Working as a bookmaker, he began to use the surname Slater but had been prosecuted twice for malicious wounding, in 1896 and 1897, although he had been acquitted on both occasions. In 1899, he relocated to Edinburgh and then to Glasgow. He claimed to be a gymnastics instructor, a dentist or a dealer in precious stones. To the police, however, he was a pimp and gangster.

A HEINOUS CRIME

In December 1908, 83-year-old spinster, Marion Gilchrist, was beaten to death in a robbery at her home on West Princes Street in Glasgow. She was alone at the time, her maid having gone out for ten minutes. Ms. Gilchrist had a large collection of jewelry (worth around a quarter of a million pounds in today's money) hidden in a wardrobe but her murderer was disturbed by a neighbor and escaped with only a brooch.

Five days after the murder, Oscar Slater left for New York. He was under suspicion because shortly before the murder someone had called at Marion Gilchrist's house asking for a man named Anderson. This was a name that Slater had used. He had also been witnessed attempting to sell a pawn ticket for a brooch. The pawn ticket was, investigating officers quickly realized, not a credible lead, as it had been sold a month prior to the murder, but they still applied for his extradition from the United States. Slater was advised the extradition request was likely to be denied, but he decided to return to Scotland voluntarily to clear his name.

SENTENCED TO HANG

Even though, at his trial, defense witnesses gave Slater an alibi for the time in question and people testified that he had announced his intention to migrate to America long before the murder was committed, he was convicted by a majority of nine to six and in May 1909 was sentenced to hang before the end of the month. A petition, signed by 20,000 helped to get his sentence commuted to one of life imprisonment just two days before he was due to hang. He would serve nineteen years in Peterhead prison in northeast Scotland.

ANOTHER CAMPAIGN

Slater had lived with a French woman and what was seen as moral turpitude outraged many Scots. Of course, there was also an anti-semitic aspect to the case and it was some of Conan Doyle's Jewish friends who asked him to take a look at it. But Slater was

A courtroom scene during the trial of Oscar Slater, May 1909.

in prison for some sixteen years before the writer stirred up interest in his case. This despite several witnesses and even police officers coming forward to contradict the evidence that had brought a guilty verdict.

Slater got a message to Conan Doyle insisting on his innocence, even after all this time. It was all Conan Doyle needed. He applied what he had learned from the case of George Edalji and launched a campaign of speeches and newspaper articles. English journalists flooded into Glasgow and two of the witnesses admitted that they had accepted bribes to ensure that their evidence pointed to Slater as the guilty party.

Ms. Gilchrist, it transpired, was not the genteel spinster that had been depicted at the time. Indeed, she was known to receive visitors late into the night. It soon became evident that the prosecution case had been

fabricated and Oscar Slater was released nineteen years after his conviction.

The release was for good conduct, as it was expressed officially. There was no apology and no compensation and Conan Doyle never heard from Slater again. It was another spectacular victory for Conan Doyle's sense of fair play.

THROUGH THE MAGIC DOOR

In 1907, Conan Doyle published *Through the Magic Door*, a collection of his essays and articles. Of course, it was not original material, but he was now approaching fifty and was slowing down a little. The last few years had turned him into a public figure and Jean joked that most people thought the writer of Sherlock Holmes was by this time dead and Sir Arthur Conan Doyle must be a politician.

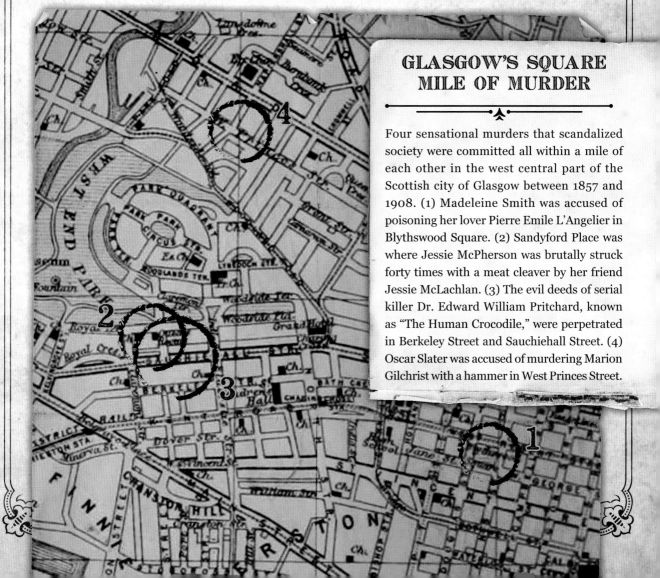

GLASGOW'S SQUARE MILE OF MURDER

Four sensational murders that scandalized society were committed all within a mile of each other in the west central part of the Scottish city of Glasgow between 1857 and 1908. (1) Madeleine Smith was accused of poisoning her lover Pierre Emile L'Angelier in Blythswood Square. (2) Sandyford Place was where Jessie McPherson was brutally struck forty times with a meat cleaver by her friend Jessie McLachlan. (3) The evil deeds of serial killer Dr. Edward William Pritchard, known as "The Human Crocodile," were perpetrated in Berkeley Street and Sauchiehall Street. (4) Oscar Slater was accused of murdering Marion Gilchrist with a hammer in West Princes Street.

GEORGE BERNARD SHAW

In 1912, Conan Doyle had a very public falling-out with the great Irish playwright, George Bernard Shaw (1856 – 1950) over the reaction to the sinking of the R.M.S. *Titanic* and the loss of 1,500 passengers and crew. Bernard Shaw wrote in May that year that the press had distorted the whole affair, describing the doomed vessel's commander, Captain Edward Smith (1850 – 1912) as incompetent. He insisted that the ship was not fit for purpose, that it had too few lifeboats for the number of people on board and that, rather than being the fine example of the British spirit presented by the press, it was, in fact, a national disgrace.

Famously, the band on the *Titanic* was reported to have continued playing as the ship went down, but George Bernard Shaw presented this not as an act of heroism, but rather, as an attempt to keep the third-class passengers on board while the ship sank, leaving room for the other classes to get away in the lifeboats.

Conan Doyle was affronted and he debated the issue at length with the playwright both in the letters pages of the newspapers and in public meetings.

CHAPTER 15

THE VALLEY OF FEAR

On the wall of Conan Doyle's study was a map of Africa — the continent fascinated him. However, as European powers scrambled for their own piece of the continent, Conan Doyle was horrified by what he saw, especially in the Congo, colonized by the Belgians. The Portuguese had claimed that it was their nation's explorers who had first visited the area and that it should, therefore, fall under their aegis.

An international conference created the Congo Free State, an immense territory, almost seventy-six times the size of Belgium, in which only 245 Europeans lived. Chief of state of the new country was Leopold II, King of the Belgians. In fact, it was set up in an odd way. The Belgian Parliament had ruled that the "union between Belgium and the new state of Congo shall be exclusively personal," making it Leopold's personal fiefdom. It was a valuable possession because of its ivory and rubber but the Belgians treated their black employees on the plantations and estates in a barbaric way. Failure to meet rubber collection quotas often ended in death. Workers were whipped or worked to death, women were raped and children were often separated from their families.

Although still exploitative, the British way was far more humane. The British realized that cruelty would not only be unethical but would fail to produce the desired results. Doctors were on hand to bring modern medicine to villagers and farming techniques were improved in order to stave off food shortages. Conan Doyle sat on several committees connected with Africa and, indeed, knew many of the doctors working there.

THE CRIME OF THE CONGO

Conan Doyle decided, against the wishes of his wife, to become involved, writing the 45,000 word booklet, *The Crime of the Congo*, sleeping less than four hours a night as he did so, and working to a daily quota of words. He sometimes worked all through the night. Jean became worried about him, of course, but he continued until he finished. It was published in 1909 to international acclaim. The illustrations were harrowing, showing Congolese people with their hands cut off. The Congo police force—the *Force Publique*—collected hands of the people they killed for failing to meet the rubber quotas. They were paid their bonus according to how many hands they had to show, so they began chopping off the hands of people who were still alive.

Sir Arthur Conan Doyle in his house at Windlesham, Surrey, 1907.

GLOBAL SUPPORT

Conan Doyle received letters of support from an astonishing array of public figures including Hilaire Belloc (1870 – 1953), President Theodore Roosevelt (1858 – 1919) and Mark Twain (1835 – 1910) congratulating him on drawing attention to the scandal but also wondering what could be done to improve conditions in the Congo. It was difficult, and Conan Doyle wanted everyone to put pressure on the Belgians in the country as well as on the government. Things did begin to change but it was only partly due to Conan Doyle's activities. The Belgian state assumed responsibility for the Congo and the situation began to improve. However, it is estimated that around ten million Congolese had died and the population was reduced to half of what it was in 1879.

AN HONORED GUEST

Sir Arthur Conan Doyle and Jean had much to celebrate at home with the arrival of their first child Denis Percy Stewart (1909 – 55). Their second child Adrian Malcolm (1910 – 70) followed a year later and a daughter, Lena Jean Annette (1912 – 97) arrived two years after that.

Conan Doyle spent his life being invited to all sorts of events and numerous countries. He became patron of several sports and he was welcome at football and rugby matches as an honored guest. He had, of course, been responsible for the development of several sports. He wrote:

> *I can claim to have been the first to introduce skis into the Grisons division of Switzerland, or at least to demonstrate their practical utility as a means of getting across in winter from one valley to another.*

(In fact, his introduction of Norwegian skis and skiing techniques helped to change Swiss attitudes to skiing.)

He rejected countless product sponsorship offers but enjoyed the recognition that fame brought. Of course, his public pronouncements on issues as diverse as Irish independence and votes for women opened

him up to danger and, having received death threats in the mail, in 1912 he was permitted a police bodyguard. No one was ever arrested but the threatening mail continued until 1918.

PROFESSOR CHALLENGER

In 1912, he published *The Lost World* which introduced the third of his major characters—Professor Challenger. Serialized in *The Strand Magazine* between April and November 1912, it was illustrated by the New Zealand artist, Harry Rountree (1878 – 1950).

The book was a great success, persuading Conan Doyle to write another Challenger story, *The Poison Belt,* published the next year. It told the outlandish tale of the world moving into a poisonous belt in space. Challenger believes it will wipe out humanity and summons Malone, Roxton and Summerlee from *The Lost World,* to his house, instructing them to bring oxygen. Challenger and his associates enter an airtight room to save themselves. When the last of their oxygen has gone, they emerge, expecting to die but, as they watch, the apparently dead people climb to their feet and get on with their lives. It had merely been a form of catalepsy that had laid them low. Humanity is shocked into placing a higher value on life.

LYNCHING SUFFRAGETTES

The Poison Belt seemed to be filled with foreboding and indeed, like many at the time, Conan Doyle was alarmed at Germany's efforts to build a strong military. The arms race was in full swing and Britain's centuries-old naval dominance was under threat. Conan Doyle was unwilling to accept what he viewed as the complacency of Britain.

Just as Conan Doyle was tiring of his own country as well as fearing for its future, an opportunity arose to leave it behind for a while. In 1914, the *Cornhill Magazine* asked him if he would like to visit Canada and the United States to write a travel article. The Canadian government also invited him to visit the National Reserve at Jasper Park in the Rocky Mountains.

The Conan Doyles' three children were deposited with friends and they sailed from Southampton on May 20, 1914, arriving in New York on the 27th. Sir Arthur Conan Doyle was just as famous in America as he was in Britain—perhaps even more so—and was immediately flooded with requests for interviews. With his trenchant views on matters such as votes for women, he could be relied upon to provide good copy. And indeed he did. He stirred up a veritable hornets' nest on May 28, 1914 with an interview in the *New York Times* saying:

Thus far ... public opinion, which usually guides the Government in England, has not demanded the entire suppression of the militant Suffragette. It has almost come to that stage now, however, and something drastic will happen, and happen soon. There will be a wholesale lynching bee, I fancy, for the English mob, when thoroughly aroused, is not a respecter of sex. If anything happens the militants will only have themselves to blame.

Headlines such as *"Sherlock's Here; Expects Lynching of Wild Women"* screamed from the newsstands and Conan Doyle was horrified at the American press's distortion of what he had said. It was even suggested that he had offered to help anyone trying to hang a suffragette. He organized an interview with the respected journalist, Louis Sherwin of the *New York Globe* to try to put the record straight. He explained how difficult the articles had made things and how embarrassed he was by them:

... it puts me in a most uncomfortable position— makes it appear that I am coming over here to say things I should not dare at home.

His time in New York was frenetic, crammed with interviews, dinners, public engagements and sightseeing. He enjoyed a private dinner with the mayor, John P. Mitchel (1879 – 1918), had a tour of the notorious Sing Sing prison and attended a baseball match between New York and the Philadelphia Athletics.

On Wednesday, June 3, he arrived in Montreal, happy to be back in Canada where he felt much more at home than in the United States. His itinerary included visits to Winnipeg, Edmonton, Algonquin Park, Ottawa and Niagara Falls, again.

THE CLOUDS OF WAR

Back in Britain, war was looming and on his return, Conan Doyle threw himself into it with his customary passion, firing off countless missives to the press and to the War Office. The Prime Minister, Herbert Asquith (1852 – 1928) was also given the benefit of his wisdom. He wrote about the need for life jackets for sailors, body armor for soldiers and, indeed, these ideas were introduced and many lives were saved.

Of course, he was too old to sign up and go to France but, using his own money, he established the Civilian Reserve which consisted of men unfit for military service. It was a good idea as the existence of these units provided reassurance for the populace and they would, indeed, have provided a measure of defense in the event of a German invasion. The War Office eventually disbanded the Civilian Defence but instituted a new volunteer army for home defense.

Characteristically, Conan Doyle signed up as a private in the Crowborough Company of the Sixth Royal Sussex Volunteer Regiment.

VISITING THE TRENCHES

He also contributed to the propaganda pamphlet *To Arms!* writing about the "swaggering Junkerdom of Prussia" and its jealousy of the British Empire. He regarded the war as a just and noble enterprise. All Britain wanted, he reasoned was a peace-abiding and reasonable Germany. To him, the war was a clear contest between good and evil and there were no prizes for guessing who was good and who was evil.

In 1915, he began writing a six-volume history of *The British Campaign in France and Flanders* which would not be finished until 1920. His research included courageous visits to the British, French and Italian front lines but he loved it, enjoying the camaraderie of the British Tommies.

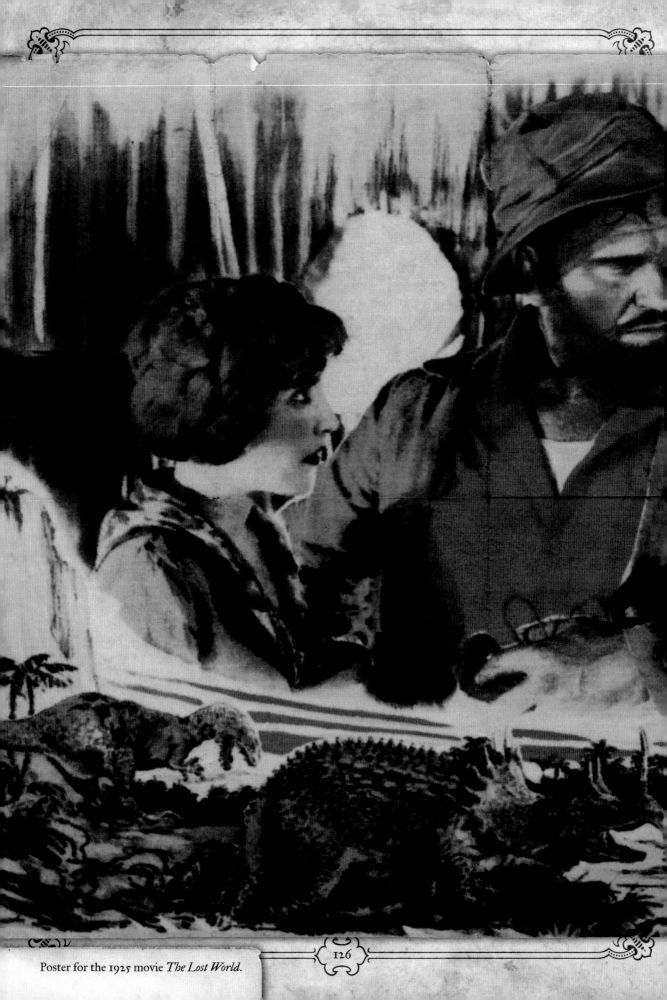

Poster for the 1925 movie *The Lost World*.

THE LOST WORLD

Edward Malone, a reporter for the newspaper *The Daily Gazette*, trying to impress Gladys Overton with whom he has fallen in love, asks his editor for a dangerous assignment. He is sent to interview the irritable explorer Professor George Edward Challenger, who has become famous following claims he has made about his recent expedition to South America. The professor is a man who does not suffer fools gladly and he has rejected the enquiries of journalists, especially as the press have called him a liar.

After a characteristically violent introduction to the professor, Malone succeeds in befriending him. Challenger tells him that another explorer, Maple White, had disclosed to him the existence of a plateau in the Amazon jungle on which prehistoric life still flourishes. Challenger invites Malone to a meeting at the Zoological Institute where he announces the discovery.

He challenges the Institute to assemble an expedition to South America to disprove his claims. His greatest detractor, Professor Summerlee, agrees to go. Malone also signs up, as does Lord John Roxton, a renowned adventurer and hunter. They find the plateau which they name Maple White Land, but they become marooned there. They are hunted by giant lizards and become involved in a conflict between humans and a people described as "ape-men." The Accala, as the humans are known, defeat the ape-men and the expedition members discover a tunnel that leads to the outside world where they meet up with a large rescue party.

Back in England, despite pictures and a report by Malone, they are largely disbelieved. But Challenger produces proof in the form of a live pterodactyl which escapes and flies over the Atlantic Ocean.

At dinner, Roxton informs the others that blue clay they had found contains diamonds worth about two hundred thousand pounds which he shares out among them. Challenger announces that he will use his share to open a private museum, Summerlee says that he will retire and categorize fossils while Roxton says that he intends to return to the lost world. Malone returns to Gladys only to learn that she has married a solicitor's clerk while he was away. He signs up for Roxton's expedition to the lost world.

Having witnessed the Battle of St. Quentin, Conan Doyle said he would never forget the horrors of the "tangle of mutilated horses, their necks rising and sinking," struggling amidst the remains of fallen soldiers. Defeats, he insisted were not the soldiers' fault. The blame lay with their superiors, or with poor planning or inadequate arms. He spent many hours talking to the men and was roundly cheered as he visited the trenches.

THE FOURTH HOLMES NOVEL

But Sherlock Holmes was once again occupying Conan Doyle's thoughts. *The Strand Magazine* had offered him a vast amount of money to write another Holmes novel and he was won over by the idea. In fact, it would be one of his greatest achievements.

The name, I think, will be The Valley of Fear. *Speaking from the present possibilities it should run to not less than 50,000 words. I have done nearly 25,000, I reckon roughly. With luck I should finish it before the end of March.*

As in A Study in Scarlet *the plot goes to America for at least half the book while it recounts the events which led up to the crime in England which has engaged Holmes's services ... But of course in this long stretch we abandon Holmes. That is necessary.*

Serialized in *The Strand Magazine* between September 1914 and May 1915, this fourth and final Sherlock Holmes novel was extremely successful, in spite of the war. It consisted of two interlinked stories. The first story is "The Tragedy of Birlstone," a straightforward country house murder story set in Sussex. The second is "The Scowrers," which is set in 1870s America dealing with the conflict between Irish miners and their English-American employers giving rise to the growth of a secret brotherhood of Irish nationalists.

HIS LAST BOW

In 1917, another collection of Sherlock Holmes stories, *His Last Bow: Some Reminiscences of Sherlock Holmes* was published. It collected seven stories including the one that lends its name to the book's title—"His Last Bow. The War Service of Sherlock Holmes." The book contains a brief preface written by "John H. Watson M.D."

The friends of Mr. Sherlock Holmes will be glad to learn that he is still alive and well, though somewhat crippled by occasional attacks of rheumatism. He has, for many years, lived in a small farm upon the Downs five miles from Eastbourne, where his time is divided between philosophy and agriculture. During this period of rest he has refused the most princely offers to take up cases, having determined that his retirement was a permanent one. The approach of the German war caused him, however, to lay his remarkable combination of intellectual and practical activity at the disposal of the government, with historical results which are recounted in "His Last Bow." Several previous experiences which have lain long in my portfolio have been added to "His Last Bow" so as to complete the volume.

The stories in this collection are:
"The Adventure of Wisteria Lodge"
"The Adventure of the Bruce-Partington Plans"
"The Adventure of the Devil's Foot"
"The Adventure of the Red Circle"
"The Disappearance of Lady Frances Carfax"
"The Adventure of the Dying Detective"
"His Last Bow. The War Service of Sherlock Holmes."
("The Adventure of the Cardboard Box" also appeared as an eighth story in later editions of the book.)

The VALLEY of FEAR

A. CONAN DOYLE

Book jacket for *The Valley of Fear.*

THE VALLEY OF FEAR

THE TRAGEDY OF BIRLSTONE

At 221B Baker Street, Sherlock Holmes is trying to decipher a coded message he has received from Porlock, an associate of Professor Moriarty. Porlock tells Holmes that he fears Moriarty's anger but he will not reveal why he has contacted him. The message warns of danger to Douglas of Birlstone but soon after Holmes and Watson learn that Douglas has been murdered.

Douglas has been killed by a shot from an American sawed-off shotgun, and beside his severely disfigured body lies a card on which is written "V.V. 341." On the windowsill is a bloody footprint and a set of dumb-bells is missing. Douglas's wedding ring was not on his finger and a bicycle is discovered hidden outside the grounds of the house. Holmes interrogates Douglas's widow and family friend Cecil Barker, and tells Watson that he believes they are in it together.

Holmes informs Watson enigmatically that he believes the key to the solution of the case is the missing dumb-bells although the police seem entirely unconcerned about them. He spends the night alone in the room in which Douglas was murdered with nothing but Dr. Watson's umbrella. The following morning, he announces that he has solved the case and requests they join him that night in a stakeout.

As they wait in the bushes outside the murder room, they see a man lean out of the window and fish an object out of the water of the moat. Confronting him, they discover him to be Cecil Barker. The object he has taken from the water is a bag weighed down with the missing dumb-bells in which they find a suit of clothing, a pair of boots, and a knife. Holmes had already discovered this bag in the water using the crook of Watson's umbrella. Everyone is amazed when Holmes announces that Douglas is, in fact, still alive and as he says this, a hidden compartment in the wall of the room opens and Douglas steps out.

Douglas explains that he had been stalked for some time by a man named Baldwin who on the night in question had tried to kill him with the shotgun. The two had struggled and the shotgun had gone off, shooting Baldwin in the face and killing him. Roping his wife and Barker into the plan, Douglas faked his own death. This was made easier by the fact that Baldwin's face had been so disfigured by the gunshot that identification was impossible. There are others who want him dead and he thought that by faking his death he might be left in peace. He gives Watson a manuscript that gives details of his past life as well as the names of those who wish him dead.

THE SCOWRERS

The second part of the novel details Douglas's life in America. A man named Jack McMurdo (we later learn this man is Douglas himself) travels to Vermissa Valley, a coal-mining area in the western United States. McMurdo expresses his hatred of the police and this attracts the attention of a man named Scanlon, a member of the Freemen, a society to which McMurdo also belongs. McMurdo joins the local lodge of the society, led by a violent man named Boss McGinty. The Freemen of this area are also called the Scowrers and they are a Mafia-like gang, who terrorize the people of Vermissa Valley. A violent man like the others, McMurdo becomes one of its more prominent members.

The Scowrers learn that a Pinkerton detective, Birdy Edwards is investigating them.

McMurdo lays a trap to capture the detective, luring him to an apartment in which Boss McGinty and several other Scowrers are hiding. But the Scowrers are surprised by McMurdo's declaration that he is, in fact, Birdy Edwards and that he joined the lodge purely to obtain information about their activities. They are arrested and McGinty and a number of others are executed because of Edwards's testimony, forcing Edwards to seek refuge by traveling to England.

Holmes warns Douglas that he must go back into hiding as Moriarty, whom Baldwin had contacted, will without doubt try to kill him. Douglas flees England but soon after Holmes receives a cryptic message: *"Dear me, Mr.*

Holmes, dear me!" Holmes deduces, sadly, from this that Moriarty has succeeded in killing Douglas. Holmes, Watson, and Inspector MacDonald discuss the possibility of Moriarty ever being brought to justice and Holmes insists that he will eventually capture him:

Barker beat his head with his clenched fist in his impotent anger. "Do not tell me that we have to sit down under this? Do you say that no one can ever get level with this king devil?"

"No, I don't say that," said Holmes, and his eyes seemed to be looking far into the future. "I don't say that he can't be beat. But you must give me time—you must give me time!"

The cipher and the man who solved it.
Illustration by Frank Wiles
from *The Valley of Fear*, 1915.

CHAPTER 16

HIS LAST BOW
SOME REMINISCENCES OF SHERLOCK HOLMES

Stories published 1908 – 17 in *The Strand*

"The Adventure of Wisteria Lodge" .... September – October 1908

"The Adventure of the Bruce-Partington Plans" .. December 1908

"The Adventure of the Devil's Foot" .... December 1910

"The Adventure of the Red Circle" .... March – April 1911

"The Disappearance of Lady Frances Carfax" .... December 1911

"The Adventure of the Dying Detective"......... December 1913

"His Last Bow.
The War Service of Sherlock Holmes" .... September 1917

"THE ADVENTURE OF WISTERIA LODGE"

This story is divided into two parts—"The Singular Experience of Mr. John Eccles" and "The Tiger of San Pedro." It begins when Mr. Eccles visits Holmes and Watson at 221B Baker Street. He is quite perturbed and wishes the two men to investigate "something grotesque." The police arrive in the midst of this to learn that an Aloysius Garcia, at whose house Eccles had been staying the previous night, has been found beaten to death. Mr. Eccles is the last man to have seen Garcia alive and tells how he had awakened to an empty house in the morning. In the second part of the book, Garcia's death is linked with a once ruthless South American dictator dubbed the "Tiger of San Pedro."

"THE ADVENTURE OF THE BRUCE-PARTINGTON PLANS"

Crime of late has been fairly petty and of little interest to Sherlock Holmes at the start of this story. Almost immediately after he has this thought, he receives a visit from his brother Mycroft who tells him of a case that threatens the security of the country. Mycroft pleads with his brother to investigate the strange death of Cadogan West whose body has been discovered on the London Underground near Aldgate station with a top-secret government document—the Bruce-Partington plans—in his pocket, but with three of the most important pages missing. It is believed that West stole the document and, before his death, sold the three pages to an enemy agent. Holmes manages to construct his case around the fact that the body was found next to a set of points on the track.

Following an illegal break-in by the great detective and his assistant, an interrogation and an impersonation, Holmes succeeds in retrieving the three missing pages for the government.

"THE ADVENTURE OF THE DEVIL'S FOOT"

Watson takes Holmes to Cornwall for some rest but they stumble upon a murder. The sister of their neighbor, Mortimer Tregennis, has been killed and her two brothers who were present have gone mad. Some movement was seen at the window before the crime and Tregennis claims it is the work of the devil. The family has been involved in a dispute about the sale of the family business and Tregennis had been estranged and, although it is resolved, he has not been living with his family.

Holmes swept his light along the window-sill.
Illustration by Frederic Dorr Steele from "The Adventure of the Bruce-Partington Plans," 1908.

Following a visit by Dr. Leon Sterndale, a famous explorer, who is irritated by Holmes's refusal to divulge his suspicions about the killer, Mortimer Tregennis is found dead.

Ashes scraped from a lamp turn out to be poisonous and that was the method used to kill Tregennis's sister and drive her brothers mad. Mortimer Tregennis had been the killer and he had used *Radix pedis diaboli* ("Devil's-foot root"). Sterndale confesses to killing Mortimer using the same method because he had been in love with Mortimer's sister for many years, but Mortimer would not permit her to marry him. Holmes is sympathetic toward Sterndale and orders him to return to Africa.

They shone a torch into the darkened room. Illustration by H.M. Brock from "The Adventure of the Red Circle," 1911.

"THE ADVENTURE OF THE RED CIRCLE"

A local landlady, Mrs. Warren, asks Holmes to investigate a mysterious lodger in her house. He had arrived several weeks previously, went out briefly on his first night, returning later in the evening, but she has not seen him since. He rings for supper to be delivered to his room and if he needs anything else, he writes single words in pencil on torn scraps of paper. The man is paying double the normal rent, but Mrs. Warren is very worried and the man's endless pacing across the floor above her is driving her to distraction.

Holmes assumes at once that a substitution has been made. The man upstairs now is not the man who first arrived. When he goes to have a look at the lodger, however, he discovers that it is a woman. Knowing this, he puts the case together with the help of the agony-aunt column of a newspaper. He uncovers two desperate refugees who are hiding from a terrible secret organization known as the Red Circle.

"THE DISAPPEARANCE OF LADY FRANCES CARFAX"

Sherlock Holmes is unable to leave London due to an urgent case in which he is involved. Therefore, he sends Dr. Watson to Europe to investigate the disappearance of Lady Frances Carfax, a spinster traveling on her own. Watson follows her movements through Switzerland, Germany and France where Holmes meets up with him and they traveled back to London together. He has discovered that Lady Carfax has had dealings with a dangerous Australian named Henry Peters, alias Dr. Schlessinger. Holmes fears that Peters/Schlessinger is capable of murder. Some of Lady Carfax's jewelry turns up in a pawn shop, sold by Peters. The next time it is Peters's wife who pawns the jewels and Holmes arranges for her to be followed.

She goes to an undertakers where she is overheard discussing an order for a coffin that is "out of the ordinary." She later goes to an address in Brixton in south London. Holmes goes to the Brixton house and finds the coffin, now containing the body of an emaciated old woman, not Lady Frances but the dead nurse of Mrs. Peters. Nothing suspicious is found in the house and Peters gloats about Holmes's failure. By the morning, however, Holmes has worked out what is going on. He and Watson rush to Brixton where they find Lady Frances in the coffin, chloroformed. Having been unable to kill her, Peters and his wife have fled. Holmes explains that he had noticed at the undertakers that it had been a very big coffin for the old lady. They were going to bury two bodies in one coffin.

"THE ADVENTURE OF THE DYING DETECTIVE"

Watson is summoned by a frantic Mrs. Hudson who informs him that Sherlock Holmes appears to be at death's door, having contracted a deadly rare disease. Holmes does not allow Watson to examine him. At six o'clock he asks the doctor to turn the gas light on, but only half way before instructing him to fetch Mr. Culverton Smith but to be sure to get back to Baker Street before Mr. Smith. When he explains Holmes's dire situation, Smith agrees to come. Watson returns to Baker Street. Believing they are alone, Smith is honest with Holmes who, it seems, has been struck by the same disease that killed his nephew Victor. Smith pockets a little ivory box he had sent to Holmes that had been fitted with a sharp spring infected with the disease, removing the evidence of his murder attempt. Suddenly Holmes sits up, no longer ill and Inspector Morton enters and arrests Culverton Smith for the murder of his nephew and for Holmes's attempted murder. Holmes has feigned the illness and had never been tricked by the ivory box.

"HIS LAST BOW. THE WAR SERVICE OF SHERLOCK HOLMES"

This story is narrated in the third person and not by Dr. Watson, one of only two in the canon to be told in this way. The First World War is about to break out and German agent, Von Bork, is preparing to leave England with a treasure trove of intelligence. His associate Baron von Herling tells him that he will receive a hero's welcome when he arrives back in Berlin and Von Bork tells him he just has one last transaction to carry out with Altamont, his Irish-American informant who is providing him with naval codes.

Altamont arrives and shows Von Bork a package but he does not trust the German, refusing to hand over the codes until he is paid. But Von Bork will not pay until he has examined what he's paying for. The package Altamont hands to him is not top-secret documents, but a book, *The Practical Handbook of Bee Culture*. As Altamont hands it to him he thrusts a chloroform-soaked handkerchief over the German's face.

Altamont is none other than the author of the book, Sherlock Holmes who has been working on this case for two years during which he has visited America and Ireland. He succeeded in identifying the security leak through which the Germans were getting their secrets and then helped arrest the agents.

After this case, Holmes retires from detective work, spending his time bee-keeping in the countryside and writing his definitive opus on investigation. His final words to Watson are ominous:

Good old Watson! You are the one fixed point in a changing age. There's an east wind coming all the same, such a wind as never blew on England yet. It will be cold and bitter, Watson, and a good many of us may wither before its blast. But its God's own wind none the less, and a cleaner, better, stronger land will lie in the sunshine when the storm has cleared.

PART FIVE

★ ★ ★

HOUDINI
AND THE
AFTERLIFE

★ ★ ★

It is an old maxim of mine
that when you have excluded
the impossible, whatever
remains, however improbable,
must be the truth.

Sherlock Holmes
"The Adventure of the Beryl Coronet"

CHAPTER 17

IS THERE ANYBODY THERE?

DEATH TAKES ITS TOLL

In October 1918, just before he was due to give a lecture on spiritualism in Nottingham, Conan Doyle received a telegram from his daughter Mary containing tragic news. His 26-year-old son Kingsley was dying of influenza and pneumonia after being wounded at the Battle of the Somme. Conan Doyle was distraught but still managed to fulfill his engagement. Kingsley eventually died on November 28, 1918.

Then, in February 1919, Conan Doyle was dealt another hammer-blow when his younger brother, Innes, who had risen to the rank of brigadier-general in the army during the war also died, again of pneumonia. These two devastating deaths were followed by a third. His mother Mary had been his counselor and he shared with her things he did not even tell his wife. She had steered him onto the correct path in many things, including his writing, during his life so far. In 1920, she died, at age eighty-three. Granted, she had been ill for some time, but it was hard for him to contemplate life without the guidance of his "Ma'am."

SPREADING THE SPIRITUALIST WORD

Conan Doyle's fascination for spiritualism had grown. "… it has grown in importance with the years, and has now come to absorb the whole energy of my life," he wrote in his memoirs. The deaths of family members plus the letters he was receiving from people grieving for loved ones lost in the war seeking guidance and answers increased his interest. He saw it as his role in life, now that he had no financial worries, to spread the word. His first book on the subject, *The New Revelation*, was published by Hodder & Stoughton in 1918

Sir Arthur Conan Doyle (center) with his son Kingsley (right) and his brother Innes (left) in 1916.

as the war was coming to an end. The book deals with the issue of the physical versus the metaphysical. It looks at death, the afterlife and communication with the spirit world.

A SÉANCE IN WALES

Conan Doyle and his wife were invited to attend a séance in Wales in 1919 in the mining village of Penylan. It featured the Thomas family who were well-known in the spiritualist world and beyond, attracting celebrities and influential people. Tom and Will Thomas had a spirit guide, known as White Eagle.

Attending this particular séance were a local MP, the chief constable of Cardiff and a number of leading spiritualists and it went exactly as a séance should. Objects, including a doll and a noisy tambourine, flew randomly around the room. Tom Thomas, who had been tied to a heavy chair, and who seemed to be in a trance, suddenly turned to Jean and asked if she felt cold. When she admitted nervously that she did, a jacket belonging to Will Thomas dropped into her lap. She donned the jacket while other objects, a guitar and a trumpet among them, took off and flew around the room.

A book entitled *An Amazing Séance and an Exposure* was written by Sydney A. Moseley about this séance. In the introduction to the book, Conan Doyle wrote:

I believe that we are dealing with a thoroughly material generation with limited and self-satisfied religious and scientific lines of thought, which can only be broken up and finally rearranged by the shock of encountering physical phenomena which are outside their philosophies. The whole campaign is, I believe, engineered from the other side, and one can continually catch glimpses of wisdom and purpose beyond that of the world. The levitation of the tambourine or the moving of furniture may seem humble and even ludicrous phenomena, but the more thoughtful mind understands that the nature of the object is immaterial, and that the real question has to do with the force that moves it.

A FIVE-HUNDRED POUND REWARD

Conan Doyle insisted that people who had never attended a séance were not qualified to be dismissive of spiritualism. Nonetheless, many, especially in the press, did their best to disprove mediums as charlatans and, worse, frauds. The editor of the *Sunday Express*, James Douglas (1867 – 1940), for instance, worked tirelessly to expose fraudulent mediums and following the séance that Conan Doyle and Jean attended, offered five hundred pounds to any medium who could prove beyond doubt that he or she had actually made contact with someone from the afterlife.

Douglas announced that he would assemble a panel that would be made up of himself, spiritualists, scientists, magicians, and clergymen who had experienced a séance. Mediums such as Tom and Will Thomas were skeptical, especially as they had endured a hard time in the past from such examinations of their work. Conan Doyle supported them in this view. The spirits were not there just to be summoned at will, they argued and if they found out that they were being used in this way, who knew if they might withdraw forever into their own world and never grace our world with their ghostly presence again?

Conan Doyle met Douglas in an effort to make the competition as dignified as possible, demanding, along with the Thomas brothers, the exclusion of one particularly cynical, disrespectful member of the jury. He also insisted he would not be taking part, deeming the whole thing to be a farce. Eventually terms and conditions were agreed by members of the jury and the mediums and the *Express* offices were chosen as the venue. The Thomas brothers were tied with thick ropes to two chairs.

Unfortunately, and probably inevitably, the outcome was inconclusive. The spiritualists in the group claimed to have felt a presence, while the non-believers saw and heard nothing. Needless to say, it was good for the circulation of the *Express*.

Douglas was no fool. He staged another test, this time featuring a professional magician who exposed numerous mediums as fraudulent over the years, but had now been converted to be a true believer. This trial was staged in the apartment of a London medium in front of seven specially chosen people. The medium described clothing belonging to the audience that they had left at home. Then, after she was bound tightly and the lights were dimmed, white vapor appeared to emerge from her, followed by a blindingly bright ray of light. But it was not enough for Douglas and the five hundred pounds remained firmly in the *Express's* bank account.

KINGSLEY'S RING

These events were of remarkably high profile, as the public was at the time profoundly interested in the veracity of spiritualism. Therefore, Conan Doyle realized he could no longer stand back and watch as his beliefs were being denounced as nonsense. He joined a committee containing some very influential people as well as the editors of *The Occult Review* and *Light,* which took another look at the medium from the second test. They locked words and articles in a box and she seemed able to read them although she apparently had never seen them before. She next described a black swan that matched a pen with the brand-name Swan in the pocket of one of those present. The next part of the trial proved extremely disturbing to Conan Doyle. She began to speak of a ring that had belonged to his late son, Kingsley. As Conan Doyle explained later to the *Sunday Express:*

She was able to tell me the initials on the ring of my boy—who died some two months ago—although the average person examining it would perhaps make nothing of it. It was so worn that it would be excusable if you could not make anything of it even if you had the ring before you. So far as the second part of the program was concerned, that is a different matter. Before a decision can be made, one must attend several séances with the same medium. One certainly saw

a floating light. But although I was sitting in the front row, and was quite close to it, I could make nothing of it. I should have to see it again before passing a definite opinion on it. In any case, I think that the proceedings were instructive and clear. But I have my doubts about the whole thing.

ANOTHER HOAX

Of course, this trial fell down for the reasons that many have before and since. It would not have been difficult to find out about Conan Doyle's family life and Kingsley's ring. He was after all a globally famous man and his life was documented in the press and elsewhere. Conan Doyle would have loved to have come out and said it was all true, but he knew it would do his reputation no good and he remained unconvinced. Just as well, as those who took part admitted a few days later the whole event had been a hoax.

THE ULTIMATE CONFIRMATION

Conan Doyle took part in another Welsh-themed séance with a well-known medium, Evan Powell. The séance involved the writer, his wife Jean and several friends as well as two fellow believers and activists on behalf of the spiritualist cause—Frank Blake and Henry Engholm. Powell was searched to make sure he was not concealing anything and he was then tied to a chair. They gave him a megaphone that had been painted with luminous color so that it was visible in the dark and then the lights were switched off.

His spirit guide, Black Hawk, then began to speak through Powell, announcing: "Leely wishes to speak with the Lady of the Wigwam." Jean was immediately of the opinion that it was her late friend Lily Loder-Symonds trying to contact her. Objects flew and moved around the room and it was impossible to divine how it was being done. What was extremely puzzling was that Conan Doyle had himself chosen the venue which was a hotel room. Therefore, it would have been impossible for anyone to come in beforehand

and set it up for fraudulent activity. For the writer, the ultimate confirmation came when he was able to speak once more to his dead son:

Then came for me what was the supreme moment of my spiritual experience. It is almost too sacred for full description, and yet I feel that God sends such gifts that we may share them with others. Then came a voice in the darkness, a whispered voice, saying "Jean, it is I." I heard the word "Father." I said "Dear boy is that you?" I had a sense of a face very near my own, and of breathing. Then the clear voice came again with an intensity and note very distinctive of my son, "Forgive me!" I told him eagerly that I had

no grievance of any kind. A large, strong hand then rested upon my head, it was gently bent forward, and I felt and heard a kiss just above my brow. "Tell me dear, are you happy?" I cried. There was silence, and I feared he was gone. Then on a sighing note came the words, "Yes I am so happy." A moment afterwards another gentle voice, claiming to be that of my wife's mother, recently deceased, was heard in front of us. We could not have recognized the voice as we could the other. A few loving words were said, and then a small warm hand patted both our cheeks with a little gesture which was full of affection. Such were my experiences.

Sir Arthur Conan Doyle with the spirit head of his son Kingsley. The photograph was taken in 1919 by William Hope, the pioneer of so-called "spirit photography." Hope was eventually exposed as a fraud in 1922.

THE VITAL MESSAGE

1919 saw the publication of Conan Doyle's second work on spiritualism, *The Vital Message*. He toured, lectured and did book-signings to promote it. The tour was extensive and exhausting and had an undoubted effect on his health. In his lectures and in interviews, he spoke about how men had ceased going to church and yet in his lectures the audience was normally fifty percent made up of men. He traveled to Northern Ireland to meet Dr. W.J. Crawford (1881 – 1920) who taught Mechanical Engineering at Queen's University, Belfast. The purpose of Conan Doyle's visit was to test a medium called Kathleen Goligher who was said to be possessed with spiritualist powers.

Kathleen Goligher.

DEALING WITH ECTOPLASM

Despite many disappointments, Conan Doyle's belief in spiritualism continued unabated. He became interested in ectoplasm, the substance that emerged from mediums when they were in a trance, a gauze-like substance that was supposed to come from the body's orifices. Spiritual beings were said to drape the substance over their non-physical bodies, enabling them to interact in the physical universe. He got in touch with Dr. Gustave Geley of the *Institut Métaphysique* in France who would become a close friend. He had been running experiments with mediums for a number of years under strict scientific conditions.

Two mediums that he had worked with were of particular interest—Madame Bisson and Eva C. In one experiment involving Eva C., she had all her orifices examined carefully before putting on a skin-tight outfit that would allow nothing to get in or out. Plasma would often appear during these tests and it seemed to be painful for the subject. It emanated from her fingers, nipples, vagina and mouth. It behaved oddly, moving around, expanding and contracting and it also adopted different shapes, even taking on the shape of a face or an arm or leg. Conan Doyle was enraptured with this information, which, of course, confirmed absolutely everything he believed.

A DEBATE IN THE QUEEN'S HALL

Inevitably, there were many who disliked the new Conan Doyle. They thought spiritualism was a distraction from what he should really be engaged upon—writing fiction. Some thought him foolish and others believed that he was dishonoring the memory of the young men who had lost their lives in the war. A man named Joseph McCabe espoused such beliefs and expressed them in Partick Burgh Hall in Glasgow in January 1920 in a lecture that he titled "Sir A. Conan Doyle's Ghosts." He said that he would very much like to debate the issues with the writer himself and Conan Doyle, was ever ready to accept a challenge.

He said he would be delighted to engage in a public discussion with McCabe.

It took place on March 11, 1920, at London's Queen's Hall. It was a sell-out and ticket scalpers were doing good business on the night. Fake tickets circulated and the real ones were selling for prices far above their face value. The audience traveled from as far away as Aberdeen in north-east Scotland and some even came from Europe to hear the two men engage in a battle of words.

McCabe opened proceedings, disparaging the founders of spiritualism, denouncing them as charlatans and even frauds. As for Sir Arthur Conan Doyle, he continued:

> I submit to this jury that, like every man who has gone into the dim supernatural world, he has lived in clouds, in a mist. Whatever other witnesses there may be, you will find that distortion of judgment, that blearing of vision, which occurs whenever a man enters that wonderful world, that world of almost unparalleled trickery in the history of man.

It was an aggressive start to the evening and there was every chance that Conan Doyle, not famous for keeping his temper, might explode. But he remained calm, rose from his seat, approached the podium and began to calmly dismantle his opponent's arguments. He dramatically pulled from his pocket a small notebook and announced to the rapt audience:

> I have the names of 160 people [in this notebook]—politicians, diplomats, authors, scientists, generals, admirals, businessmen and artists who believed without any doubt or question in the truth of spiritualism. Were these men fools or dunderheads? When these grand sailors led ships into deadly battle against Germany's navy were they idiotic and impractical? When these cabinet ministers decided on affairs of state that could affect the world were they uneducated or callow?

He went on to say that many people had taken the trouble to do a lot of work in the area of spiritualism and those who have not are unqualified to criticize. He drew a spontaneous round of applause before going on to defend the men who had fostered the interest in spiritualism that McCabe had criticized.

The audience moved further onto Conan Doyle's side. He discussed the nature of plasma and ectoplasm, described Dr. Geley's experiments with Madame Bisson and Eva C., and introduced the writings of the German spiritualist investigator, Dr. Albert von Schrenck-Notzing (1862 – 1929).

There was at that point an interruption from McCabe who claimed that Eva C. was what is called a "ruminant," the type of person who can swallow things and regurgitate them so that they emerge from her mouth. He belittled everyone that Conan Doyle had mentioned, saying they were all co-conspirators.

There was booing from the floor and McCabe was losing the argument. The debate raged on, and when it ended, it appeared that Conan Doyle received the biggest cheer.

Joseph McCabe (1867 – 1955).

CHAPTER 18

ENCOUNTERING HARRY HOUDINI

AN AUSTRALIAN TOUR

Conan Doyle was invited to tour Australia, a huge and expensive undertaking, especially if, as he insisted, his wife and children accompanied him. But there was a consensus among the organizers that there was a considerable profit to be made. Thus, in August 1920, the Conan Doyle family set sail for Australia, arriving five weeks later. He spoke in Adelaide, Melbourne and Sydney where 3,500 people attended.

THE COTTINGLEY FAIRIES

It was while he was in Australia that he wrote a letter to the physicist and spiritualist Sir Oliver Lodge (1851 – 1940) explaining that he had seen a set of photographs purportedly depicting fairies. The editor of *Light* had told him about the photographs that had been taken by two cousins from Bradford, Elsie Wright (1901 – 88) and Frances Griffiths (1907 – 86).

In mid-1917 Frances Griffiths, who was then nine, was staying with her mother at the house of Elsie Wright, then sixteen, in the village of Cottingley in West Yorkshire. There was a stream at the bottom of the garden where the girls often played, mainly, they claimed, because of the fairies they saw there. To prove the truth of what they were saying, Elsie borrowed her father's camera, and, supposedly, took some snaps of the fairies. The resulting picture, developed in Elsie's father's own darkroom, showed Frances behind a bush on which four fairies appeared to be dancing. But Mr. Wright was aware that his daughter knew her way round a photographer's studio and dismissed the dancing fairies as cut-outs that she had

Frances Griffiths and the "Cottingley Fairies" photograph, 1917. Sir Arthur Conan Doyle considered the picture genuine, but it was made with paper cut-outs and hatpins.

fashioned. Two months later they came back with another photograph, this time showing Elsie sitting on the lawn, her hand reaching out to a gnome who was about a foot tall. Arthur Wright still thought the girls had tampered with the photographs but his wife Polly believed them to be real.

THE THEOSOPHISTS' CYCLE OF EVOLUTION

In mid-1919, Polly Wright attended a lecture on "Fairy Life" at the Theosophical Society in Bradford and showed her daughter's two photographs. They were then displayed at the society's annual conference several months later where they were seen by Edward Gardner, a leading theosophist, who believed them to be significant for the movement. One of the central tenets of theosophy was that humanity is involved in a cycle of evolution, moving toward perfection. Gardner said:

... the fact that two young girls had not only been able to see fairies, which others had done, but had actually for the first time ever been able to materialize them at a density sufficient for their images to be recorded on a photographic plate, meant that it was possible that the next cycle of evolution was underway.

FAKE OR FACT?

Edward Gardner sent the pictures to Harold Snelling, an expert in photography, who was of the opinion that they were genuine, that there was no evidence of any kind of "studio work or card or paper models." Gardner began to use the pictures in his lectures around the country.

Sir Oliver Lodge dismissed the photographs as obvious fakes. Conan Doyle was horrified. He could not understand firstly, how two ordinary girls in the north of England could have falsified the images, and secondly, why they would want to. Further credence was given to the photos when film-manufacturing company Kodak examined

them and said there was no evidence they had been tampered with.

While he was in Melbourne, Conan Doyle learned that more photographs had been taken that showed fairies. He resolved to dig deeper into this matter on his return to Great Britain. Another campaign beckoned. From Australia, however, he moved on to New Zealand where he lectured and met more spiritualists and mediums.

FAIRIES IN *THE STRAND*

Sir Arthur Conan Doyle had been commissioned by *The Strand Magazine* to write an article on fairies for the Christmas 1920 issue and asked Edward Gardner for permission to use the girls' photographs in the article. Bizarrely, Arthur Wright refused payment, not wishing the images to be "soiled" in any way, if they did indeed prove to be genuine.

Conan Doyle, on his return to Britain, resisted requests for more fiction and rejected the notion of writing more Sherlock Holmes stories. Indeed, his next book reflected his recent life. *The Wanderings of a Spiritualist*, published in 1921, describes his tour of Australia and New Zealand, detailing the places he visited and the people he met, although he does take time to expand upon his spiritualist beliefs as well.

In 1922, Conan Doyle published an account of the Cottingley Fairies in *The Coming of the Fairies*. The fairy episode was very damaging to his reputation and credibility and it would be many years before the girls, by that time women, admitted that the pictures were not real. They had meant it only as a bit of fun and it had got out of hand.

MEETING HARRY HOUDINI

Then, Conan Doyle's wife Jean suddenly mysteriously developed psychic powers, making contact with her own brother as well as his son and brother-in-law. Conan Doyle immediately told a new friend, the world-famous magician and escapologist, Harry Houdini (1874 – 1926).

Conan Doyle and Harry Houdini met for the first time in 1920 when the escape artist was visiting England and quickly became good friends. Of course, they disagreed fundamentally about spiritualism. Conan Doyle wrote to his friend:

> I see that you know a great deal about the negative side of spiritualism —I hope more on the positive side will come your way. But it wants to be approached not in the spirit of a detective approaching a suspect, but in that of a humble religious soul yearning for help and comfort. These clairvoyants, whose names I have given you, are passive agents in themselves and powerless. If left to themselves they guess and muddle—as they sometimes do. When the true connection is formed, all is clear.

HOUDINI'S MOCKERY

Houdini came to stay with the Conan Doyles and they all got on famously, the magician entertaining with his tricks but also proving witty and articulate in conversation. The writer and the magician discussed spiritualism deep into the night and took walks arguing about it. The Conan Doyles returned the favor when they next visited the United States, Sir Arthur was particularly impressed with Houdini's vast library of books on the occult and psychic matters. They attended a séance in Atlantic City at which Jean Conan Doyle was the medium.

She gave Houdini messages from his late mother with whom he had been trying to communicate since her death. Conan Doyle had always believed that Houdini must himself have psychic powers and when the magician was handed a pencil and paper, he wrote the name *"Powell."* Conan Doyle took it to be a message from Dr. Ellis Powell, an old spiritualist friend of his who had just died. Houdini was less convinced by the evening, however.

The Conan Doyles gave Houdini a letter, purportedly written to him in English by his mother in her spirit form which was signed

with a cross. The magician pointed out that firstly, being a practising Jew, she would never have used the Christian symbol of the cross. Secondly, he said, she could not write a word of English. Conan Doyle was annoyed and an argument ensued. When the writer asked him why, if it was all phony, he had written the name of his recently deceased friend, Houdini replied that at the time he had been thinking of a magician of his acquaintance whose name was Powell.

A mocking article published by Houdini about the séance hurt Conan Doyle deeply. He regarded it as insulting to Jean and wrote to the magician:

> I have no fancy for sparring with a friend in public, so I took no notice. But, none the less, I felt rather sore about it. You have all the right in the world to hold your own opinion, but when you say that you have had no evidence of survival, you say what I cannot reconcile with what I saw with my own eyes. I know by many examples the purity of my wife's mediumship, and I saw what you got and what the effect was on you at the time. You know also that you yourself once wrote down the name of Powell, the one who might be expected to communicate with me. Unless you were joking when you said you did not know of this Powell's death, then surely that was evidential.

END OF A FRIENDSHIP

It was the end of a beautiful friendship and from then on relations between the former friends were marked by rancor and bad feeling. It was a situation that Conan Doyle always regretted although it had really been Houdini who sparked the bad feeling. The writer had responded to Houdini's criticism of his deeply held beliefs in a fairly mild manner but Houdini had been angry. Perhaps he had longed for there to be truth in spiritualism and his disappointment was too great for him not to vent his anger.

HARRY HOUDINI

Born in 1874, Erik Weisz was one of seven children of a rabbi from Budapest whose family emigrated to the United States in 1878. At age thirteen, he moved with his father to New York where he did odd jobs before becoming a trapeze artist while waiting for the rest of the family to join them.

Fascinated by magic, Weisz developed a stage show and called himself "Harry Handcuff Houdini." He was joined by his wife Wilhelmina, known onstage as "Bess." He became known for his escapes using handcuffs and began to tour America and Europe, becoming the highest-paid entertainer in American vaudeville. His escape tricks became increasingly elaborate involving straightjackets, packing cases nailed shut with him inside and water-filled tanks. He had a talent for picking locks and was also exceedingly strong.

By 1912, his act had reached its pinnacle with the Chinese Water Torture Cell. In this stunt, Houdini was suspended by the feet and lowered upside-down into a locked, water-filled glass cabinet. In order to escape, he had to hold his breath for three minutes. Audiences marveled and he continued to perform the trick until his death in 1926. He also flew planes, starred in several films and published several books.

Houdini also became a fervent campaigner against what he viewed as the chicanery of fraudulent mediums and campaigned against spiritualism wherever he went, exposing numerous charlatans. This did not stop him from agreeing with his wife that the first of them to die would attempt to communicate with the other from beyond the grave. Their experiment was a failure.

He died from acute appendicitis in 1926 reportedly after being caught unawares by a punch from a McGill University student who was testing Houdini's much-vaunted ability to be able to take blows to the stomach. Houdini had no time to say that he had to prepare himself first.

MRS. HUDSON

"Her cuisine is limited but she has as good an idea of breakfast as a Scotchwoman."

Sherlock Holmes
"The Adventure of the Naval Treaty"

Mrs. Hudson is the landlady of 221B Baker Street, a lady who often argues with Holmes about the tidiness of his rooms. But, as Watson tells us in "The Adventure of the Dying Detective," she puts up with a great deal:

Not only was her first-floor flat invaded at all hours by throngs of singular and often undesirable characters, but her remarkable lodger showed an eccentricity and irregularity in his life which must have sorely tried her patience. His incredible untidiness, his addiction to music at strange hours, his occasional revolver practice within doors, his weird and often malodorous scientific experiments, and the atmosphere of violence and danger which hung around him made him the very worst tenant in London. On the other hand, his payments were princely. I have no doubt that the house might have been purchased at the price which Holmes paid for his rooms during the years that I was with him.

The landlady stood in the deepest awe of him and never dared to interfere with him, however outrageous his proceedings might seem. She was fond of him, too, for he had a remarkable gentleness and courtesy in his dealings with women.

In "A Scandal in Bohemia," Holmes gets her name wrong: "When Mrs. Turner has brought in the tray I will make it clear for you." Needless to say, this has sent Sherlockians into a frenzy over the decades.

AGE IS CATCHING UP

Sir Arthur Conan Doyle was getting older and acknowledged that he was not as strong as he once was. But he still worked long hours and, although he was not writing as much, he remained an avid traveler. He went to Canada in 1923 and met local spiritualists. But he also attended a baseball match on Dominion Day, between Winnipeg and Indianapolis. As a result, he wrote to the newspapers when he returned home extolling the virtues of the game, describing it as the game of the future. He wrote ceaselessly to newspapers of all sorts on all kinds of topics, some important and some fairly whimsical. He also, to the eternal gratitude of his legions of fans, returned at last to Sherlock Holmes for one last hurrah.

THE CASE BOOK OF SHERLOCK HOLMES

The Case Book of Sherlock Holmes appeared in 1927, published in Britain by John Murray and in America by George H. Doran. It consisted of stories published in *The Strand Magazine* between October 1921 and April 1927:

"The Adventure of the Mazarin Stone"
"The Problem of Thor Bridge"
"The Adventure of the Creeping Man"
"The Adventure of the Sussex Vampire"
"The Adventure of the Three Garridebs"
"The Adventure of the Illustrious Client"
"The Adventure of the Three Gables"
"The Adventure of the Blanched Soldier"
"The Adventure of the Lion's Mane"
"The Adventure of the Retired Colorman"
"The Adventure of the Veiled Lodger"
"The Adventure of Shoscombe Old Place."

Several of the stories are on a par with Conan Doyle's earlier work, but the collection as a whole is regarded as weaker than most of the rest of the Sherlock Holmes canon.

In 1927, he published another book on spiritualism, *Pheneas Speaks*. In it his dead friends return to life and confirm that everything Conan Doyle believes is true. Needless to say, it was criticized by reviewers.

CHAPTER 19

THE CASE BOOK OF SHERLOCK HOLMES

Stories published 1921 – 27 in *The Strand*

"The Adventure of the Mazarin Stone" . . . . October 1921

"The Problem of Thor Bridge" . . . . February – March 1922

"The Adventure of the Creeping Man" . . . . March 1923

"The Adventure of the Sussex Vampire" . . . . January 1924

"The Adventure of the Three Garridebs" . . . . January 1925

"The Adventure of the Illustrious Client" . . . February – March 1925

"The Adventure of the Three Gables" . . . . October 1926

"The Adventure of the Blanched Soldier" . . . . November 1926

"The Adventure of the Lion's Mane" . . . . December 1926

"The Adventure of the Retired Colorman" . . . . January 1927

"The Adventure of the Veiled Lodger" . . . . February 1927

"The Adventure of Shoscombe Old Place" . . . . April 1927

"THE ADVENTURE OF THE MAZARIN STONE"

This story is an adaptation of Conan Doyle's play, *The Crown Diamond* and is written in the third person, one of only two Sherlock Holmes stories to be written thus, the other being "His Last Bow." Holmes is commissioned to recover the priceless crown diamond, the Mazarin Stone. The action takes place in one room (as does the play) and Dr. Watson features only fleetingly. It focuses on the recovery of the stone.

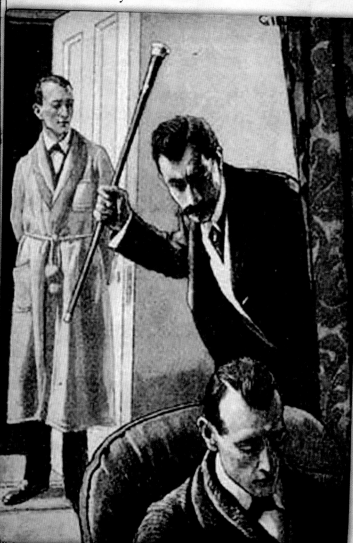

His thick stick raised, he approached the silent figure. Illustration by Alfred Gilbert from "The Adventure of the Mazarin Stone," 1921.

"THE PROBLEM OF THOR BRIDGE"

An American former Senator, Mr. Neil Gibson, commissions Holmes to investigate the death of his wife and prove that the couple's governess, Grace Dunbar, is innocent of her murder. Holmes takes the case on, even though he and Gibson do not see eye to eye. He quickly disproves the evidence against Miss Dunbar and, using a chip in the stone balustrade of Thor Bridge and Watson's revolver, he demonstrates that Mrs. Gibson has, in fact, not been murdered but has committed suicide. Jealous of Miss Dunbar's relationship with her husband, she tried to make it appear to have been murder and to pin it on the governess.

"THE ADVENTURE OF THE CREEPING MAN"

Holmes is asked by Mr. Trevor Bennett to investigate the strange behavior of his employer, Professor Presbury. He has been very moody and after disappearing for a few weeks to Prague, had returned a changed man, furtive and sly. He has also begun to crawl around on his hands and feet. Furthermore, his dog has suddenly turned against the professor. Presbury has been receiving odd packages and Bennett wonders if this odd behavior might have something to do with them. Holmes deduces that while abroad the professor has become addicted to a drug that makes him behave like a monkey.

"THE ADVENTURE OF THE SUSSEX VAMPIRE"

Mr. Robert Ferguson is convinced that his Peruvian second wife has been sucking their baby son's blood. Sherlock Holmes is dismissive of the notion of vampire activity but despite this, he accepts the case and before even visiting Ferguson's house he has worked out that it has nothing to do with the supernatural. The culprit, Holmes announces, is Jack, Ferguson's 15-year-old son by his first wife. Jealous of the new arrival, Jack has been firing poison darts at his baby brother's neck. The baby's mother has been sucking the poison out of her baby's neck, rather than biting him to suck his blood.

"THE ADVENTURE OF THE THREE GARRIDEBS"

Nathan Garrideb has been contacted by an American named John Garrideb who has told him that if they can find a third male person of the name Garrideb, they stand to inherit five million dollars each. Holmes is visited at Baker Street by John Garrideb who is displeased that Nathan Garrideb has involved a detective in the case. Nonetheless, he accepts Holmes's help. He has to or he will be found out for he has hatched a scheme to ensure that Nathan is out of his accommodation for a while. He says he has found a third Garrideb and dispatches Nathan to Birmingham to meet him. Holmes consults with the police and learns that John Garrideb is not actually the man's name. He is a killer and when they confront him as he attempts to force open a trapdoor in Nathan's rooms, he opens fire, hitting Dr. Watson in the leg. Watson explains how upset Holmes is that his friend has been wounded:

It was worth a wound—it was worth many wounds—to know the depth of loyalty and love which lay behind that cold mask. The clear, hard eyes were dimmed for a moment,

and the firm lips were shaking. For the one and only time I caught a glimpse of a great heart as well as of a great brain. All my years of humble but single-minded service culminated in that moment of revelation.

The killer is captured and the trapdoor hides a room containing a printing press and piles of counterfeit banknotes that had been put there by a previous occupant.

"THE ADVENTURE OF THE ILLUSTRIOUS CLIENT"

The agent of an illustrious client engages Sherlock Holmes to help prevent the marriage of Violet de Merville to Adelbert Gruner, an Austrian baron suspected of having murdered his first wife. Miss de Merville is completely smitten, however, and will have none of it. Holmes's job seems almost impossible until he is introduced to Kitty Winters, who was

He realized that two pistols were pointed at his head. Illustration by Howard K. Elcock from "The Adventure of the Three Garridebs," 1925.

the baron's former mistress. From her he learns of a diary kept by the baron that lists the numerous women with whom he has consorted. Holmes hopes that it will help convince Miss de Merville that she should not marry Gruner. When Watson reads that Holmes has been attacked and badly beaten by two men and is near death, he rushes to Baker Street only to learn that his friend has exaggerated his injuries to imply that he will be unable to do anything for a while. Watson visits Gruner posing as a connoisseur of Chinese pottery and while he is trying to sell a piece to the baron, Holmes breaks in and steals the diary. After he shows it to Violet, the wedding is canceled.

"THE ADVENTURE OF THE THREE GABLES"

Mary Maberley of Harrow Weald has written to Sherlock Holmes asking for his help but he is then visited by Steve Dixie, a ruffian, who warns him to stay away from Harrow Weald. Holmes threatens to unmask Dixie's involvement in a murder case and learns that his boss Barney Stockdale must be involved in whatever is going on at Mary Maberley's house. He visits Harrow Weald and learns that a rich woman has tried to buy the elderly Mrs. Maberley's house and all its contents. It is immediately obvious to Holmes that she wants something in the house. Mary Maberley's late son had been involved with the wealthy lady at one time and had written a novel about the relationship in which it was obvious who the main characters were. She does not want it published and wants to secure the only remaining manuscript. Holmes persuades the wealthy woman to write a cheque for five thousand pounds to Mrs. Maberley in return for his silence about the affair.

"THE ADVENTURE OF THE BLANCHED SOLDIER"

Unusually, Sherlock Holmes assumes the role of narrator in this story. James M. Dodd is searching for a missing friend, Godfrey Emsworth, and suspects that something sinister is going on at the Emsworth family home. Recently, for instance, when he had been staying there, he awoke in the middle of the night to see Godfrey's face pressed against the glass of his bedroom window. Rushing outside, he found no sign of his friend. Next day, Dodd saw a well-dressed man leaving an outbuilding. Looking through a crack in the shutters, he is certain he sees Godfrey and beside him the well-dressed man who is reading. Godfrey's father finds him and orders him to leave. Godfrey's parents have told him that they have dispatched their son on a round-the-world trip but James suspects that to be a lie and that Godfrey is hidden somewhere on the estate. Holmes visits the estate and deduces from the publication that the man was reading that Godfrey has contracted leprosy while fighting in the Boer War in southern Africa and his family wish to keep his illness secret. All ends happily when it is discovered that Godfrey is only suffering from a milder form of the disease.

"THE ADVENTURE OF THE LION'S MANE"

Now retired and living in Sussex, Sherlock Holmes narrates this story. He tells us this is because "the good Watson had passed almost beyond my ken. An occasional weekend visit was the most that I ever saw of him." The tale begins with Holmes telling us:

After my withdrawal to my little Sussex home, when I had given myself up entirely to that soothing life of Nature for which I had so often yearned during the long years spent in the gloom of London.

He relates his involvement in solving the murder of Fitzroy McPherson, science master from the nearby preparatory school, The Gables. In fact, Holmes is present when the man, his body covered in red welts, staggers from a bathing pool in agony. In his dying words he mentions a lion's mane. Holmes uncovers a number of suspects but finds it difficult to come up with a solution to the case.

Then, McPherson's dog is found dead with the same symptoms as the science master. The police want to arrest Ian Murdoch, a maths teacher at The Gables who had once been a suitor of the beautiful Miss Bellamy, McPherson's fiancée. They believe he may have killed McPherson out of jealousy. Murdoch appears with the same red welts that McPherson and his dog had and when Holmes goes to the bathing pond, he spots the killer—a deadly Lion's Mane Jellyfish.

"THE ADVENTURE OF THE RETIRED COLORMAN"

Josiah Amberley, a retired art dealer engages Sherlock Holmes to investigate the disappearance of his wife who is believed to have run off with their neighbor, Dr. Ray Ernest. The couple have taken with them a considerable amount of cash and securities. Holmes is not terribly interested until he discovers that Amberley is not what he seems. The solution he believes lies somewhere at Amberley's home and to gain entry, he sends Amberley out of the city on a false errand with Watson watching over him before breaking into his client's house. He discovers that Amberley has murdered the missing couple. He knows this because his alibi does not hold up—his seat at the Haymarket Theater had been unoccupied on the night in question. There had been fresh painting done to decorate Amberley's house and

Holmes deduces that it has been used to cover the smell of gas which Amberley had used to kill his wife and her lover.

"THE ADVENTURE OF THE VEILED LODGER"

One of the more unusual Sherlock Holmes stories, this one deals with a decades-old unsolved murder case. Mrs. Merrilow visits Holmes to tell him about her lodger, Mrs. Ronder, who has a severely disfigured face. She shouts out *Murder!* in the night and is ill and wasting away. The lodger tells Mrs. Merrilow to mention the name Abbas Parva to Sherlock Holmes. This recalls to the detective a case where a circus lion had escaped and attacked two people, killing one.

The man sprang to his feet with a hoarse scream. Illustration by Frank Wiles from "The Adventure of the Retired Colorman," 1927.

Mrs. Ronder was the survivor and the dead victim was her husband. There are many inconsistencies in the case.

Holmes and Watson visit the veiled Mrs. Ronder who explains to them that her husband had been a cruel and callous man and she had a lover, the circus strongman, Leonardo. She and Leonardo hatched a plan to get rid of her husband. At a Berkshire village named Abbas Parva, Leonardo smashed Mr. Ronder's skull with a club with nails hammered into it that made the wounds resembling those made by a lion's teeth. Leonardo freed the lion to enhance his story but it attacked and mutilated Mrs. Ronder who has wanted to unburden herself of the story before killing herself. Holmes talks her out of suicide.

He looked over his shoulder with a face as if he had seen the devil coming out of hell.
Illustration by Frank Wiles from "The Adventure of Shoscombe Old Place," 1927.

"THE ADVENTURE OF SHOSCOMBE OLD PLACE"

Mr. John Mason, head trainer at Shoscombe Old Place horse racing stables consults with Sherlock Holmes regarding his master, Sir Robert Norberton who, in his opinion, has gone mad. He thinks this because Sir Robert has argued with his sister, Lady Beatrice, and given away her prized spaniel. He acts oddly in other ways and meets with a strange man at the old crypts. Furthermore, burnt human bones have been found in the furnace at Shoscombe. Holmes and Watson go to Shoscombe and stay at an inn, the owner of whom now owns Lady Beatrice's prize spaniel. Holmes takes it for a walk and releases it as Lady Beatrice's carriage comes out. It runs toward the carriage but then retreats in terror. Although the carriage contains only her ladyship and a maid, Holmes hears a male voice call out *"Drive on!"*

In the crypt Holmes finds a coffin with a recently dead body in it. Sir Robert arrives and he takes them back to the house to explain everything after Holmes tells him he has worked most of it out anyway. Lady Beatrice had died of dropsy a week previously but he was keeping her death secret to keep creditors at bay while he waited for the Derby when he believed his horse would win and be able to pay off everything. To hide her body in the crypt he and the maid's husband had to dispose of an older body—hence the burned bones. Each day the maid's husband, dressed in her ladyship's clothes, took her place in the carriage which explains the masculine voice Holmes heard. Fortunately, Sir Robert's horse wins the Derby and he manages to pay his debts. The police decide to take no action against him.

CHAPTER 20

THE DESCENDING SPIRAL

STILL TRAVELING

Conan Doyle's health was beginning to trouble him. He suffered from dizzy spells and now and then lost the feeling in his right leg. Sleep was also proving difficult. But still he traveled even though his friends and his doctors advised that he should not subject himself to such stresses. The fall of 1928 saw him, Jean and their three children setting sail for South Africa, Kenya, and Rhodesia. South Africa of course took him back to the dark days of the Boer War. Although most people were friendly enough, he did encounter hostility from those who saw him as a messenger of imperialism who had defended the concentration camps and the slaughter of women and children. He was, as ever, speaking about spiritualism and interviews mostly covered that and Sherlock Holmes and the resurgence of Germany.

WORRYING ABOUT EUROPE'S FUTURE

Conan Doyle worried continually about what was happening in Germany and was alarmed by letters from his spiritualist friends there. He also had a number of Jewish friends who made their fears clear to him. He wrote to MPs and managed to arrange for a refugee from Germany to find a place to live in London. He also delivered a series of lectures on the subject "The Future of Europe," that brought up the dangers that were facing Jews. He recommended that Britain should build up her armed forces and look toward mechanized warfare.

SCANDINAVIA

In 1929, Conan Doyle visited Scandinavia and Holland and that same year he published *The Maracot Deep and Other Stories,* another in the vein of *The Lost World,* but without its charm. The title story involves a gang of explorers in a diving bell and an underground city. Professor Challenger reappears in the story "When the World Screamed." He believes that the world is a living organism and drills to the heart of the planet where he finds a breathing, shining mass. When one of his companions thrusts the point of a harpoon into this substance, the planet lets out a shout.

Sir Arthur and Jean Conan Doyle in Stockholm, Sweden, 1929.

AN EERIE COUGH

Meanwhile, the letters continued to flow from his prolific pen, written at a specially created desk that was just the right height to allay the neck and back pain from which he now suffered. He wrote of a strange experience when in the middle of the night he heard footsteps outside his bedroom door and then a cough. When he opened the door there was no one there. He then received a letter from a medium who said that she had dreamed of visiting him around the time he heard the footsteps and had administered some healing treatment to him. She had also coughed in exactly the way he had described. Conan Doyle was excited by this:

> These are the facts, and they seem to me beyond all range of coincidence, and to present a very clear case of bi-location. Mrs. Leonard was sleeping at Kenley but undoubtedly her double or etheric body had visited me at Crowborough.

There was a torrent of letters on this matter, some supporting, some derisive. Others put forward alternative explanations for the incident. Some even said he had perhaps been visited by an angel giving him advance notice of his death.

A HEART ATTACK

Sir Arthur Conan Doyle's health was by now not good at all. He coughed a great deal and he was not sleeping. Unusually, he became irritable. One day, he was suffering from cramp in his arm and the following day he had a heart attack. He was rushed to hospital but was soon home again. He was told that next time it might be fatal and was warned to slow down. Naturally, he took no notice and was soon back at his desk writing letters.

ON THE EDGE OF THE UNKNOWN

Conan Doyle did get better to the extent that his doctors gave permission for him to attend the Armistice Day Memorial Service at the Royal Albert Hall in the morning and at the Queen's Hall in the evening. He gave a speech from a balcony wearing only a thin suit and coat amidst a snowfall and a biting wind. The following day he had to be helped out of bed but he still went out debating spiritualism and promoting his last book, *The Edge of the Unknown*, a collection of fifteen essays on spiritualism. He had to be helped home from his last engagement and was barely able to speak and unable to move. They gave him oxygen to ease his breathing.

Sir Arthur Conan Doyle with his son Adrian (left) and Major Alfred H. Wood (right), 1930.

DEATH IS NOT THE END

On the morning of July 7, 1930, Sir Arthur asked for his bedroom window to be opened so that he could hear the birds singing. He explained to his family that they would all meet again. Death was not the end. Jean held his hand and at 9:15 a.m. that morning he squeezed her hand and passed into what he truly believed was the next world. His last words to Jean were "You are wonderful." He was seventy-one years old.

Sir Arthur Conan Doyle's funeral took place four days later. It was a warm summer's day and he had insisted that there be no mourning. His headstone was of solid British oak and the inscription read:

Steel true, blade straight.

Sir Arthur Conan Doyle, February 5, 1930, a few months before his death.

PART SIX

★ ★ ★

THE SHERLOCK HOLMES LEGACY

★ ★ ★

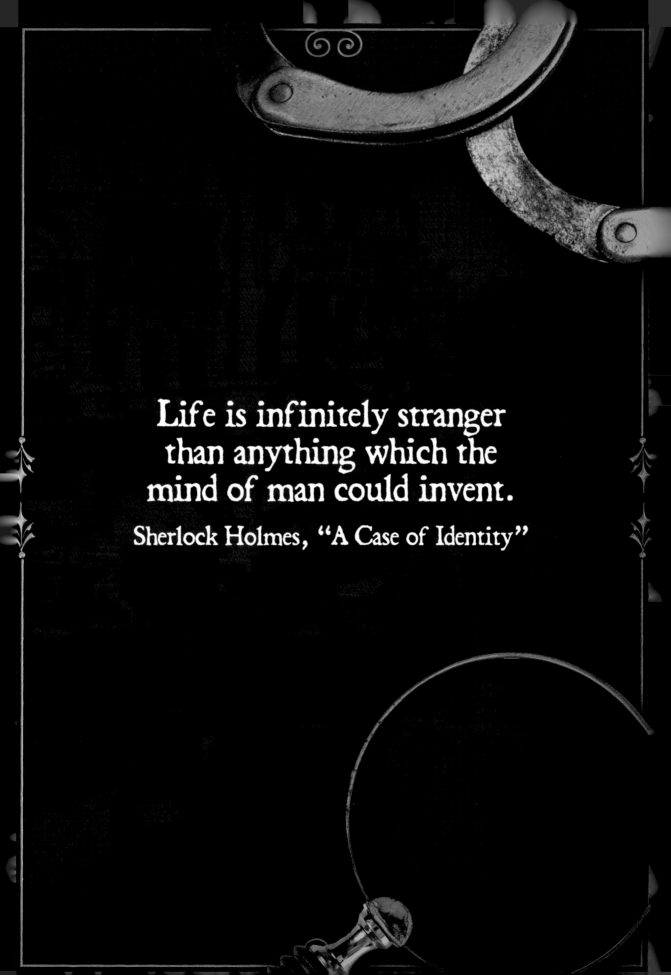

Life is infinitely stranger
than anything which the
mind of man could invent.

Sherlock Holmes, "A Case of Identity"

CHAPTER 21

THE RIVALS OF SHERLOCK HOLMES

Fictional detectives started following in the footsteps of Sherlock Holmes even before Holmes wrestled with Professor Moriarty at the Reichenbach Falls. With Holmes out of the way, supposedly dead, these imitators became known collectively as the "rivals of Sherlock Holmes." Most of them were almost immediately forgotten, but a few have stayed with us over the years.

The comparisons were fairly obvious. The detective had nothing to do with the police and there was usually an associate who was similar in temperament and behavior to Dr. Watson. The detective would have a special talent, like Holmes, such as scientific investigation or deductive reasoning. His or her investigative methods would appear brilliant to other people such as police officers or their Watson-like associate. They would possess quirky character traits and pastimes and they would live in isolation at accommodation that was similar to Holmes and Watson's rooms at 221B Baker Street. In fact, only when the hard-boiled detective stories of the 1920s appeared did the detective story progress away from the Sherlock Holmes prototype.

MARTIN HEWITT

The closest imitation of Holmes can be found in Arthur Morrison's popular stories featuring Martin Hewitt, a lawyer who, like Holmes, possesses a brilliant talent for deduction. Immediately after Holmes's apparent demise, the editors of *The Strand Magazine* started publishing Morrison's stories to fill the gap left by Holmes.

Morrison made efforts to divert attention from the similarities to Sherlock Holmes. Where Holmes is tall, Hewitt is only of average height. He is also stout where Holmes is lean and, unlike Holmes, he has a good relationship with Scotland Yard. Hewitt is also a fairly happy and cheerful individual which Holmes certainly was not.

DR. JOHN EVELYN THORNDYKE

Dr. John Evelyn Thorndyke was a Holmes-like detective created by R. Austin Freeman, appearing in 21 novels and 38 short stories between 1907 and 1937. Thorndyke focuses on science and forensic crime scene analysis to solve his cases. In fact, he carries with him a portable crime scene laboratory. There is, of course, an assistant, Dr. Jervis who acts as narrator. Lestrade is represented by Superintendent Miller and Thorndyke lives at a notable address—5A King's Bench Walk,

Arthur Morrison (1863 – 1945).

Inner Temple, in central London's legal district.

Like Holmes, much of his time is spent proving the police wrong. Like Holmes he is tall, naturally athletic and a committed bachelor and he is also something of a polymath. But there is a major difference in the form of the stories. Freeman created what is known as the "inverted" detective story by which the commission of the crime is shown or described at the beginning and the second part explains the detective's attempt to solve the mystery. Known as a "howcatchem" this is the opposite of the "whodunit" style of Conan Doyle in which the full details of the crime and its perpetrator are not revealed until the end of the story.

DIXON DRUCE

The fictional detective Dixon Druce was one of the more popular Sherlock Holmes substitutes in *The Strand Magazine* after the Reichenbach Falls. What was different about Druce was that the stories were written by a woman, L.T. Meade, one of the few successful woman mystery writers of her time. Dixon Druce was the manager of Werner's Agency and Eric Vandeleur, police surgeon for Westminster, was his "Watson." Unlike Watson, however, Vandeleur does not chronicle the stories. Druce does that for himself.

PROFESSOR AUGUSTUS S.F.X. VAN DUSEN

Professor Augustus S.F.X. Van Dusen, PhD, LLD, FRS, MD, is known as the "thinking machine," and features in a series of short stories and two novels written by American writer Jacques Futrelle (1875 – 1912). The stories were originally published in Philadelphia's *Saturday Evening Post* and the *Boston American*. The professor solves mysteries with the unswerving use of logic and has his friend Hutchinson Hatch as his "Watson." Futrelle died at age thirty-seven on April 15, 1912, on board the RMS *Titanic*.

MAX CARRADOS

In 1914, while Holmes was still alive and well and appearing in *The Strand Magazine*, the English writer Ernest Bramah (1868 – 1942) started writing detective stories featuring Max Carrados, a blind detective. The influence of Sherlock Holmes is evident and a former lawyer named Carlyle fills the Watson role, running the detective agency. Carrados has developed his surviving senses to such effect that people often fail to realize that he is blind. It is his extraordinary powers of perception that distinguish Carrados. Bramah wrote stories about him until 1934.

CARNACKI THE GHOST-FINDER

If Bramah pushed the Sherlockian limits with his blind detective, English fantasy writer, William Hope Hodgson (1877 – 1918) took it even further with his creation of Thomas Carnacki, a detective of the occult and supernatural phenomena. He appeared in six short stories in *The Idler* magazine

L.T. Meade was the pseudonym of Elizabeth Thomasina Meade Smith (1844 – 1914).

and *The New Magazine* between 1910 and 1912. Dodgson was his Watson-like associate and it is he who narrates the adventures and who lives in an apartment in Cheyne Walk in Chelsea, west London. William Hope Hodgson died in World War I at age forty.

LOVEDAY BROOKE

At least Loveday Brooke was a different gender to Sherlock Holmes. This lady detective was the brainchild of the British writer, Catherine Louisa Pirkis (1839 – 1910). She launched her creation in the first of seven short stories in February 1893, published in *The Ludgate Monthly* some ten months prior to Holmes and Moriarty engaging in their fight to the death. Unlike other female detectives appearing at the time, Loveday did not rely on her good looks and feminine wiles. Instead, she utilized the same tools as Sherlock Holmes—logic and minute observation. She made careful examinations of crime scenes and more often than not was at odds with the police's interpretation of the evidence. She is a spinster and past thirty but her maturity and life experience land her a job with a flourishing detective agency in Lynch Court whose owner describes her as:

HE INTRODUCED HIMSELF.

Loveday Brooke (left) was one of the first female fictional detectives. Illustration by Bernard Higham from *The Experiences of Loveday Brooke, Lady Detective* (1894).

> *The most sensible and practical woman I ever met ... she has so much common sense that it amounts to genius—positively to genius.*

THE OLD MAN IN THE CORNER

British author and playwright, Baroness Emmuska Orczy (1865 – 1947), creator of the Scarlet Pimpernel, invented a detective who worked from an armchair. Known as "the old man in the corner," he positions himself in an armchair in the corner of a London teashop and, using Holmesian deduction, solves the crimes that he reads about in the newspapers. Miss Polly Burton, a journalist, is his associate. She habituates the teashop where she invariably discusses a crime with the old man and during their conversation he solves the mystery. After half a dozen stories, published in 1901 in *The Royal Magazine*, she assumes the Watsonian role of narrator. Interestingly, in these stories, no perpetrator is ever brought to justice.

LADY MOLLY OF SCOTLAND YARD

Baroness Orczy also created the detective Molly Robertson-Kirk who first appeared in 1910 in the hugely popular book *Lady Molly of Scotland Yard*. Her principal tools were her intelligence and her deductive skill, but her cases were usually solved by her interpreting evidence of a domestic nature that would be foreign territory to her male counterparts. At the end of the book she leaves the police force to marry her fiancé.

THE DESCENDANTS OF SHERLOCK HOLMES

Edgar Allan Poe invented the detective novel when he introduced the world to his intriguing character C. Auguste Dupin who first appeared in the short story "The Murders in the Rue Morgue." But if Poe was the inventor, it was Sir Arthur Conan Doyle who established the detective novel as a truly popular literary genre, loved by millions and inspiring and influencing countless other writers who went on to create some of the most memorable and best-loved characters in fiction.

HERCULE POIROT

Agatha Christie (1890 – 1976), the best-selling author of all time, introduced her famous fictional Belgian detective, Hercule Poirot, in her first book, *The Mysterious Affair at Styles*, published in 1920. Like Holmes, Poirot has an amanuensis, Captain Hastings, who chronicles Poirot's cases like Dr. Watson. Hastings is, like Watson, a retired military man and shares many of Watson's personality traits. By no means a genius, Hastings, like Watson, often makes a seemingly trivial point that illuminates a case for his associate. Like Holmes, Poirot is an advocate of the human rational faculty and he uses Hastings as a foil, much as Holmes uses Watson. Furthermore, Poirot even has a mysterious brother with an exotic name—Achille. There is even an equivalent of Conan Doyle's Inspector Lestrade in the form of Inspector Japp. Christie has acknowledged her debt to the Sherlock Holmes stories:

> *I was still writing in the Sherlock Holmes tradition—eccentric detective, stooge assistant, with a Lestrade-type Scotland Yard detective, Inspector Japp.*

Poirot featured in 33 novels and 51 short stories between 1920 and 1975 and the stories continue to be adapted for television, film and the stage.

FATHER BROWN

G.K. Chesterton (1874 – 1936) was a big fan of Sherlock Holmes and wrote several essays on the great detective. He also wrote a series of short stories featuring a short and unremarkable Catholic priest named Father Brown. The first story, "The Blue Cross," was published in June 1910 in Philadelphia's *Saturday Evening Post*. It was published in *The Story-Teller* magazine in London a few months later. Father Brown has the knack

of being able to look deep into the human soul and, like Holmes, has a nemesis, M. Hercule Flambeau and a Lestrade-like figure in Aristide Valentin, head of the Paris Police. Father Brown differs from Holmes in his methods, relying, more often than not, on intuition rather than deduction.

LORD PETER WIMSEY

Lord Peter Death Bredon Wimsey is the creation of English writer, Dorothy L. Sayers (1893 – 1957), who described her character as a melange of Fred Astaire and Bertie Wooster. He is an upper-class amateur sleuth and in the first few novels something of a clown. As the stories continue, however, his character becomes more rounded and the plots evolve into compelling "whodunits." His Watson is his valet and former army colleague, Mervyn Butler, and Inspector Charles "Parker Bird" Parker often helps out. Later, he is assisted by the woman who would become his wife, Harriet Vane.

Agatha Christie's Belgian detective Hercule Poirot, played by David Suchet in 1992.

CHAPTER 22

HOLMES ON THE PAGE

In the same way that fans of the great horror writer, H.P. Lovecraft, have taken his themes and developed them, creating what is known as the Cthulhu Mythos, many authors have written further Holmes adventures in the style of pastiches and parodies.

CONAN DOYLE'S SELF-PATISCHE

Conan Doyle can be said to have created pastiches of Holmes himself. His 1898 story "The Lost Special" mentions an "amateur reasoner" who remains unnamed but is obviously to be identified by readers as Sherlock Holmes. The same happens in some other Conan Doyle stories such as "The Field Bazaar" and "The Man with the Watches." "How Watson Learned the Trick," a wry tale written in 1924 for Queen Mary, wife of King George V, provides an entertaining parody of the Holmes-Watson breakfast scene.

FAN FICTION

Even while Holmes and Watson were still in situ at 221B Baker Street, magazines and newspapers were publishing pastiches and parodies of the Sherlock Holmes tales and with the death of Sir Arthur Conan Doyle in 1930 and the certain knowledge that there would be no more Sherlock Holmes stories, other writers began penning their own versions. It is worth noting that nowadays, via the internet, we can enjoy the phenomenon of "fan fiction" whereby fans of a writer create their own stories using the characters and situations of that writer. Sherlock Holmes remains one of the most popular vehicles for fan fiction. One expert has identified around 8,000 examples of Holmes parody and pastiche and that figure is constantly being augmented.

THE UNDOCUMENTED CASES

The original stories themselves provide opportunities for the writer of a brand new Sherlock Holmes story. The Holmes expert Philip K. Jones lists 126 undocumented cases that are mentioned in the sixty Holmes stories and these at least give the prospective writer a start. Of course, there are, literally, thousands of writers who have decided to conjure up an entirely new story and these have expanded in some cases into eras and genres that would undoubtedly shock Sir Arthur Conan Doyle.

THE LOST CHRONICLES

But, there are also pastiches written in the style of the original that take place in the Victorian or Edwardian eras. Denis O. Smith is highly regarded as a writer of Holmes pastiches, as evidenced by his 1982 story "The Adventure of the Purple Hand" which can be found in *The Lost Chronicles of Sherlock Holmes*. In this tale, malaria-suffering tea-importer, Mark Pringle, calls Holmes in to investigate a series of incidents involving an overheard conversation between his wife and a stranger, a figure seen crossing his garden after dark and a five-fingered purple handprint that has appeared on his garden wall.

Conan Doyle's son, Adrian Conan Doyle, has even taken up the challenge. In partnership with the well-known American mystery writer, John Dickson Carr, he published the collection of short stories *The Exploits of Sherlock Holmes* in 1954.

In 2011, with the approval of the Conan Doyle estate, the well-regarded children's writer, Anthony Horowitz wrote a Sherlock Holmes novel, *The House of Silk*. A sequel titled *Moriarty* was published in 2014. It was not the first time the estate had authorized a pastiche. In 2005, Caleb Carr's *The Italian Secretary* was approved by them and Lyndsay Faye's 2009 novel *Dust and Shadow: An Account of the Killings by Dr. John H. Watson*, pitching the great detective against Jack the Ripper, was also approved.

RETIREMENT AND BEEKEEPING

Holmes was revived by American crime writer, Laurie R. King, in her Mary Russell novels, a series of thirteen historical mysteries the first of which was *The Beekeeper's Apprentice*. Holmes is semi-retired in Sussex when an American girl meets him. He trains her in the art of being a detective and they subsequently marry.

The author of *The Mysteries of Pittsburgh* and *Wonder Boys*—Michael Chabon—published a novella called *The Final Solution* in 2004 that features a retired detective with an interest in beekeeping. He becomes involved in the case of a missing parrot owned by a nine-year-old Jewish refugee from Germany.

Holmes is also getting old in Mitch Cullin's 2005 novel *A Slight Trick of the Mind* set two years after the end of the Second World War. At the age of 93, Sherlock Holmes comes to terms with a life lacking in emotion. The book was later made into the successful film *Mr. Holmes* (2015), starring Sir Ian McKellen.

INSPECTOR LESTRADE AND MYCROFT HOLMES

Other characters from the Sherlock Holmes canon get their own chance to shine in a number of novels. Inspector Lestrade strikes out on his own in seventeen books written by M.J. Trow, beginning with *The Adventures of Inspector Lestrade* in 1985. And Irene Adler features in a series written by Carole Nelson Douglas.

Mycroft Holmes has also been the protagonist in a number of books—a series of four titles by Quinn Fawcett and

Enter the Lion, a 1979 publication by Michael P. Hodel and Sean M. Wright. Somewhat bizarrely, former NBA star Kareem Abdul-Jabbar joined forces with screenwriter Anna Waterhouse to pen the 2015 novel *Mycroft Holmes*.

The Baker Street Irregulars are showcased in Anthony Boucher's 1940 work, *The Case of the Baker Street Irregulars*. Hired as technical advisers by a film producer, the Irregulars investigate the mysterious murder of a heavy-drinking ex-private detective turned hardboiled mystery novelist and screenwriter at 221B Romualdo Drive.

Sir Ian McKellen played a 93-year-old Sherlock Holmes in the 2015 movie *Mr. Holmes*.

ALTERNATIVE PASTICHE

Many authors have taken Sherlock Holmes into other worlds that Conan Doyle would have had great difficulty recognizing. The huge success of Nicholas Meyer's mid-1970s pastiche, *The Seven-Per-Cent Solution*, took Sherlock Holmes pastiches in an entirely fresh direction. Based on Conan Doyle's "The Final Problem," in Meyer's book, Holmes joins forces with Sigmund Freud, the founding father of psychoanalysis. This led to other authors making unlikely pairings for Holmes. Among the historical figures with whom he has thrown in his lot are Albert Einstein, Bram Stoker, Gilbert and Sullivan, Harry Houdini, Lillie Langtry, Grigory Rasputin and Teddy Roosevelt, not to mention numerous members of the British Royal Family and many important politicians.

IMPROBABLE HOLMES

An excellent anthology is *The Improbable Adventures of Sherlock Holmes* published by Night Shade Books. Twenty-eight stories can be found in this book, the contributors drawn from the worlds of science fiction, crime fiction and science fantasy. Each story pits Holmes against the horrific forces of H.P. Lovecraft's Cthulhu Mythos.

A STUDY IN EMERALD

In Neil Gaiman's story which won the 2004 Hugo Award for Best Short Story, the tables are turned and Moriarty is the detective while Holmes is the criminal. Elements of Conan Doyle's *A Study in Scarlet* exist alongside Lovecraftian tropes. The narrator has been brutally injured and tortured in the war against "gods and men of Afghanistan." The killer who scrawls *"Rache"* onto the wall of the room in which the body is found, is deduced by the "consulting detective" to be a multi-limbed alien from Germany and the Queen is one of Lovecraft's Great Old Ones who, having defeated humanity 700 years previously, now rule the world.

ZOMBIES VS VAMPIRES

Holmes sometimes pops up in bizarre situations in pastiches. Loren D. Estelman's 1979 novel *Sherlock Holmes vs Dracula* sees him take on Dracula who is on the rampage in London. Estelman followed that with *Dr. Jekyll and Mr. Holmes*. Holmes flies through a wormhole into 1980 to investigate UFO sightings in *The Case of the Cosmological Killer: The Rendlesham Incident*. Barrie Roberts brings Holmes to life in *The Further Adventures of Sherlock Holmes: The Man From Hell*, a collection of stories that range from the beginning of his career to extraordinary encounters with Martian invaders.

In *Victorian Undead: Sherlock Holmes vs Zombies*, written by Ian Edgington and illustrated by Davide Fabbri, Holmes and Watson tackle a zombie outbreak orchestrated by Professor Moriarty that threatens to overwhelm London.

HUNTING JACK THE RIPPER

Holmes and Jack the Ripper have faced each other countless times in the world of the Sherlock Holmes pastiche. Holmes was working as a consulting detective during that time and it is inevitable, therefore, that authors should involve him in solving the notorious case.

Some of the better pastiches in this vein are Ellery Queen's 1966 novelization of the film of the same name, *A Study in Terror*. Jack the Ripper features in *The Return of Moriarty* (1974) by John Gardner and in William S. Baring-Gould's 1962 biography of the great detective—*Sherlock Holmes of Baker Street*—Holmes's involvement with the Ripper case is discussed. Michael Dibdin pitches Holmes against the Ripper in *The Last Sherlock Holmes Story* and in Nick Rennison's biography of the great detective, *Sherlock Holmes: The Unauthorized Biography*, Holmes's brother Mycroft conveys a request from the higher echelons of government for him to investigate the Ripper killings. In all there are around forty books in which Sherlock Holmes hunts Jack the Ripper.

CHURCHILL AND THE MARTIANS

Real characters and events figure in Sam North's *The Curse of the Nibelung: A Sherlock Holmes Mystery*, published in 2005. Eighty-six-year-old Holmes is sent with Watson to Nazi Germany by Winston Churchill to help uncover a terrible secret. Meanwhile, the world of H.G. Wells meets Sherlock Holmes in Manly W. Wellman's *Sherlock Holmes's War of the Worlds* (1975) in which the detective resides in a London occupied by Martians.

SHERLOCKIAN PARODIES

A successful parody is created through love for the character Sherlock Holmes as well as a deep knowledge of the canon. And there are many of them.

The very first full-length parody was James Francis Thierry's *The Adventure of the Eleven Cuff-Buttons*, published in 1918 and featuring the detective Hemlock Holmes. One of the most unlikely parodies, however, was written by John Lennon for his 1965 bestseller, *A Spaniard in the Works*. The book included the Holmes spoof, "The Singularge Experience of Miss Anne Duffield," featuring the detective Shamrock Wolmbs.

James M. Barrie, writer of *Peter Pan*, was a good friend of Conan Doyle. In 1893, he gave Conan Doyle a copy of his book *A Window in Thrums*. On the flyleaf he had written a parody of Sherlock Holmes—"The Adventure of the Two Collaborators." This is regarded as one of the finest Sherlock parodies ever written. It tells the story of the ill-fated relationship of the two men.

Three of Robert L. Fish's thirty-two Sherlockian parodies,

written from 1959 to 1981, have won Edgar Allan Poe Awards from the Mystery Writers of America. "Schlock Holmes" is assisted by Dr. Watney and lives on Bagel Street. John Ruyle has penned twenty-four Sherlockian parodies featuring the character Turlock Loams. Printed in beautiful limited editions, they are highly collectible. Among the titles are "The Adventure of the Five Buffalo Chips," "The Adventure of the Frying Detective," and "The Adventure of the Cardboard Lox."

Issue #1 of the "Baffling New Adventures of Sherlock Holmes," 1955.

CHAPTER 23

HOLMES ON THE STAGE AND SILVER SCREEN

PUTTING HOLMES ON THE STAGE

The hunger for more Sherlock Holmes adventures after his apparent death at the Reichenbach Falls in 1893, and Conan Doyle's reluctance to revive him, led to unlicensed theatrical adaptations much to Conan Doyle's annoyance. It was an inevitable transition, given the crisp and effective dialogue and the tight plots of the stories. The colorful characters also lent themselves brilliantly to being dramatized. Realizing the financial opportunity afforded by putting Sherlock Holmes on the stage, Conan Doyle began work on the first official theatrical appearance of the great detective.

THEATRICAL PIRATES

However, before Conan Doyle's own venture got off the ground, Holmes made two unauthorized stage appearances. The earliest play featuring the great detective was Charles Rogers's *Sherlock Holmes*. Rogers's standard fare was Victorian melodrama and this play did not disappoint. Conan Doyle hated it. In the play, Dr. Watson is married to a woman named Amy but it seems that Sherlock Holmes is also in love with her. There is a Jack the Ripper-style villain and a wide range of implausible plot twists. Rogers had used the flimsy Victorian copyright laws to his advantage. By writing a new plot not based on any previous Sherlock Holmes story, Conan Doyle was powerless to put a stop to the unofficial performances by Cordyce & Hamund's Company at the Theater Royal in Glasgow, Scotland, in 1894.

Seymour Hicks' *Under the Clock* was another unlicensed Holmes production from 1893 that was billed as an "extravaganza." It was a one-act musical parody written by Hicks (who played Watson) with Charles Brookfield who played Holmes. Conan Doyle was reportedly greatly angered by these pirated portrayals.

SHERLOCK HOLMES : A DRAMA IN FOUR ACTS

In 1899 the most famous stage production of Sherlock Holmes premiered. It started out in 1897 as "The Strange Case of Miss Faulkner" written by Sir Arthur Conan Doyle as a play in five acts featuring Sherlock Holmes and Dr. Watson. Conan Doyle approached the English actor Herbert Beerbohm Tree to play Holmes. But the two men disagreed over the characterization and so the writer offered the Holmes role to Sir Henry Irving instead whom he had collaborated with before. Irving turned it down. Finally A.P. Watt, the literary agent, introduced Conan Doyle to the American theatrical producer Charles Frohman who suggested that Holmes should be portrayed on stage by the much respected American actor William Gillette.

Gillette quickly decided that the play needed a complete rewrite and got Conan Doyle's approval to start a new script. Gillette kept the characters but devised a totally new play which he wrote in a month. Then disaster struck. A fire broke out in Gillette's San Francisco hotel and the script along with Conan Doyle's original were both destroyed. Gillette set to work on a new script which he amazingly completed in a week.

In May 1899 William Gillette was invited to meet Conan Doyle at Undershaw in Crowborough to discuss the play. Legend has it that Gillette got off the train dramatically in full Holmes attire complete with deerstalker

WILLIAM GILLETTE

Conan Doyle was well aware that the demand for Sherlock Holmes stories would be insatiable and dramatic productions would try to fill the gap. He decided, therefore, to write his own play. His agent sent the completed work to theater producer Charles Frohman. But Frohman felt that it needed the input of someone with experience in writing for the stage. William Gillette (1853 – 1937) was suggested and Conan Doyle agreed. Gillette, an American actor-manager, playwright and stage manager wrote a version based on "A Scandal in Bohemia," "The Final Problem," and *A Study in Scarlet,* so Conan Doyle was credited as co-author of the play, even though Gillette had written it and added many new elements.

The play—*Sherlock Holmes: A Drama in Four Acts*—toured America after its Broadway run of 260 performances and then Gillette took it to Australia. It played in London (200 performances) and toured Great Britain. Gillette is estimated to have performed as Sherlock Holmes around 1,300 times in the next thirty years, a portrayal that helped to cement the modern image of the detective. His use of the deerstalker hat and the curved calabash pipe, for instance, established these as essential props for anyone taking on the role of Sherlock.

William Gillette also portrayed Holmes in a 1916 seven-reel silent film—*Sherlock Holmes*—directed by Arthur Berthelet. The film was long thought to have been lost but turned up in 2014 at the *Cinémathèque Francaise* and is now being restored. It is thought that this is the only filmed record of William Gillette playing his signature role.

Gillette announced his retirement many times throughout his thirty-year acting career. In 1929, age seventy-six, he started the final farewell tour of *Sherlock Holmes* in Springfield, Massachusetts. Originally scheduled for two seasons, the tour ran on until 1932. He died on April 29, 1937, age eighty-three, in Hartford, due to a pulmonary hemorrhage and was buried in the family plot at Riverside Cemetery, Farmington, Connecticut.

hat, pipe and a large magnifying glass with which he began to study Conan Doyle closely. Eventually he announced solemnly in Holmesian tones that the astonished Sir Arthur Conan Doyle was "Unquestionably an author!" The two men swiftly struck up a friendship which lasted until Conan Doyle's death in 1930.

Sherlock Holmes: A Drama in Four Acts opened at the Garrick Theater on Broadway, New York on November 6, 1899 and was performed for seven months until the following June before going on a nationwide tour of America. Eventually the tour came to the Lyceum Theater, London in September 1901 before touring the major cities in England and Scotland. Alongside Gillette in the touring company from 1903 to 1906, playing the minor part of Sherlock Holmes's page Billy, was a young actor who would later became world famous—Charlie Chaplin.

Any remaining misgivings Sir Arthur Conan Doyle may have had about the production diminished as soon as the huge financial success of the play became obvious. In a letter to Gillette, Conan Doyle wrote:

> *I consider the production a personal gratification ... My only complaint is that you made the poor hero of the anemic printed page a very limp object as compared with the power of your own personality which you infuse into his stage presentment.*

THE ADVENTURE OF THE SPECKLED BAND

Sir Arthur Conan Doyle again turned his hand to writing for the stage with *The Adventure of the Speckled Band*, first performed in 1910 and featuring a live snake at its climax. Holmes was played by H.A. Saintsbury (1869 – 1939) who had already played him in Gillette's play. It is estimated that Saintsbury played Sherlock Holmes more than 1,400 times. Popular Shakespearian actor Lyn Harding stole the show as the villain of the piece, Dr. Grimesby Rylott (using a different spelling from the book). The play was a huge success.

AWARD WINNING DRAMA

1978 saw the stage adaptation of *The Sign of the Four* in Paul Giovanni's *The Crucifer of Blood* which was the recipient of four Tony Awards. *Sherlock's Last Case*, written by Charles Marowitz, opened on Broadway in 1987 with Frank Langella as Sherlock. A black comedy, the play features a death threat against Holmes by Moriarty's son. At one point, Watson turns against Holmes and imprisons him. Steven Dietz adapted William Gillette's play and *Sherlock Holmes: The Final Adventure* opened in 2007. A melange of "A Scandal in Bohemia" and "The Final Problem," it won an Edgar Award for Best Mystery Play.

MR. HOLMES GOES TO THE MOVIES

Sherlock Holmes is reckoned to have appeared in more films than any other character in cinema history. He has been depicted 254 times and played by more than 75 actors including Sir Christopher Lee, Charlton Heston, Peter O'Toole, Christopher Plummer, Peter Cook, Roger Moore, John Cleese, Robert Downey Jr., and Sir Ian McKellen.

SILENT HOLMES

Sherlock Holmes's first appearance on celluloid lasted just thirty seconds. *Sherlock Holmes Baffled* was produced in 1900 by the American Mutoscope & Biograph Company. It was made to appear on Mutoscope machines in arcades and was viewable by only one person at a time. It shows a burglar being interrupted by a cigar-smoking Holmes and then vanishing several times to the bafflement of the detective.

There were a number of silent Sherlock Holmes films, one of which starred John Barrymore, one of the greatest film actors in movie history. In 1922, Barrymore played the great detective in an adaptation of William Gillette's play *Sherlock Holmes*. It was notable for some scenes being filmed on location in London. Lost for decades, this gem was rediscovered in the mid-1970s.

CRIMINALS, BEWARE THE HAWK-LIKE EYE!

THE UNDYING SHERLOCK HOLMES: MR. SAINTSBURY
IN "THE SPECKLED B

H.A. SAINTSBURY

Sherlock Holmes as portrayed on stage by H.A. Saintsbury in 1910. Charlie Chaplin said of Saintsbury in 1964: "Mr. H.A. Saintsbury ... was a living replica of the illustrations in *The Strand Magazine*. Of all those who played Holmes, he was considered the best, even better than William Gillette ..."

EILLE NORWOOD

During the golden age of the silent movie in the 1920s, as filming techniques became more sophisticated, so did the plots and the acting. One man is notable for having played Sherlock Holmes forty-seven times on film between 1921 and 1923 in forty-five two-reelers and two feature films. English actor Eille Norwood (1861 – 1948) was sixty years old when he first played Sherlock Holmes. His performances impressed Sir Arthur Conan Doyle who said: "His wonderful impersonation of Holmes has amazed me." He learned to play the violin and shaved his hair so that he more closely resembled Sidney Paget's vision of Holmes. Sadly, very few examples of his work have survived.

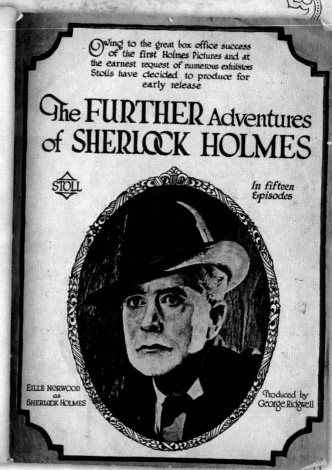

Owing to the great box office success of the first Holmes Pictures and at the earnest request of numerous exhibitors Stolls have decided to produce for early release

The FURTHER Adventures of SHERLOCK HOLMES

STOLL

In fifteen Episodes

EILLE NORWOOD as SHERLOCK HOLMES

Produced by George Ridgwell

TALKING HOLMES

When sound was introduced and talking pictures arrived, Sherlock Holmes came into his own on film. By the early 1930s, the talkies were a global phenomenon and in 1931 a version of Conan Doyle's stage play *The Speckled Band* was produced with Lyn Harding as the nasty Dr. Grimesby Rylott and Raymond Massey as Sherlock Holmes. Unfortunately, the film is marred somewhat by the director Jack Raymond's decision to turn 221B Baker Street into a busy modern detective agency.

In 1933, Reginald Owen, a rather plump individual, was miscast as Sherlock Holmes in *A Study in Scarlet* which had little connection with the original. It was not a success. However, another of the great Sherlocks, Arthur Wontner (1875 – 1960), was about to star in a run of five Holmes films from 1931 to 1937.

Wontner's first film in 1931 was *The Sleeping Cardinal,* an original story. This was followed by *The Missing Rembrandt* (1932) in which Holmes tracks down the evil Baron von Guntermann—"the worst man in London." *The Sign of Four* was released in 1932. *The Triumph of Sherlock Holmes* (1935) was an adaptation of *The Valley of Fear* involving a deadly American secret society and Professor Moriarty. *Silver Blaze* (1937) adds to the original story with the character of Henry Baskerville and Moriarty who is running an illegal betting scam. Wontner was lauded by Vincent Starrett (1886 – 1974), author of *The Private Life of Sherlock Holmes* (1933):

No better Sherlock Holmes than Wontner is likely to be seen and heard in pictures, in our time.

But of course there were many more versions of Sherlock Holmes to come.

BASIL RATHBONE

Basil Rathbone (1892 – 1967) created possibly the greatest of all the Sherlock Holmes movie portrayals. Born in South Africa, Rathbone's family returned to England when he was three years old. He fought in the First World War, achieving the rank of captain but had already launched his acting career before the war, appearing in *The Taming of the Shrew* in 1911. He was successful after the war and began to work frequently in the United States.

His film career before Sherlock Holmes included *David Copperfield* (1935), *Captain Blood* (1935), *A Tale of Two Cities* (1935), *Romeo and Juliet* (1936), and *The Adventures of Robin Hood (1938)* playing the villainous Sir Guy of Gisbourne. He also appeared in several horror films including *Son of Frankenstein* (1939). Nonetheless, it is for his Sherlock Holmes that Rathbone is best remembered. With Nigel Bruce as his Watson, he starred in fourteen Holmes films as well as hundreds of radio shows. With an angular face and crisp vocal delivery, he was the perfect Holmes.

One of the best of his movies is undoubtedly the first of his Sherlock Holmes films *The Hound of the Baskervilles* (1939). When it turned into a runaway success, the studio decided to make a sequel and so a series began. The stories were initially set in the Victorian era but with the outbreak of the Second World War, and a move of the series from 20th Century Fox to Universal Studios, they began to take

place against the background of that conflict. Thus, in *Sherlock Holmes and the Voice of Terror* (1942) Holmes and Watson try to foil a Nazi radio broadcast and in *Sherlock Holmes and the Secret Weapon*, they race against the Nazis to secure plans for a new bomb sight. The last of Rathbone's Sherlock Holmes films was *Dressed to Kill* in 1946.

Despite his film success—he was nominated for two Academy Awards and won three stars on the Hollywood Walk of Fame—Rathbone insisted that he wished to be remembered for his stage career. He always said that his favorite role was that of Romeo, not Sherlock Holmes. Basil Rathbone died suddenly of a heart attack in New York City on July 21, 1967 at age seventy-five.

WHAT YOU DON'T KNOW ABOUT SHERLOCK

THE PRIVATE LIFE OF
SHERLOCK HOLMES (1970)

Starring Robert Stephens as Holmes and Colin Blakely as Dr. Watson
and set in the years before World War I, the film features German
spies, a British Navy submarine disguised as a sea monster, Queen
Victoria and Holmes's brother Mycroft in a complex espionage plot
which ends with Sherlock Holmes seeking comfort in drugs and his
violin. The current *Sherlock* writers Steven Moffat and Mark Gatiss
credit *The Private Life of Sherlock Holmes* as the inspiration for
their award-winning TV series starring Benedict Cumberbatch.

OLIN BLAKELY Produced a
R CONAN DOYLE Music by MIKLOS ROZSA

HOLMES HAS MADE A GREAT MOTION PICTURE.

THE MIRISCH PRODUCTION COMPANY
presents
BILLY WILDER'S

THE PRIVATE LIFE OF SHERLOCK HOLMES

anything but elementary

ed by BILLY WILDER Written by BILLY WILDER and I.A.L. DIAMOND

ALL AGES ADMITTED
rental Guidance Suggested

Filmed in PANAVISION® COLOR by DeLuxe®

United Artists
Entertainment from
Transamerica Corporation

THE HOUND OF THE BASKERVILLES (1959)

In the next twenty years, with the arrival of television, there were only two major Sherlock Holmes films. British horror film company, Hammer, produced *The Hound of the Baskervilles* in which Peter Cushing took the role of Holmes, with André Morell as Watson. Being a producer of horror films, Hammer embellished the production with some added elements such as human sacrifice and a tarantula, but the film works very well.

A STUDY IN TERROR (1965)

"Here comes the original caped crusader!" shouted the PR campaign for *A Study in Terror*, borrowing from the very successful *Batman* television series of the time. John Neville played Sherlock Holmes and Donald Houston took the role of Dr. Watson. The pair investigate the Jack the Ripper Murders in glorious Technicolor.

THE PRIVATE LIFE OF SHERLOCK HOLMES (1970)

In 1970 the great director Billy Wilder made *The Private Life of Sherlock Holmes* with British stage star Robert Stephens playing Holmes and Colin Blakely as Watson. The pair deal with a case involving midget acrobats, a missing husband, Trappist monks, the Loch Ness Monster, a German spy plot, dead canaries and a copper ring that has turned green. Understandably, the film was a flop although its reputation has grown among Holmes aficionados over the years.

THEY MIGHT BE GIANTS (1971)

George C. Scott plays a man who is mentally ill and believes himself to be Sherlock Holmes. Dr. Watson, played by Joanne Woodward, is his psychiatrist in this entertaining but strange film. As the psychiatrist is drawn into her patient's delusion, she becomes involved in a real mystery.

THE ADVENTURE OF SHERLOCK HOLMES' SMARTER BROTHER (1975)

Following on from his comedy success starring in Mel Brooks's *Young Frankenstein* (1974), Gene Wilder wrote, directed and starred in *The Adventure of Sherlock Holmes' Smarter Brother*. Wilder plays Sigerson Holmes, younger brother of the detective. Tired of being overshadowed by his famous brother, he sets up his own detective agency. Sherlock sends a case to Sigerson and he works with Sergeant Orville Sacker of Scotland Yard, played by Marty Feldman at his brilliant best, to solve the case.

THE SEVEN-PER-CENT SOLUTION (1976)

Sigmund Freud joins forces with Holmes in an adaptation of the bestselling novel *The Seven-Per-Cent Solution* which was scripted by the novel's author Nicholas Meyer. In a terrific Hollywood blockbuster, Nicol Williamson stars as an eccentric Sherlock Holmes while Alan Arkin takes the Freud part. Robert Duvall plays Dr. Watson, Vanessa Redgrave is Lola Devereaux and Sir Laurence Olivier takes the role of Professor Moriarty.

THE STRANGE CASE OF THE END OF CIVILIZATION AS WE KNOW IT (1977)

Monty Python's funny walks man, John Cleese, plays Arthur Sherlock Holmes, grandson of the original detective in this low-budget Sherlockian romp. The splendid Arthur Lowe plays a wonderfully inept Watson. Moriarty's grandson announces that the world will end in five days and Arthur is called in to stop him.

THE HOUND OF THE BASKERVILLES (1978)

The third Holmes comedy of the decade, this disaster of a film starred Peter Cook as

Arthur Wontner, played Holmes on screen from 1931 to 1937. Critics thought at the time that no better Sherlock Holmes would ever be seen.

Sherlock and his comedy partner, Dudley Moore, as Watson. Even an astonishing cast of British comic talent, including Terry Thomas, Prunella Scales, Max Wall and Kenneth Williams could not save this self-indulgent mess.

HOLMES FILMS OF THE 1980s

As the years passed, Sherlock Holmes seemed to become more attractive to television producers than those of the cinema. In the 1980s there were still a number of Holmes films being produced, however. *Young Sherlock Holmes* (1985) had Holmes and Watson meeting at boarding school and Holmes taking on a wicked Egyptian cult. In 1986, Sherlock became a mouse in the Disney film *The Great Mouse Detective*, based on Eve Titus's books. Michael Caine plays Sherlock and Ben Kingsley is Watson in *Without A Clue* from 1988. In this strange version of the Sherlock Holmes world, Watson is the brilliant detective while Holmes pretends to be the great detective in public but is in reality no more than a drunk.

ROBERT DOWNEY JR. AND JUDE LAW

Sherlock Holmes returned to the big screen in 2009 in the Guy Richie-helmed *Sherlock Holmes*, a blockbuster that focuses on Holmes's physical skills such as martial arts, fencing and boxing. In 1891, Holmes and Watson are hired by a secret society to stop a plot to expand the British Empire by what appear to be supernatural means. Nominated for two Oscars, the film spawned an equally successful sequel, *Sherlock Holmes: A Game of Shadows* that hit cinemas in 2011. A third film starring Downey Jr. and Law is now in the pipeline.

MR. HOLMES (2015)

Sir Ian McKellen starred as an aged, retired Sherlock Holmes, suffering from early dementia, in *Mr. Holmes*, an adaptation of Mitch Cullin's 2005 Sherlock Holmes parody *A Slight Trick of the Mind*. The film was well-received by critics and public alike.

ROBERT DOWNEY JR.

JUDE LAW

SHERLOC

SHERLOCK HOLMES (2009)

Jude Law (left) as Watson with Robert Downey Jr. as Sherlock Holmes. Downey is a martial arts enthusiast, and was inspired by the Baritsu mentioned in the 1903 story "The Adventure of the Empty House." The star also revealed his thoughts about playing the role: "Holmes is such a weirdo ... when you read the description of the guy—quirky and kind of nuts—it could be a description of me."

RACHEL McADAMS   MARK STRONG

K HOLMES

221B

THE GREAT GAME

Also known as the Sherlockian game, the Great Game is indulged in by Holmes scholars trying to resolve anomalies and clarify issues in the Sherlock Holmes stories that are merely implied. The game involves treating the stories as if they are not fiction. It began in 1902 in essays by Arthur Bartlett Maurice and Frank Sidgwick and soon Sherlock Holmes experts began to emerge.

The priest and detective story-writer Ronald Knox provided the first piece in the genre of mock-serious critical writing on Sherlock Holmes in "Studies in the Literature of Sherlock Holmes" and the American writer Christopher Morley was the founder in 1934 of the Baker Street Irregulars, an organization of Holmes enthusiasts that exists to this day. In her book *Unpopular Opinions*, British crime writer Dorothy L. Sayers included several essays on Sherlock Holmes. She explained The Great Game in her introduction to the book:

The game of applying the methods of the "Higher Criticism" to the Sherlock Holmes canon was begun, many years ago, by Monsignor Ronald Knox, with the aim of showing that, by those methods, one could disintegrate a modern classic as speciously as a certain school of critics have endeavored to disintegrate the Bible. Since then, the thing has become a hobby among a select set of jesters here and in America.

In response to Knox's essay, Cambridge University Professor Sydney Roberts wrote a booklet entitled *A Note on the Watson Problem*. S.C. Roberts published a complete biography of Dr. Watson and the "Game" began.

American writer and journalist Vincent Starrett was an early player, writing *The Private Life of Sherlock Holmes* in 1933. Starrett was one of the founders of The Hounds of the Baskerville (sic), a Chicago chapter of the Baker Street Irregulars.

Participants in the Game attempt to explain away anomalies in the stories. One of the most obvious ones involves the location of the wound Dr. Watson suffered in Afghanistan. In *A Study in Scarlet* it is said to be a wound to the shoulder but in *The Sign of the Four* it is in his leg. Watson's Christian name also provides a matter for discussion. He is "John" in *A Study in Scarlet* and "The Problem of Thor Bridge" but by the time we get to "The Man with the Twisted Lip" he is being called "James."

Taking the game to its extreme are a couple of biographies of Sherlock Holmes. William S. Baring-Gould's *Sherlock Holmes of Baker Street* appeared in 1962 and Nick Rennison's excellent *Sherlock Holmes: The Unauthorized Biography*, a book rich in historical context and fascinating insights, was published in 2007.

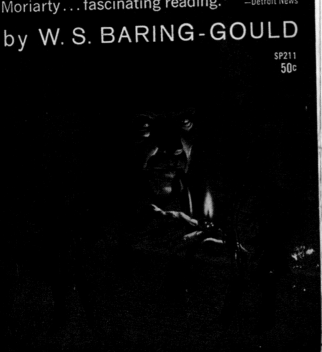

Book cover for *Sherlock Holmes of Baker Street* (1962).

CHAPTER 24

HOLMES ON TELEVISION AND COMPUTER GAMES

When the National Broadcasting Company began trialing television in New York in 1937, the very first "teleplay" broadcast was a dramatic production of the Sherlock Holmes story "The Three Garridebs."

It would not be until after the war that Holmes would again appear on TV. In March 1948, *Tea-Time for Baker Street* was broadcast in Detroit. Holmes and Watson are engaged on a case leaving their landlady Mrs. Hudson and her friend Mrs. Wiggins to solve a crime.

THE NEW ADVENTURES OF SHERLOCK HOLMES

Running from 1954 to 1955, this was the first Sherlock Holmes series and the only American one until *Elementary* of 2011. Ronald Howard, son of the British actor Leslie Howard, took the role of Holmes and character actor H. Marion Crawford played Watson. It ran for 39 episodes. Although many of the episodes were based on Conan Doyle's original stories, a number were original and played for laughs.

SHERLOCK HOLMES

The BBC's 1964 – 65 series was intended to be the most accurate production of Sherlock Holmes to date. Douglas Wilmer, a true Sherlockian, was taken on to play Holmes and Nigel Stock played Watson. Wilmer was a good Holmes, depicting the detective in all his complexity and Nigel Stock re-established Watson as a serious individual, closer to Conan Doyle's version. When Wilmer turned down the opportunity to continue in the role after the thirteen episodes of the first series, the BBC turned to Peter Cushing who had already starred as Holmes in *The Hound of the Baskervilles*. Cushing was, like Wilmer, a Holmes aficionado, to the extent that he was in the habit of changing the script to ensure it was faithful to the original.

THE ADVENTURES OF SHERLOCK HOLMES AND DR. WATSON

Between 1979 and 1986, Soviet television produced a series of five films at the Lenfilm movie studio, split into eleven episodes, starring Vasily Livanov (1935 – age 81) as Sherlock Holmes and Vitaly Solomin (1941 – 2002) as Dr. Watson. Later, a cinematic adaptation was made based on the 1986 episodes. A street in old Riga doubles as Baker Street. On February 20, 2006 Livanov became an Honorary MBE (Member of the Order of the British Empire) "for service to the theater and performing arts."

SHERLOCK HOLMES (GRANADA TELEVISION)

A wealth of British television talent was assembled for Granada television's series that ran from 1984 to 1995 and showed 41 of the 60 stories in the Holmes canon. A "bible" entitled *The Baker Street File: A Guide to the Appearance and Habits of Sherlock Holmes and Dr. Watson* was even compiled that served as a guide to the habits, mannerisms and personality traits of characters. In the search for authenticity, no detail was too small. It was hugely successful, viewed in 50 countries. The actor chosen to play Holmes was Jeremy Brett (1933 – 95) of whom *The New York Times* said:

> *Mr. Brett was regarded as the quintessential Holmes: breathtakingly analytical, given to outrageous disguises and the blackest moods and relentless in his enthusiasm for solving the most intricate crimes.*

HOUSE (2004 – 12)

Not so much a series about Sherlock Holmes as a homage to him. British actor Hugh Laurie stars as medical doctor Gregory House (his surname a subtle play on Holmes) who, like Sherlock, uses deductive reasoning and psychology to solve his cases. There is much about this show that is respectfully borrowed from Sherlock Holmes—Dr. House is always reluctant to take on cases that fail to interest him; he is addicted to the drug Vicodin; his address is apartment 221B; as well as his asocial behavior, his musical talent and his effortless skills of deduction.

SHERLOCK (2010 – PRESENT DAY)

It seemed that Jeremy Brett had created the ultimate Sherlock and no one would ever rise to such heights again. But then in 2010 Benedict Cumberbatch came along and gave us a Sherlock Holmes for the twenty-first century.

Created by Dr. Who writer Steven Moffat and Mark Gatiss who plays Mycroft in the series, the three seasons of *Sherlock* have been garlanded with awards and nominations including BAFTAs, Emmys and a Golden Globe. Set in modern-day London, the series has a number of crimes and perpetrators but Holmes is still engaged in his battle with Professor Moriarty, chillingly played by Andrew Scott. At Holmes's side is Watson, engagingly played by Martin Freeman.

ELEMENTARY (2012 – PRESENT DAY)

Johnny Lee Miller stars as Sherlock Holmes in this update of Conan Doyle's stories. Holmes is a recovering drug addict and former consultant to Scotland Yard who helps the NYPD solve crimes. Dr. Joan Watson is played by Lucy Liu. She has been hired by Holmes's father to help his son stay sober but works with him on cases. A female Moriarty is played by Natalie Dormer and Rhys Ifans takes the role of Mycroft Holmes. The series has been praised for its innovative approach, the performances and the writing.

Granada TV's *Sherlock Holmes* (1985) starring Jeremy Brett (left) as Sherlock Holmes and David Burke as Watson.

THE GAME'S AFOOT!
SHERLOCK AND GAMING

Sherlock Holmes was made for gaming and numerous companies have used the characters of Conan Doyle's stories to create fascinating and challenging games. We only have space to discuss a few in these pages.

The first Sherlock Holmes game arrived in 1984. Developed by Melbourne House, a company famous for its *Lord of the Rings* games, it allowed players to control Holmes by text commands and there were no graphics. In 1987, Infocom released another text-based adventure game—*Sherlock: The Riddle of the Crown Jewels*.

The first game on CD was published by Icom in the 1990s. *Sherlock Holmes: Consulting Detective* was ninety minutes long and shot with a real cast, although the actors were amateur. Players had to solve fake logical riddles. It developed into a trilogy and survived long enough to be issued on DVD as well.

Electronic Arts began publishing a series called *The Lost Files of Sherlock Holmes* in 1992 with "The Case of the Serrated Scalpel," in which Holmes has to solve the case of a brutally murdered actress. "The Case of the Rose Tattoo" followed in 1996, but the acting was poor and the plot was labored.

Ukrainian group Frogwares have made games based on the works of Jules Verne and Bram Stoker. They are the producers of the award-winning series, *Adventures of Sherlock Holmes*, made for Windows, Nintendo, PlayStation, Wii and Xbox. Kerry Shale is the voice of Holmes in most of the games.

The player controls Holmes or Watson in either a first or third-person perspective in a game that is mainly made up of puzzles to be solved, using Holmes's characteristic deductive reasoning or with the assistance of Dr. Watson. Clues and evidence are hidden throughout the environment in which the game takes place. When clues are discovered, they are taken back to 221B Baker Street or elsewhere and examined under a microscope or chemically separated. The gamer travels across the world.

Titles include *The Mystery of the Mummy, Sherlock Holmes versus Arsène Lupin* and *Sherlock Holmes: The Devil's Daughter*.

Benedict Cumberbatch's BBC series has also spawned a range of games that can be found online and on the official *Sherlock* app.

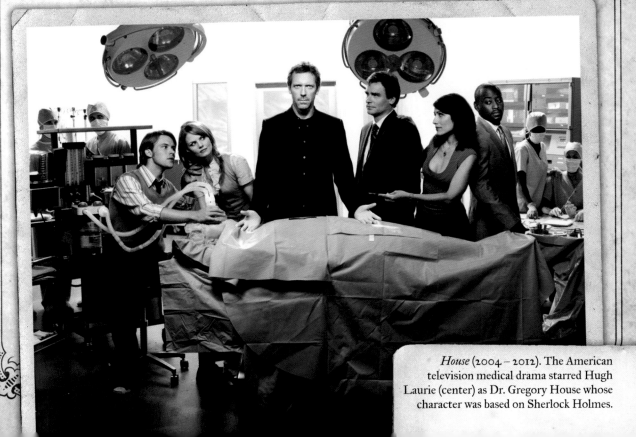

House (2004 – 2012). The American television medical drama starred Hugh Laurie (center) as Dr. Gregory House whose character was based on Sherlock Holmes.

FAREWELL TO THE STAGE

WILLIAM GILLETTE

in His Famous Creation

SHERLOCK HOLMES

by William Gillette & Sir Arthur Conan Doyle

DIRECTION of
A·L·ERLANGER &
GEORGE C·TYLER

Steele

WEEK, BEGINNING
MON. JAN. 13

ORE
TINEE SATURDAY ONLY

PRINTED IN

WILLIAM GILLETTE'S
FAREWELL TOUR

Playbill from Ford's Grand Opera House,
Baltimore during William Gillette's
Farewell Tour in January 1930. Illustration
by Frederic Dorr Steele. Gillette was
by this time seventy-seven years old.

FURTHER READING

This chronicle of the life and times of Sir Arthur Conan Doyle and Sherlock Holmes is designed to be an informative and entertaining introductory text. There are other more academic publications available should the reader wish to delve more deeply. Publications that were especially useful during the preparation of this book are listed below and contemporary newspaper and magazine articles are cited at the point where they appear within the text.

Baring-Gould, William S. (1995) *Sherlock Holmes of Baker Street, the Life of the World's First Consulting Detective.* London: Random House

Bunson, Matthew E. (1995) *Encyclopedia of Sherlock Holmes: A Complete Guide to the World of the Great Detective.* London: Pavilion Books

Campbell, Mark (2012) *Sherlock Holmes.* London: Pocket Essentials

Conan Doyle, Sir Arthur (2007) *Memories and Adventures: An Autobiography.* London: Wordsworth Literary Lives

Conan Doyle, Sir Arthur & Baring-Gould, William S. (ed.) (1992) *The Annotated Sherlock Holmes: The Four Novels and Fifty-six Short Stories Complete.* London: Random House

Conan Doyle, Sir Arthur & Hodgson, John A. (Ed.) (1994) *Sherlock Holmes: The Major Stories with Contemporary Critical Essays.* Boston: Bedford

Coren, Michael, (1995) *The Life of Sir Arthur Conan Doyle.* London: Bloomsbury Publishing

Costello, Peter (2006) *Conan Doyle, Detective.* London: Robinson

Dickson Carr, John (2003) *The Life of Sir Arthur Conan Doyle.* New York: Avalon Publishing Group

Lellenberg, Jon, Stashower, Daniel & Foley, Charles (2009) *Arthur Conan Doyle: A Life in Letters.* London: Harper Press

Lycett, Andrew, (2007) *Conan Doyle: The Man Who Created Sherlock Holmes.* London: Weidenfeld & Nicholson

Norman, Andrew (2009) *Arthur Conan Doyle: The Man Behind Sherlock Holmes.* Stroud: The History Press

Pugh, Brian W., (2011) *A Chronology Of The Life of Arthur Conan Doyle. A Detailed Account Of The Life And Times Of The Creator Of Sherlock Holmes.* London: Andrews

Rennison, Nick (2005) *Sherlock Holmes: The Biography.* London: Atlantic

Smith, Daniel (2009) *The Sherlock Holmes Companion: An Elementary Guide.* London: Aurum Press

Wagner, E. J., (2006) *The Science of Sherlock Holmes: From Baskerville Hall to the Valley of Fear, the Real Forensics Behind the Great Detective's Greatest Cases.* Chichester: Wiley

SHERLOCK (2010 – PRESENT)

Benedict Cumberbatch (left) and Martin Freeman as
Holmes and Watson with the London skyline behind
them. In-keeping with Conan Doyle's original character
who used every contemporary tool available to solve the
crimes, Benedict Cumberbatch's Sherlock uses texting,
the internet, and GPS, to catch the villains. Martin
Freeman's modern day Watson has returned from
military service in Afghanistan, the same war zone the
original Watson has served in over a century before.

INDEX

Page numbers in italic denote an illustration

Quarto is the authority on a wide range of topics.

Quarto educates, entertains and enriches the lives of our readers—enthusiasts and lovers of hands-on living. www.quartoknows.com

This edition published in 2017 by
Chartwell Books
an imprint of Book Sales
a division of Quarto Publishing Group USA Inc.
142 West 36th Street, 4th Floor
New York, New York 10018
USA

ISBN-13: 978-0-7858-3501-1

10 9 8 7 6 5 4 3 2 1

Printed in China

Picture Credits

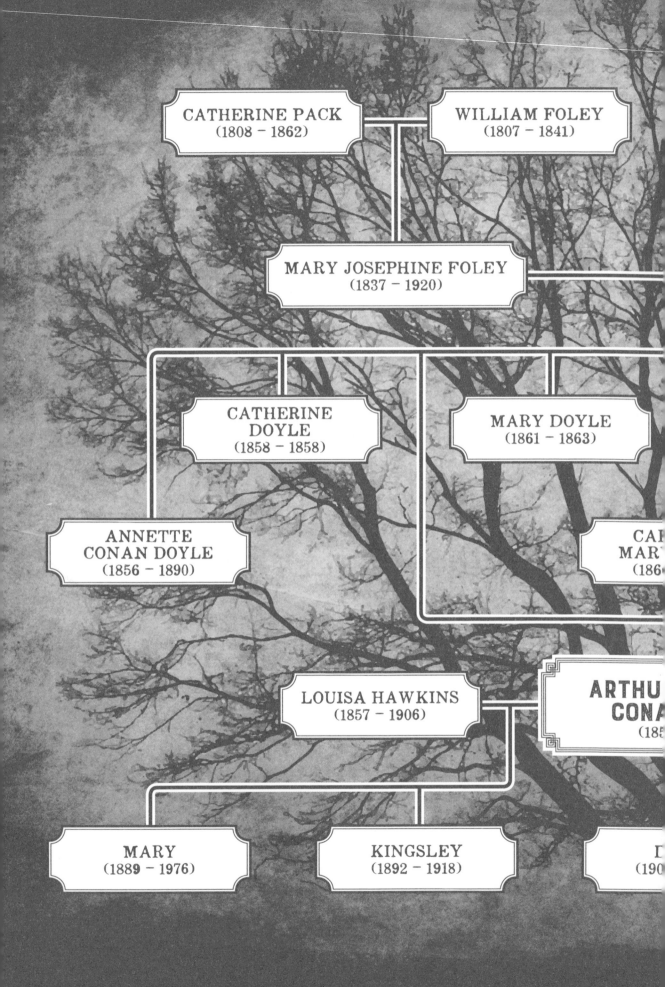

CATHERINE PACK
(1808 – 1862)

WILLIAM FOLEY
(1807 – 1841)

MARY JOSEPHINE FOLEY
(1837 – 1920)

CATHERINE
DOYLE
(1858 – 1858)

MARY DOYLE
(1861 – 1863)

ANNETTE
CONAN DOYLE
(1856 – 1890)

CA
MAR
(186

LOUISA HAWKINS
(1857 – 1906)

ARTHU
CONA
(185

MARY
(1889 – 1976)

KINGSLEY
(1892 – 1918)

D
(190